UNDETECTABLE

CASEY CHARLES

RUNNING WILD

RUNNING WILD PRESS

Paperback ISBN: 978-1-955062-97-8
eBook ISBN: 978-1-955062-98-5

INVICTUS

Out of the night that covers me,
    Black as the pit from pole to pole,
    I thank whatever gods may be
For my unconquerable soul.

         — WILLIAM ERNEST HENLEY (1875)

Memoir partakes of masochism, even as it seeks catharsis.

CONTENTS

INTRODUCTION

During my early years as an assistant professor at the University of Montana, I hired one of my older students to paint my house. His family owned a painting business. We became fast friends that summer, and he invited me and some of his buddies to raft the Alberton Gorge one day in early July. The Gorge is a narrow section of the Clark Fork west of Missoula with sufficient constriction and gradient to turn the wide ambling green river into a channel of whitewater that runs through a beautiful canyon made of purple rock. Kent had his own boat, a 10-foot inflatable raft. He assured us he was an old hand at navigating the river, even when the high water of the early season gave the flow an extra speed. Four or five of us piled into the boat with paddles, life jackets, and a lunch cooler after we carried it from the parking lot down to the Cyr Bridge put-in off Highway 90. A gorgeous Montana summer day it was, and we hankered for a fun ride.

The Gorge has Class I to III rapids generally, never reaching the higher, more dangerous waves and drops, but in early summer the volume of the water moving through the tightened canyon gave the current a swift kick. We weren't a quarter mile into our steerage before our overloaded boat flipped, and all of us fell into the river at the beginning of a set of major rapids, flailing away with lifejackets, bathing suits, shoes, and in some cases a paddle. Our raft was on its own. I'm a strong swimmer, so my first reaction was one of odd exhilaration, "a go-with-the-flow" feel, thinking I could easily maneuver myself into slower water near the shore. No sooner did that thought cross my mind than I got hit with a wave and pulled under for 15 seconds before bobbing up to gasp for air with my life jacket around my ears. I tugged on my paddle in an effort to steer myself toward the bank, but as soon as I made headway, I was pulled under again by a rapid, this time for a longer stretch.

It took a while to realize that I might be in danger, as strange as that might seem, but I am a competent ocean swimmer. I came up for air again and struggled toward shore before the next wave hit. Over and over—10 times dragged under by the river god, knocking my old Keds on rocks now and again but mostly just losing breath, fatigued every time the life jacket buoyed me up from the froth. After a while, I started to realize I was not only getting water-logged, but also losing strength. It dawned on me that the Gorge was wearing me down, luring me into succumbing to its power, like some domineering lover. I started to get scared, reaching for breaths when I came up, getting slapped with waves, swallowing water. At some point, I realized that I might never get to shore; the force of the current seemed insurmountable. A couple of times I stopped paddling when I came up, stopped trying to rudder myself to the slow water, which was out of reach. A couple of times I let the river take me down between waves, let the Clark Fork have its way, while a heavy resignation swept over me.

The thrill turned to dread, the dread to disbelief. Roseate cliffs moved before my eyes as I was pulled along by the velocity of the flow, my neck almost choked by the life jacket. Would I ever get to the bank, I wondered. But there was no time to do much wondering, since another wall of cold water soon swamped me, requiring the sheer struggle for air, the utter fight to breathe. A physical push of adrenalin suddenly kicked in—what adrenalin was left in my soaked body. A deep reach into the muscle of survival, one I almost never had to use. I tried to move to the side, tried to grab boulders stuck in the slow water, reached toward a rock with one hand, my paddle still in the other.

There is no explanation for how I ended up sitting on the bank in the sand minutes later. I can't recount what pushed me to safety, what combination of will and instinct, raw and painful, drove my refusal to surrender, what low gear I found in my strained engine. I had survived. I was tired, my friends had been following me down the bank on foot, having gotten out earlier. I told them I was okay. I sat on the beach for minutes, shivering in the sun, spooked by the near occasion of drowning.

This book is not about rafting; it's a story about survival. Yet, when I told my friend, an author, that I was writing a memoir about living with the human immunodeficiency virus (HIV), he wanted to know what I meant by survival. So many memoirs portray women and men facing the slings and arrows of outrageous fortune, he said in so many words, but no one ever talks about what makes people want to survive—what drives a woman living in a Kenyan slum with a broken immune system, no job, and a violent husband to keep going, to seek help and get healthy? What has compelled me to just keep coming up for air in the face of heartbreak, infection, mental breakdown, and drug failure?

Putting together the story of my three decades living with HIV in a privileged stratum of America has not led to some formula for survival in the face of adversity, some key to staying alive through faith or love or community. Not to discount these factors, this book instead approaches survival through a kind of *via negativa*, as the mystic monks would have it, through a refusal to look beyond the experience itself. What got me safe to shore in the gorge ultimately was not prayer, instinct, a paddle maneuver, not even some ironclad will. The drive to survive kicked in when I faced the peril head-on, when I gave up approaching the river as a ride or fate or even just a physical challenge. I saw the deadly current for what it was; I saw myself for what I was: afraid, angry at my leaden arms, on the verge of surrender. HIV survival depends on luck, strength, support, and material circumstance, I told my friend, but it also requires a raw honesty about the blood, sweat, and tears—the stigma and shame—the money and politics—that comprise the story of one of the most devastating pandemics in world history.

What struck me as I began to outline my life as a white upper middle-class Montanan with HIV was not just the privilege of my socio-economic position in the world but also the atypicality of the trajectory of my life as a gay man who could not find his way out of the closet until his late 20s, who, when he did come out, fell deeply but dangerously in love. In many ways, I am a second-generation survivor of the acquired immunodeficiency syndrome (AIDS)—I never lived in West Hollywood, the Castro, or Chelsea. I did not have the chutzpah to be out and proud at Stonewall or City Hall in San Francisco. I did not work with Shanti or fight with the Gay Men's Health Crisis in the 80s. I cannot count myself as part of that dramatic and tragic generation of men and women who fought for their lives in the 1980s, whose stories have generated a literature of memories that my tamer tale cannot compete with.

Yes, I have watched my friends Tom and Dallas die; I sat in group with men who suffered from lymphoma and wasting, but I was not in the thick of it on Noe Street; I did not wear tight jeans and bomber jackets, my hair cut short, my t-shirt tight, snorting poppers and letting myself fool around all night in the dark rooms South of Market. With some guilt, I must disown any serious affiliation with the true sufferers of this plague, the vanguard of gay liberation who fought the stigma, cursed heartless Reagan, yelled at the NIH, the churches and vulturous media even as these championed men lost weight in and out of hospitals, treated for chlamydia, cytomegalovirus (CMV), gonorrhea, syphilis, amoebas, crabs, Hepatitis B and C.

I was not there, or if I was, in 1982, I was belatedly and conflictedly undergoing the kind of coming out *sturm und drang* that was by then old hat for the Edmund Whites, Paul Monettes, and Michael Callens of the world. At that point, I was practicing law, going out with Sue Frattini, and secretly falling in love with straight tennis players in the Rose Garden of North Berkeley. I was on the downlow at Peet's Coffee on the Northside, taking a Greek man home for some afternoon delight when no one was looking, slinking down to the White Horse whenever I had the conflicted nerve. When I finally did come out in the late 80s, when I moved East and fell deeply and unabashedly in love, I faced the greatest challenge of my life. Love became a death sentence, HIV another closet, survival a way of life.

Behind the times, I was in my twenties too much of mensch to be part of the scene, unworthy of the Larry Kramers of the world. Yes, I eventually picked up a frayed copy of Louise Hay; I went through the COenzyme Qs, wheat grass, and antioxidants. I meditated, visualized, stretched, ran, lifted, swam, and read. But I never learned to love myself. I loved to write, knew how to throw things at walls, how to yell and scream loud enough to send the dogs out of the house and the neighbors into their yards. I knew how to be pissed and depressed, pay thousands of dollars for therapists I thought were nice but ineffective. I just have never gotten to this place of self-love and *joie de vivre* that some associate with long-term survivors. Obviously. I will never make peace with the cruel fate that made my love lethal. The more I delve into my past, the more regrets and self-recriminations—once buried in protective self-defense—now emerge. Can this self-critique be positive for the Positive? I don't know. This question loomed as I tried to recount, refresh my jaded recollection, tried to bring back what is at some level lost forever, but still persisted as a record of tortured resolve, a testament to endurance in the face of my fated love story and its aftermath.

Some of my disclaimer does admittedly participate in the rhetorical figure of *occupatio*, I confess—my father's favorite preamble to the toasts we were forced to make on our feet during every major holiday or minor saint's day on the Catholic *Monitor's* calendar, his prologue consisting of that shopworn disclaimer "unaccustomed as I am to public speaking," the usual introduction to one of his lengthy encomia to his family and the principles of equality and diligence which he championed. While I have unabashedly been willing to make hay when the sun did not shine, to capitalize or at least attempt to craft an *objet d'art* out of my star-crossed narrative, fashioning drama out of the specter of the ultimate dénouement, namely death, I have continued to take some umbrage with the gay glitterati who insist that joining the AIDS club has brought new meaning and spiritual awakening to their lives, given them a renewed sense of belonging and camaraderie. Yes, I am always happy to find a fellow HIVer on the Hollywood Squares of Scruff or Grindr on occasion, but I am not, consciously at least, someone who subscribes to the notion that HIV has brought enlightenment, belonging, or renewed purpose to my life. Living with this retrovirus is about as much fun, about as entertaining, enlightening, and edifying as trying to hang a shower curtain from those stubborn rungs that refuse to unclip three feet above your head, the entire metal circle upon which they hang ready at any minute to fall to the tub, doing this chore as you wait for water to boil.

Without denying my own peculiar form of tough-luck realism, I cannot take issue with the brave men and women (and today the transmen and transwomen) who fought heroically for their lives before PCP prophylaxis or KS diagnoses were even available, back in the days of GRID and ARC, the days of a gay plague when 25-year-old men woke to soaked sheets and sore throats that would never leave them, when nodes grew beneath their square jaws or under their toned biceps, the days of *The Body and Its Dangers* and *Sea of Tranquillity*, to name a few of the masterful fictions that have emerged from the gay plague.[1]

People ask me—friends, that is, and enemies who remind me of myself—why I am writing this story, why am I beating the dead horse of AIDS tales, what I hope to prove or show or elucidate with this re-creation of a blocked past, a past not really worthy of the Magic Johnsons and Greg Louganises of the world. During these years of limbo, awaiting the opportunity of some infection, I once found myself in a multiplex in Beaverton, Oregon, crying and sweating through *Philadelphia*, the theater packed with people. "City of brotherly love, don't turn your back on me, I don't want to be alone," I heard Neil Young sing, his soundtrack un-writable, untranslatable into anything but tears. That night, in the car after the show, my t-shirt wet with sweat, I realized that solitude was probably the most real, excruciating, deeply complex reality in my life. HIV brought that aloneness into focus, forced me to face it, spell it out, live through it.

Can this fractured memory be anything more than another stone added to the cairn of selfies in suffering, another Instagram post of wasted cheekbones? How is this attempt at nonfiction more than another indulgence in solipsistic navel gazing, another "look at me" set of signifiers for your eyes to skim on your Kindle Reader? When people ask what compels, what drives my exposition, I can only say I don't know for sure. I tell them I am exploring my recalibration from a death sentence to the chronic guts of survival, giving me the opportunity, as the years pass, to watch the CEO of Apple come out of the closet, watch undetectable guys bareback again with erotic abandon. But I cannot in good or bad conscience, to borrow Nietzsche's more accurate assessment of that mental function, claim some revelatory resurrection by pharmaceuticals, cannot elaborate upon the miracle of my continued existence, for one ineluctable reason: I never in fact looked death in the face other than to tell death, like John Donne did, to die.

I have never really contemplated what death means; I refused to surrender to the incomprehensibility of eternity—that implacable nothingness which I tried religiously to ignore, stave off, fence out by means of pills, brown rice, and sobriety. I have run from dying men in support groups as I have run from the dying man in me, so when years later I moved to Mexico for a year with six months' supply of my drug cocktail, I was not rejoicing in my survival. I did not make an about face, for there never was a face to turn about; it has always been a face of desperation and fear, a face of perseverance in the face of rejection and self-doubt, an outward arrogance masking a deep insecurity.

If the truth be known, the truth—the very *sine qua non* of the memoir genre with its insistence on accuracy to some unrecoverable event—is not only at some level unknowable but actually not particularly earth shaking. This then my story of the Walter Mitty homo, wedded to the hackneyed truth of folding laundry and sponging countertops, making a queen-sized bed for a mid-sized queen, who was not really even a queen, rather a cisgender Eddie Bauer wannabe fly fisherman who just happens to like to kiss not the sky like Jimi Hendrix but the guy next store, the straight guy next store with his snowshoes and Tacoma pickup. I am not the stuff of Oedipus or Antigone, not even the non-stuff of temperance minded Guyon nor pious Aeneas. I was not molested nor rehabbed nor incarcerated, not a political prisoner nor a trophy owner. I am not Bruce Springsteen. I come from the suburbs and went to state schools. I am not a bestseller. You want the truth, you want reality, you want to know what it's like to crawl through the rabbit holes of oblivion toward some ashy scatter over the Bitterroot River? You want reality?

Faced as I soon became with the fear and loathing of my struggle, not in the dramatic whitewater of a narrowing gorge, but in the flat, slow stretches through years of rejection, infection, and stigma, I came to realize that HIV survivors are hardly a homogenous bunch, that my story, no matter how inimitable in its inner workings of queer neurosis, is in many ways hardly reflective of the varieties of HIV experience. Over the decades, I have met men and women who have survived class IV and V rapids, whose socio-economic circumstances shed an entirely different light on the agony of survival. At home, on apps, in groups, on the net, I have encountered positive men and women who have overcome tuberculosis and pneumonia, who have faced a level of shunning that made my travails pale beside their resilience in the face of poverty, prejudice, and medical neglect. Their ordeals are the matter-of-fact counterpoint to my often-caustic ruminations about my quixotic life, steeped in a sarcasm that barely conceals the raw emotions which inexplicably bring me back to my father's dual injunctions: leave the world a better place than you found it, and don't give up. I hope this HIV story can perpetuate his advice—words we all can survive by.

THE RAMBLE

(1989-1990)

1
MIDTOWN

I felt rather queer jogging up 5th Avenue from Times Square in my unsupportive running shorts that summer, but once I'd hooved past those curvaceous horse rumps at the foot of Central Park, my attire seemed more appropriate. Through the dappled light of canopied trees, past prams and cane-carrying septuagenarians who occupied the precious shade of those deep green benches (what a color, what a delight those thick-coated slats!), I jogged up the promenade with my inimitable clomp. It must have been mid-morning, must have been before noon, an hour before the Borinqueño picnics and white-skinned volleyballers had rolled out in full force, not as hot and humid as it would turn later on that July day in 1989. I wound my way through the maze of The Ramble, though I had no idea I was in The Ramble. I knew only I was jogging and getting lost in New York, New York, which was all someone like me could really hope for, a parvenu from Buffalo enchanted with the notion of being in the thick of it, in the thick air of a malodorous Midtown dorm room with its Kafkaesque cockroaches and permanent odor of take-out Chinese, where I was incarcerated during a ten-week intensive Latin workshop at CUNY in the Grace Building across from the debt ticker. So, yes, it was exciting—even if it was summer in the city. In a daze, I floated over the lovely asphalt walkways through thickets of leaf-life, until a sudden flash of red drew my eyes from my sneakers.

I kept that flag for many years, his red t-shirt. I am not sure I ever wore it. It was perfect on him, on his tall lanky torso, light olive skin tanned under sun. Those pale plaid shorts and beautiful long legs. He was walking on a path above me when I noticed his rich lips and aquiline nose, his black-coffee eyes. There was something fated in the viscera of that moment, in the pulse of my attraction to the fragility and finesse of his stride. His look slowed my pace to a walk and then, like a dove homing, I glided by him with a grin and paused to look back over my shoulder and catch his glance.

We both knew; our hearts beating on the bench where we sat—me, a cramming student again, and Gilberto, an immigrant from Rio who worked the night shift on Macy's loading docks outside Newark in his new country. We walked back together to my particle-board dorm room, where I showered as he waited on my single bed until I came out with a towel. He took off his shirt, his body built on dance and labor, thin and ripped at the same time. And what was I then but a runner and machine-toned generic white man who happened to look like some forgettable movie star? We had no problem getting off, Gil and me, those afternoons during my struggles with declensions.

There is another inevitability in life besides death and taxes; it is called desire. That memory of fullness in search of itself. That need met in a heart's thump on a green bench, knees tapping in the big city, with Frankie shouting "New

York, New York" hopelessly into some microphone of the mind. In The Ramble famous for gay *liaisons dangereuse*, a danger discovered in that fateful decade to be as real as death. Need, want, drive, desire—the rungs of a psychoanalytic lexicon. There is no synonym for love. Gilberto's love was the fifth largest country in the world. Maybe I'm hiding behind flippancy, filtering memory of a park's light in smelly Midtown through a rosy lens.

New York is famous for bad pizza, for delis in corner stores. We stood in line at Sbarro's on the corner of 7th Avenue and West 46th, ordered a slice of floppy pepperoni after making love on a stained mattress in my spartan room with its view of a brick wall, while the air conditioner rattled. We faced each other across a plastic table under fluorescent light. Gilberto's heels twitched in anticipation of my rejection of his English, my Spanish insulting his Portuguese. We moved from one form of intercourse to another, even though the first consisted of no penetration, and the second started and stopped around who we were, where we lived, what we did to survive as gay men from different continents, different classes and cultures. I was a doctoral student learning to read Ovid in ten weeks under the exacting tutelage of classicists. Gilberto lived in Little Brazil, a part of Newark called Ironbound, where he rented a dorm room in a clapboard boarding house, shared with four or five other guys.

He had come to New York originally with his friend and ex-lover Victor to sell coat art in fashion centers, but then on impulse and enchantment, he decided to stay in the States and give up on Victor. Determined to make it in America, Gil found work in a Macy's warehouse, taking orders from a sadistic foreman during swing and night shifts.

At SUNY Buffalo, I had returned to school to study literature, an ex-lawyer in love with Shakespeare and Sidney, who had come that summer to Manhattan to brush up on Latin and run away from the man I left in Buffalo, the man who came with me from Berkeley. He had sacrificed California to my stubborn pursuit of English, and followed me, after, by some strange but telling convergence of 1985 events, I had in the matter of six months announced to my family that I was part of another family (the gay one), left my sputtering law practice, applied to PhD programs, and packed up my Honda Civic to shuffle off to Buffalo, an improbable move from America's most intriguing and queer city to the abandoned bricks of the Rust Belt. Leaving law and family behind, I had come out at last.

Gil and I, both in our 30s somewhere, were hooked by the lure of our limbs. He was intrigued by his white American in running shoes and my privileged study. I was fascinated by my love of Iberia and its colonies. Not that Brasileiros were Latinos. I learned that in a hurry. I learned how hard it was to say *não*.

That summer we met on his days off. He drove his Honda under the Holland Tunnel and parked it somewhere on the west side in Midtown. We walked to the Metropolitan Museum or the Whitney. We took the subway to Greenwich Village. We saw big movies on big screens—*Die Hard*—and saw art house films like *Pauline at the Beach* in Soho theaters. We ate John's pizza. Gil lay on his back stretched out on my sad single bed with his beautiful stomach muscles and his uncut penis as I on my side watched his body with an absorption both insatiable and fulfilled simultaneously. As if I'd reached the summit of a peak to find an alpine meadow in sunshine. I learned how to *falar* (and *fodar*) a little as I fell in love with his body and language.

But we were busy; we didn't have free time. I was putting in 12-hour days on grammar and vocabulary; he was rotating long shifts unloading polyurethane couches. He came from Vila Velha, north of Rio, wanted to be a dancer, went into the military as required, knew he was gay early, taught English in Rio, lived with his cousin on the hill that divides Copacabana and Ipanema until he decided to come to the other United States. I told him I dreamed of swimming in the bays of Brazil.

2
UPPER WEST SIDE

"I met someone. He's Brazilian."

"Wherever did you find the time, my boy?" Josh asked. He sat beside me on the couch outside the classrooms on the 17th floor of the Grace Building in Midtown across from Bryant Park. We were early for our morning lesson in demonstrative adjectives (*hic, haec, hoc*). Josh was the oldest of the twenty students at the Latin/Greek Institute—charming, brilliant, well-connected, arch, gay as New York. "*Ave*," he would greet us in the morning. We with our regular coffees and toasted bagels. He in pressed cuff khakis and the light starch of a button-down Brooks Brothers blue oxford, his penny-loafers shining with a glow that matched the polish of his mind, even at the ripe old age of 69—a number I only discovered later, after I received the nod to visit his Upper West Side flat, where his parents, German Jews, had cultivated the gargantuan genius of their physically diminutive child. He had published espionage novels under a pseudonym; had an MBA, JD, MSW, and PhD. He counseled AIDS patients in his latest incarnation as a social worker. Polymath, violinist, Jungian, historian, trustee of international foundations, this five-foot-six dapper peripatetic befriended me for some reason—boyish good looks, runner's body—his motivation escaped me, but I welcomed his attention.

For whatever reason, be it caritas or cupiditas, platonic or erotic trajectories—the two of us became fast friends, Jew and gentile, 60 something and 30 something, quick read and drudge, gay man and gay man. Josh queried me further about Gilberto as he prepared coffee for us in his meticulous little slip of a kitchen, pristine in its black and whites, a table for two at the window.

"Where did you meet this hot Brazilian?" he asked me, as he ground his beans for the French press.

"I was running in the park," I said. "A couple of Sundays ago."

"In The Ramble, I take it," Josh said.

"The Ramble?" I asked, unfamiliar with gay geography.

"My dear man, that wooded section of the Park is the most notorious pick-up spot for gay men in the country. The police have been pulling overexposed homosexuals out from behind those bushes since time immemorial."

"Maybe I read about it somewhere," I said, feeling stupid. Though sufficiently randy, I was on the periphery of the gay loop, an ingénue, only glancing at Damron Guides on occasion at Moe's on Telegraph Avenue. I had fooled around in Berkeley and a little in San Francisco before I moved to Buffalo with Jack, the lover I met at the White Horse in Oakland, but I was still filling out my gay card.

"So, you have fallen madly in love with a passionate Brazilian—in between ablatives, I take it. How perfectly romantic. If you don't mind my impertinence, would I be presumptuous to surmise that you secreted him into your dorm room for a tryst of some sort?"

"That's correct, counselor." We were both ex-lawyers, enjoyed our interrogations, though Josh's were much more frequent than mine—given his wit.

"Need I remind you, my dear man, that one out of every three men that come to The Ramble is now infected with the HIV virus. I assume that you have both been tested." My heart skipped a quick beat before I dismissed my interlocutor's warning. Surely Josh could not be suggesting that I had become so promiscuous as to expose myself in a South of Market bath house to the prodding of some popper-popping Castro clone.

"Yeah, well, Jack and I got tested after we got together, and then again recently we did."

"Thank goodness. Aaannd..."

"Gil says he did before he came to the U.S. We talked that through after our first *tête à tête*, as you might call it."

"My dear man, call it what you will. Call it your first fuck, for all I care. I couldn't be happier for you. I am curious primarily to make sure you avoid this scourge. I trust you are both using condoms, if I may continue my unseemly prying. Protection is essential these days. Need I tell you I'm counseling 15 dying men in a support group at St. John's right now, spending hours in the hospital. They're all dying of pneumonia, unless they get the drugs in time. Sometimes it's too late. K.S.—Kaposi's sarcoma, dementia. You wouldn't believe what is happening to these beautiful young men. They're skeletal. *The Times* just reported that there are almost 400,000 cases of AIDS in the state of New York, and most of them, I can assure you, are not intravenous drug users. Over a million people are infected in the United States. The devastation is real and, to be honest with you, heartbreaking. I just don't think I can lead another support group for a while after this one ends. I don't have the stamina. We're all scared to death right now —literally."

I was rather flabbergasted and moved, not by Josh's command of statistics, but by the compassion of his social work. He, a man I associated with string quartets at the Yale Club and editorials in the *Times Literary Supplement*, shared with me his voluntary care for the sick and dying, only blocks from his home.

"Well, Gil and I, thankfully, are being safe. We haven't even done anything that requires a condom at this point."

"Thank God. Just be careful, I beg you," he stated, using the heel of his hand to slide the plunger through the glass sleeve of his coffee press. Cups and saucers had been carefully placed at the petite two-top below the kitchen window.

3
KEARNY, NEW JERSEY

My summer of love ended. I moved back from Midtown Manhattan to Buffalo, back to my new place on the West Side of the Queen City now that I had officially separated from Jack. My new boxcar apartment in another burnished brick building featured a view of Lake Erie from the large kitchen where a blonde table and chairs became the meeting place for my intermittent social life. Furnished with garage sale bargains in Cheektowaga and West Seneca, the so-called snowbelt, my two-bedroom upstairs flat featured an Indian blue bathroom and an inoperative fireplace with a mantle where Mauricio, the orange Persian, perched in splendor over an oval hook rug. The floors were, disappointingly, a flecked tile from the Fifties, but the ceilings were coved and high. Given these ample if rough-edged digs, I had no excuse, except the pull of my Brazilian in New Jersey, not to tackle my hellish dissertation.

Back to my new solo life, back to my cubicle in the library, head buried in endless romances, as I explored the dialectic of love and desire, the longing subject in quest of fullness the other can never bring. In late September, I decided I had to see him, had to buy a plane ticket to Newark for a weekend with Gilberto in his new basement apartment—a converted garage, nicely carpeted, a raised bed with a curtained corner that served as bedroom. The fullness I felt with Gilberto in bed as I learned more Portuguese and we read Machado de Assis in some uncanny way put my theories into practice. Gil had given English lessons in Brazil, and I longed to learn his tongue, longed to say *tudo bem, tudo joia* with the carefree insouciance of a Carioca. We spent hours in that bed holding on to one another, watching people blow up on television, indulging our appetites for lovemaking and Gil's version of *feijoada*, which was really just rice, beans, and ground meat with a ton of salt and a small slice of carrot on the side. Maybe a tape of Caetano Veloso in the speakers with a dash of Sonia Braga.

Gil's low-ceilinged new apartment on the outskirts of Newark gave him an autonomy he relished, though the commute to work was longer, the rent higher than the boarding house in Ironbound. For us, Gil's garage apartment came to feel like a hideout during my visits, a refuge where we spent hours on his mattress falling in and out of sleep, in and out of kissing and watching and dreaming and ejaculating ecstatically on stomachs, on sheets, on thighs on t-shirts and towels. Sometimes I felt like I was suffocating under his insatiable need to touch, hug, and rub, lock lips and tie up limbs. I felt like I needed to come up for air, to rise, shower, drive to a park. Gilberto's body was a dream—lithe, muscular, brown, defined. His uncut penis was perfectly proportioned, perfectly shaped, beautifully erect. His smile after we made out told me he could never get enough of my worked-out body, my generic light-skinned American cut, my hairy chest.

One night my lover quietly raised the question of fucking. He wanted to know what I thought about it. I was happy the way things were. I was a cuddler, a hugger, a kisser—a white-bread vanilla gay adolescent pushing forty. Jack and I had fooled around with intercourse after a while together. It was fun but not essential. Gil mentioned it as something to try. We were watching a rerun of *Cheers* when the subject arose. I felt like John Lennon putting up with Yoko in an Amsterdam hotel. We had been in bed for what seemed like forever, rising to piss and eat ice cream, returning to television and more erections. I had turned into a cliché, embodied lyrics that had begun well before Ovid and now occupied songbooks of pop stars. I was emotional, blind, brainwashed, smitten and stricken. Attached. Unable to keep up with Gil's sexual energy, I was worn down after a weekend with him, even if we emerged now and again from our love cave to drive over to Manhattan and walk the park, go to a film, head to the Village.

I can't remember exactly when we began penetrating, when I became so overwhelmed by his insistence that I gave into his burrowing, totally open to his embraces. Before we began, I headed over to the health center in Buffalo for a blood draw and waited two weeks for the results, fearful for the first few days, as I thought back to what we or I had done over the past year. Most gay men still live from test to test, but back then before rapid HIV testing, I would sit in a room full of strangers waiting for a nurse to open a folder and announce the news, thinking about saliva and random semen on a hangnail. We were waiting for a vaccine, for a cure from the CDC or the NIH. We still are. We tried to have faith in Anthony Fauci; we still do. But none of this really fazed me once the negative result sent me on my way again, flying US Air to Newark, Gil there at the airport waiting for me, his beat-up Honda in short-term parking. He drove with Brazilian abandon to his den, where we found our way under the sheets pdq.

Forgotten were the Perry Ellises and the Rock Hudsons,

the rumored Nureyevs and the Arthur Ashes still alive, the
Liberaces and the Freddie Mercuries. These AIDS stories were
in the papers, on the news. They had nothing to do with us,
ensconced as we were beneath a ranch home in a Newark
suburb, a stack of two-and-a-half-star videos (*Rambo 3, The
Accused, Coming to America, Naked Gun*), maybe a novel or a
set of essays to grade in my composition class. By then—was it
November? —we were going at it both ways, holding our shots
until we cleared out. Never had bottoming felt that good.

Our bower of bliss was interrupted halfway through fall by
the appearance of Victor, Gil's ex-partner (business and love),
mentor, friend, erstwhile sugar daddy. Victor was shorter,
stockier, more European in his Borges-like looks. His deep-set
eyes dominated his stocky face. A wonderful man—urbane,
particular, disdainful of all things boorishly American. He
looked to France for culture, where he sold many of his painted
leather jackets for money good enough to buy his apartment in
the hills between the two most famous beaches in the world—
the immaculate Ipanema and the popular Copacabana. Victor
was more relaxed, more sardonic, more irreverent than
Gilberto. I liked having him around except when it was time for
us to make love behind the curtain. while V slept on the couch
and listened to my stifled groans and Gil's sighs.

Victor, in spite of our discreet squeaks of pleasure, must
have felt similarly ill at ease witnessing his ex-lover fuck around
with some enchanted gringo. I was getting in over my head, Vic
explained to me, one Saturday when Gil went to work. His ex,
he warned me, had spent many nights in the movie theatres
and fleabag hotels of Rio's Botafogo district, getting fucked by
sailors and salesmen. Victor told me about our mutual friend's
rather rapacious sexual appetite and the lengths to which he
had apparently gone to satiate that hunger. Was he trying to
make me suspicious, trying to drive a wedge between me and

15

Gil? Was he jealous? Or was he apprising me of another part of my beautiful Brazilian man, who could dance and sing and spread his legs? I listened as Victor described the pick-up culture in downtown Rio—late at night where guys would hang and hook up.

I listened but did not register. I didn't believe V was jealous. He was much older than Gilberto. They were cousins, business partners. Victor had nurtured or at least tempered Gil's coming out, though still not to his parents. Later, when Gil and I stayed at his parents' house in Vila and slept in the same room, there were never any questions about our "orientation," as queer as that might seem to our out-and-proud gay culture. Vic and Gil had been together for many years—maybe since Gil was 17 or 18, so at play in Victor's disclosure, to my mind, was more a caveat about his insatiability or his checkered past, about their open or forced open relationship, than the work of a green-eyed monster.

These words to the wise evaporated when Gilberto and I wrapped our arms around one another, when we were inside each other, when I began to cry as we spooned before nodding off. My attitude toward "homosexuality" in college and even later when I staved off a fascination with men boiled down to the question I once and a while asked my girlfriends: what do they do? The thing-in-the-hole mentality seemed clearly to mean one thing in one particular hole—the *membrum virile* in the *vagina*. Other holes and other things did not enter my "get laid" mentality. But soon the allure of male anatomy began to trump my rather missionary sensibilities, especially when I looked through magazines or watched Charlton Heston movies (O Chuck, if you only knew!). I digress to note my rather sexist approach to man-on-man play later, when I came out and fell in love with erections and pectorals. I sensed that the rectum for many gay males, except possibly those who honestly understood themselves as unabashed bottoms (more power to them), tended to represent the anatomical locus where gay sex faced gender norms in a dramatic way.

Once fucking became part of my queer experience, I had to face the categorical either/or of gay culture: top or bottom, man or woman, straight-gay or gay-gay—so that my sexism, to the degree it equated passive intercourse with the feminine, was strangely conflated with internalized homophobia. In this case, phobia seemed particularly apt. To relax enough to allow a guy to occupy my anal cavity was for me scary and emasculating; I felt allured and ashamed.

This stimulating hole had become for me a point of condensation for all the fears I had about my reception in the real world as a fag, as butt-fuck, sissy, asscrack, bent piece of shit. Only with Gil, was I able (a little) to give up all my rectal-phobia that accompanied my sexuality. To this day, I hook in as Versatile in part because Gil— "taught" might not be the right word, nor "forced,"—wore me down into discovering not that the rectum was a grave as Leo Bersani argued in his famous essay, but that the anus, should one be able to relax the sphincter (an art in itself), was a kind of paradise in spite of the end of Dante's *Inferno*. Anyway, like so many other anatomical areas—like nipples and tongues and eyes—the rectum turned out to be another erotogenic zone. Of course, I was conflicted about entering and being entered, squeamish about a cavity that serves most centrally as an evacuation passage, but the point here was that Gilberto fucked me a lot; he never came inside me but he fucked me a lot and I loved it and I usually ejaculated big time within a New Jersey minute of his gentle entrance.

Too much information? Is my reader a balls-out gender-fucking queer or some more sedate happily married, gay-friendly couple interested in the evolution of circuitous lives? It doesn't matter. The upshot of these intense weekends in Kearny, New Jersey, came with my rather impetuous decision to shuffle out of Buffalo again for a while, sublet, and move down to the Garden State and start a life with the new love of my life. Call it a whim, an impulse, something crasser in terms of pleasure if you wish, but blindly following my heart or head, my penis or the abhorrence of the vacuum of my solitude, at the end of that fall semester, I up and moved down to Northern Newark near the Orange Street stop of the old streetcar. Gil and I shacked up, as my late father would call it. From San Francisco to Buffalo to Newark—my itinerary in the late 80s mapped volumes, as it were, spoke rather obviously in support of the lyric that there was no valley low enough to keep me from getting to my Gil.

I walked four blocks to the old Northern Newark streetcar that took me down to Penn Station, under the Hudson up to 34th, where the sidewalks of New York led me to the dissertation slash research room at the New York Public Library near Times Square. The long commute afforded me enough time to read *Middlemarch* while bumping bodies and averted gazes. Gil and I had signed a month-to-month on a nice upstairs apartment. He went to work in Passaic and I to NYC, wearing kid gloves to check out first editions. If the truth be known I was just posing, trying to be cool. I loved the old library with its high ceilings and exhibits. I could have written my thesis anywhere, but the notion of ordering books from the closed stacks through the antiquated system of pneumatic tubes, the idea of being in New York sitting on those steps with the lions couchant, the idea of working out at 24 Hour Fitness, crowded and full of Italian men with soft skin, dark hair, and alarming chests. The allure of the vegan Zen restaurant where brown rice and tofu became sexy, those peanuts honeyed in the hot woks of the cart men with their tasteless pretzels—it all seemed so new and different for a man trying to be hip, trying to avoid the improbabilities of my affair.

Gil and I wintered over, playing house, fucking one another like bunnies, sitting at the counter of a local Greek restaurant in Kearny that exuded deep heterocentricity. We had no friends to speak of. Gil had his immigration lawyer who—with his influence—worked to procure him a green card. He was seeing a priest and being a good citizen. He patiently took shit from his foreman at Macy's. There was Josh of course and my buddies in Buffalo. I filled in Josh on my excitements and misgivings, on Gil's penchant for sitcoms and endless reclination, on his nascent suspiciousness. His inquiries into my movements in Manhattan, his heavily salted ground beef that spent too many days on the back burner. Josh, an infinitely compassionate man, was not about to inform me I was both in over my head and barking up the wrong tree, though he would never mix metaphors, and in fact would be loath to employ such bromides, especially ones pertaining to a natural world he might visit in a pit helmet but never integrate into his high-church English. Josh listened; we laughed. He did meet Gil; we did have an afternoon at Riverside Park or a tea somewhere near the Cathedral—St. John the Divine. (I vaguely recall a dense Linzer torte outside a cavernous café on Amsterdam Avenue.) Josh probably surmised that Gil and I had very little in common ultimately beyond the bedroom and learning language, but he was not about to confront me with that knowledge in any direct way. Not that I would have heeded him if he had.

4

JOG, MEMORY

This next section of my remembrance remained blank for a long time, a stretch of white space, testimonial to my suspicion about the accuracy of language to capture memory. I finally realized that words, however slippery, were all I had to recreate what happened, to fill in the stubborn blanks of my story.

I am not sure whether or not I even went to the New York Public Library that spring day in 1990—wildly bright in the afternoon, nimbus clouds floating over a true-blue sky. I know I ran in Branch Brook Park around four. Our local green space spread its long patchwork down the hill from our flat in Northern Newark—the park narrow in places, wider in others as it opened to gardens and baseball fields. Busy roads intersected sections of lawn. I wore blue shorts and a white t-shirt—my uniform for running—thick cotton sopped with sweat down my spine. The six-mile workout was usually stop-and-go because of boulevards I had to cross. I was a slow runner, steady, dogged, unhappy with a body I fought to maintain its semblance of definition sufficient to pass the gay buff test.

"The body is the temple of the soul," I remembered hearing from some handsome sports announcer in Oakland during the Berkeley days. I wanted to make my temple worth admiring by my soulmate Gil, I told my sweating self as I jogged uphill. Suddenly a competing notion came to my grad-student mind. Wasn't the soul the prison of the body, according to queer theorist Michel Foucault? His competing notion would stick with me for longer than I imagined that day, that afternoon, in the sharp, clear, windswept air of an overcrowded eastern seaboard suburb, my body occupied by a foreigner.

In short, I wanted to get in shape, and aerobic exercise served as the best way to ward off flab while at the same time allowing me to ingest large quantities of Häagen Dazs ice cream. Running brought me outside as well, and the outside had always served as a remedy to my malaise of fear and shrinking. That low-grade dissatisfaction with undetectable progress towards fame, completion, orgasm, happiness, tenure. Hence the huffing and puffing across sidewalks, dirt paths, lawns, pounding pavement, overcoming that initial nausea and inertia and falling into some semblance of stride, encouraged by the day's gusty perfection—seventy degrees, fresh between fronts, pine boughs bowing to Boreas, as Jack in the Box wrappers tumbled down roads with the randomness of a lottery called life.

I can only guess with retrospective imprecision which mental channels needed to be turned down or switched off that day: a persistent misgiving about my future compatibility with a high-strung Brazilian man whose intensity was simultaneously compelling and exhausting; the usual perseveration over the unfinished dissertation. Was I in the library for research or was I just finding an excuse to shack up with Gilberto and get the hell out of Buffalo? In short, I was bucking headwinds—the entire impracticality and distractedness of my current trajectory and local habitation in the bowels of Newark's North Ward. Where was I and how did I get there? These the preoccupations mitigated if not allayed by the current demands of breathing, I hoofed up a hill to the stretching place, a bench inside the caged bullpen of a baseball diamond where, as habit would have it, I stretched hamstrings and calves before heading out to the field to lie prone on the grass in corpse pose—*savasana*—as the yoga people call it.

At last, I wiped my brow with the front of my T, took a swig of water from a dribbling fountain, and found my way out to left field, where the grass, newly mowed, spread like a soft carpet under frigate clouds that floated across the sky—a regatta of white masts before my out-stretched arms. What a day, what a sky, what a memory—I exclaimed to myself. An inner trigger recalled thick towels on the pier at Lake Tahoe, summers in August, freckle-faced and nose peeling—those days of mountain sun in the Sierras, drying off from a cold swim, shy with my paperback or comic book, alone with Lucky, our German Shepherd mix who was my best and only friend. The sky evoked granite boulders of the lake I loved more than any place in the world. On my back, I looked up, remembering.

Those minutes were an endorphic interlude between sit-ups and stretches on the empty field, minutes that conjured images of a cold, clear lake, a summer sun warm when clouds stopped teasing. In spite of the complications of my career shift at 35 years of age, in spite of my improbable but deeply tangible love affair with Gilberto—I felt my body aching for the West, for the laconic nonchalance of California. Yet in the abeyance of these longings, I also felt a certain contentment with *being there*—even if there was of all fucking places–New Jersey. I felt myself indulge in a Ram Dass moment of (dare I use the word) "happiness" for fear of some jinx, felt at that moment fitted to a

time and place, tired and sore and relaxed and relieved by
aerobic exercise and its perspective.

Maybe I pulled a few strands of grass and threw them in
the air, maybe I rolled over into a child's pose, circled my shoulders or rolled my neck. I rose finally from the presence of that
anatomical chapel that reeked of damp sweat and walked
finally a few blocks to the stairs of our house, a two-story row
home hardly twenty feet from the almost identical structure
beside it. Stairs led up to the front door that opened on to a
hallway, where a steep flight toward our second story flat
ascended in angular darkness to the front door, opened with a
key secured in the hidden pocket of my nylon running shorts.

I entered the living room. The beige wall-to-wall carpet,
the amulet hung on the door frame to ward off the residue of
domestic turmoil from previous tenants, the futon loveseat
diminutive in the corner beside a table for the television. To my
surprise, the spaciousness of this unlived-in living room did not
on this weekday afternoon lie in the semi-darkness of its usual
somber disuse in spite of its newness—its recent paint job, its
clean carpet. The room was alive with light and noise, TV
tuned loudly to *The Golden Girls*. Shows like *Cheers* and *Sein-
feld* gave Gilberto an education in Americana—its language, its
humor, its foibles, its *All in the Family* ridiculous bigotries.
These shows gave him vocabulary and distracted him from
what must have been the unnerving anxieties of being a
Brazilian in Newark, New Jersey. Gil, an immigrant in a
country whose ideological creed on the Statue of Liberty
masked the deep xenophobia of second-generation Germans
and Cubans who wanted walls across our borders to keep "ille-
gals" at bay.

I was pleased but startled to find Gil on the carpet
watching television at 5 in the afternoon.

"Hey," I said, closing the door. "What are you doing here?"

23

He didn't turn down the television; he didn't take his eyes off the screen.

"*Oi*," he said, looking up at me, nervously, Gilberto with his striking beaked profile, his dark eyes the color of an eddy in a mountain river.

"Did you get off work?" I asked, coming further into the room, standing before him in my t-shirt, colorless where sweat drenched the whiteness. "What a great day," I told him. "So sunny, incredibly clear."

He raised himself up and sat cross-legged on the carpet. He was deeply flexible. "I had to meet with the priest who wrote a letter for the green card."

"Did your application come through?" I asked. He had taken the citizenship test, been to the immigration lawyer, filled out the paperwork, received the medical exam.

We were waiting to hear about approval of his permanent residence status. He had contacted a priest, who wrote him a letter of recommendation. We were both waiting in anticipation, hoping the papers would come through, since the lawyer had the "inside track" with her contacts at the INS.

I don't know exactly what happened next. That's why I have hesitated to write. I've blocked it. I'm not sure why such a momentous moment should require fabrication to recreate—why memory should fail. I know the TV was on; I know Gil did not get up from his cross-legged position on the rug. I stood near the door while he remained seated, half looking at the screen as he spoke. Camera cuts of the sitcom distracted our words. I could tell he was angry, somehow belligerent, or skeptical about what he had to tell me. He somehow felt (I am guessing) he had been dealt a bad hand by fate, felt the process had betrayed him. The fault, if there was a fault, resided not in himself or me but in those who informed him his application was denied. The world had conspired to kill his joy.

"I can't stay in this stupid country," he said, staring at Bea Arthur and Betty White in their Miami living room. "I can't get the green card."

"Why?" I asked, more solicitous now, more puzzled, sympathetic. "What happened?" I asked, realizing intuitively that his fixation on the screen, his failure to make eye contact, was sending me a serious message, through paradoxically distancing—the isolation that shame brings to us all.

"The test," he said. "The blood test. They say I have it." He did not mention any acronym; he didn't have to. My heart—like a rubber ball pushed down underwater in a pool and then released—suddenly thumped against my chest. In a flash of strange disjunction, danger and distress, a moment of pure fear, flushness, a moment of turning around and pacing. A moment of pure self-preservation glimmered in hope across my untested self. Maybe I don't, was all I thought. Maybe I would get lucky. Only the thumping was indisputably attestable, that and the afternoon slant light that angled in from a jog's memory, that and the laughing *Golden Girls*, Gil was angry. He fidgeted, tapped his feet, refused to look at me. Love had revealed itself as deadly.

"But I thought you were tested before in Brazil," I protested. "I thought you were negative."

"Their test shows I have this thing," he said. "I cannot stay here. I have to go home." He was more indignant than sad. I stood stunned, unable to collapse onto the rug and hug him. Unable to do anything but pace, analyze, ask questions, begin my retreat into self-absorption.

"How can you be positive?" I asked. "You told me you were negative when you came to New York, and I was tested before I met you. There has to be some mistake." Gilberto looked at me blankly, then returned to the television show, unwilling to engage. Both of us in the living room reacted to the news of his diagnosis with the most callous mundanity imaginable. Gil fixated on the plot of his re-run. I stood standing, looking down and over toward him, beginning to sink under the weight of his disclosure. I leaned against the wall, turned and faced it, pressed my forehead against the newly painted sheetrock. I looked around the room, searched for some way to undo our dialogue. Some way to negate chronology, to undermine the findings of a microscope.

"I will have to get tested," I said to him finally, after a moment of silence in the amber dusk, its rays diffusing the sharpness of the Mitsubishi picture. I paced over the carpet, flashed on Victor's warning months ago when we talked in the Kearny basement apartment about Gil's history, about his naiveté, about his voracious need for dick, brilliant in its Brazilian freedom, but unconcerned about the implications of its exuberance, a kind of fey willfulness about the primacy of pleasure. Surely, though, Victor's admonishment and my sudden recall were nothing but the rearing of the ugly of head of American Puritanism. Gilberto loved me; he would never intentionally hide the truth. He would never willingly put my life in danger in order to pursue our passion.

Perhaps these ruminations, so consuming in the aftermath, did not come to me at that moment but only later—all at once on a subway or in reflection after my trip across the Hudson to get tested. I don't know. What I know is that I felt a jolt, a quake, to my existence. I felt a sudden crack in the fictional stability of my secure, smug white American male world. Not so much shaken but warped, terrified by the prospect of my decease. The Fool in the Tarot. Me—leaving San Francisco and the law office—to start a new career and finally be with a guy. To pursue my desire at last only to be stymied by the prospect of a fatal disease. My new start a dead end.

"We have to get you to a doctor," I said. "We have to find

out what your status is for sure. We have to find out." I moved automatically into caretaking mode, emotionless and unexpressive. I had to assume a virtue even if I had it not. I had to comfort my lover. He was in another hemisphere, newly diagnosed, an illegal immigrant, a gay man in his thirties. He needed me, and my own hurt for now would be suppressed by losing myself in him. Gilberto would become my focus. My *Golden Boy* for now.

5

SNAPSHOT—1990

The timeline: In 1990, 8 to 10 million people worldwide were estimated to be living with HIV, the incurable retrovirus that attacked the immune system and led to fatality from AIDS. Between 500,000 and a million had died from AIDS since the counting began in the 1980s—18,447 in the United States, most of them gay men, including in this year Halston the designer and Keith Haring pop artist. In this year Ryan White, the 18-year-old hemophiliac, died, and Congress named their AIDS bill after the young heterosexual. In San Francisco, activists at the International AIDS Conference protested the government's immigration ban on people with HIV. The FDA approved AZT, a drug for treatment of the disease, and the American with Disabilities Act outlawed discrimination against the disabled, including those disabled by AIDS.[1]

6

UPPER EAST SIDE

That spring of 1990 found me on the Upper East Side in the waiting room of a daylight brownstone, anxious to see the doctor in his starched white coat—sterile and polite. How thick the black paint on the metal fence above a clipped privet hedge at the office entrance, how empty the waiting room and yet how perfect the testing recommendation from my friend Joshua, who counseled men dying in the anterooms of St. John's. I was hoping against hope I must have known when I rolled up my sleeve.

Gil and I never did come inside each other even if we didn't use condoms. Maybe pre-cum was not as infectious. Was that possible? Didn't Gil tell me in Sbarro's while we ate slices of pepperoni the summer we met; didn't he tell me in broken English, tell me he was safe? He said he had been tested in Rio, I remembered distinctly. He told me he had been tested before coming to the US, told me he was negative. *He told me*—the three words repeated in my head like scratched vinyl. I knew in that sterile office, even as my blood leaked into the test tube, that I would live forever with the conviction that it was Gil's fault. He was the cause of my imprisonment with the deadly virus that would hound me for so many years. My new long-time companion.

I sat in a daylight doctor's office only a block or two from Central Park, the very place I had met the wonderful guy who harbored a deadly virus unwittingly or not, a lover who I was destined to blame as the destroyer of my life, wiping my hands of complicity. I had to face the reality that even if the dropping-like-flies 80s had come to a close, I would probably still join the unable-to-survive days of Perry Ellis and Arthur Ashe, those pre-*Philadelphia* days when people were expiring left and right, when support groups were standing room only, the ones peopled with men enduring neck goiters and buffalo humps and skeletal torsos and cytomegalovirus, blindness and dementia. I was scared.

Back to the waiting room of a daylight brownstone only blocks from the Metropolitan Museum of Art, me nervous to see the doctor who—with his syringe and gray hair, his immaculate manners, the reserve of his location, his Henry-James formality—noticed how much sweat I emitted. How anxious I was even to ask for the blood to be assayed, how my tacit admission of sodomy somehow put me on that map of opprobrium.

The doctor tried to calm me down. He told me to wait a week or two for the results, told me to be patient, but not in any dogmatic way. He was diplomatic and annoyed that his friend Josh had sent me to him, annoyed that this mixed-up Buffalo scholar from California, this ungrown-up, shy, arrogant, frightened man should be there sweating on his spotless and meticulous porcelain table.

7

CHELSEA

After my HIV test, a fait accompli, I put my head down and continued to work. I dragged Gilberto to a doctor in the Village who drew blood and scarred his inner arm to see how quickly he would heal. Gil was afraid of being deported. We both were not talking about the future.

His T cell (CD4) count was down around 200 (close to an AIDS diagnosis). Anxious and shocked, we sat beside each other on the plastic seats of the PATH from Newark to Manhattan, stared at the silver hand rails, scarves tied beneath the chins of clutch-pursed grandmothers. We stared at the self-conscious boys in their untied big shoes and baggy hoodies. We watched overcoats, bumped shoulders as we rocked across the toxic Jersey shore, full of reeds and ducks destined for cancerous ends. There was nothing to say. We couldn't stop taking care of one another—at least not for now, even if I was already feeling I had to find a way out.

Was it after walking home from the Bloomfield stop on the old Newark railway car that the phone call came in from my white-coat physician late in the day, Gil at work? Was it June

1990 when I found myself—frightened, spent, and shocked, sitting before a Jungian on the Upper West Side—the therapist Josh arranged for me to see after I told him I was positive? Only Josh, Victor, and Gil knew at that point. I had no one else to tell. No one I trusted. In an office like a living room with lots of symbolic pictures, a large round man listened to my fear and shame. He was gentle and detached like the doctor who gave me the news.

My desperation was quiet, unremarkable, my anger submerged. I started doing all the right things—the support groups, the Coenzyme Q. I avoided grapefruit juice. I contemplated wheat grass and meditation. I attended meetings at the Gay Men's Health Crisis in Chelsea. I had been told I might live to see 2000—if I took care of myself. My panic was catatonic, zombiesque, seething. I became, almost automatically, the Kinks' well-respected man, "doing the best things so conservatively." But out of my eyes came the bitter stare, cursing some improbable and imaginary "fate." The glassy verge of desperation, rage, and panic held back by the white dam of my eyes.

Both Gil and I were determined to eschew the newly approved but notorious drug AZT, with its body-destroying side effects. Both of us were unwilling to consider Interferon or anything else Pfizer was touting in the news. I read whatever I could find in the *Gay City News*, from materials available at the GMHC in the West Village, the old brownstone where freaked-out queers congregated. During one meeting, at least a hundred guys packed into an upstairs room to hear experts talk about helper cells, pneumonia tests, about cat feces and toxoplasmosis, about saliva and swollen nodes. Among hoodies and thin men wrapped in big coats, I heard about Reagan's callousness, about herpes and shingles, sex and suicide. About the dark days in the Village. I went to talks about unstudied retroviruses, viruses that attacked the very cells that fight off viruses, breaking down the body's defenses, leaving me open to 23 opportunistic infections, vulnerable to flus and bugs that hid in crab and raw egg, in other human bodies. I went to doctors, took incomprehensible notes, tried to find out all I could, tried to be rational and level-headed. I suppressed the shame and fear and blame and head-banging that seethed beneath my shock and disbelief at the pronouncement of my death sentence.

8

THE RED SEA

For decades, AIDS has been one of the leading causes of death in the world.[1] Replication of the human immune-deficiency virus (HIV) leads to the set of opportunistic infections that comprise the acquired immunodeficiency syndrome (AIDS).

HIV is a retrovirus. Viruses like influenza are parasites that cannot live by themselves but must occupy other cells to replicate and survive. By contrast, a retrovirus is made up of RNA rather than DNA (deoxyribonucleic acid). DNA is the protein-based material that contains the blueprint or guidelines that allow an organism to function, while RNA (ribonucleic acid) is a single stranded protein that carries out the DNA's instructions, making sure the material of cells produces blue instead of brown eyes. Retroviruses have the disadvantage of having to turn themselves into DNA within the host cell they attack before they can replicate.

HIV is an RNA-based retro-parasite virus that attacks the cells in the body that fight off pathogens like viruses, destroying those CD4 white blood cells that protect immune function.

HIV is inimitably a virus that attacks the virus fighters of the human body; it is in that sense a kind of meta-virus. The killing effect leaves the body defenseless to the syndrome of diseases like pneumocystis and toxoplasmosis and dementia that make up the opportunistic infections we know as AIDS.

The HIV virus is only detectable through an electronic microscope because it is 100-150 billionth of a meter in size, 4 millionth of an inch, or $1/70^{th}$ the size of a CD4 white blood cell. It is super small and contains a viral core or envelope which harbors a bullet-shaped capsule comprised of two RNA strands and the enzymes or proteins needed for replication once the HIV virus attaches and fuses with the larger CD4 cell.

The biology of HIV is complicated and riddled with jargon, specialized language that requires training to understand. This complexity in itself is highly symbolic of the formidable challenge that the virus has presented to the world on fronts as varied as economic, social, political, sexual, geographic, and religious. Etymologically, the HIV complex has or comes with (com) many threads (plex).[2]

These tangles are illustrated by the three enzymes (molecules that accelerate chemical reactions) HIV needs to complete its replication: 1) transcriptase, 2) integrase and 3) protease. Drugs that attack the virus called fusion or entry inhibitors like Fuseon do the work of preventing the HIV virus from attaching to the receptors that protrude like ship-rope rungs from the CD4 cells. Other drugs attack the virus after it enters the host cell and is in the process of trying to zip its RNA into the DNA of a host CD4 cell with the help of transcriptase, which is a kind of zipper end where strands of the HIV RNA and the CD4 DNA can dock and merge. So NNRTI and NRTI drugs (non-nucleoside and nucleoside reverse transcriptase inhibitors) do the work of either making the zipper dock difficult to fit or replicating a whole bunch of zipper docks to slow and confuse the RNA to DNA process. AZT (azidothymidine), which is also known by the generic name Zidovudine and the brand name Retrovir, is a nucleoside analog reverse transcriptase inhibitor (NRTI) of historic importance for its overdosage in the early stages of the pandemic. It is now part of certain highly active antiretroviral therapy (HAART) or cocktail which in various formulas combines different drugs to limit replication of a virus that multiplies in the millions within the body. These drugs not only have brand and generic names, but they also have abbreviations and chemical names. Even the therapies are complex in their identification.

Protease inhibitors are another form of antiretroviral therapy that prevent the scissoring process whereby the new strands of the virus created in the host cell must link together in order to form another bullet capsule on its way to other CD4 cells. Atazanavir, for example, also known as Reyataz, is a protease inhibitor approved by the FDA in 2003 and marketed by Bristol Myers. As part of a once-a-day HAART regimen, patients combine Reyataz with Epzicom, which is an NRTI (not a protease inhibitor but a reverse transcriptase inhibitor).

The test for HIV detects antibodies in fluids or the bloodstream. Infectious viruses display proteins called antigens and the immune system produces immunoglobulin, Y-shaped proteins which identify and neutralize the virus. 97% percent of hosts display antibodies within three months of contraction of the virus. Rapid testing now takes less than 30 minutes, though in 1990 the blood test could take up to two weeks for results.

Once I tested positive in 1990, the doctors drew more and more blood. Having HIV drains the system of a supply of blood, but the red stuff replenishes itself quickly, even though the process is positively vampiric. My soul is the color of red meat, sometimes darker, sometimes the color of a room inside of a whorehouse. I prostitute my Red Sea to the electron microscopes in distant cities that charge by the minute and support lab technicians and doctors who drive SUVs and take their children to Maui for 10-day vacations. Microscopes open up a world of life within the blood lake. They count the number of clusters of differentiation 4 (CD4) cells that exist in a milliliter of my blood, which is only a small part of the finger-like tube with the colored tab the lab tech extracts through a needle in the crux of my needle-marred arm.

CD4 is a glycoprotein that attaches to the surface of T helper cells, monocytes, macrophages, and other dendritic cells. The CD4s are messengers that tell CD8 cells to kill pathogens like viruses and bacteria in the body. Individuals usually have between 500 and 1200 of these proteins in a slice of blood on a glass plate under a microscope. My count hovered around 400 to 600. If below 500 and positive, I became immune-compromised. If less than 200, I would get an AIDS diagnosis, a further stigma that opens up a world of disability, susceptibility, hatred, and latex.

The CD4 count was the signature indication of one's health in the HIV circle for any number of years. I waited a couple of weeks to discover how long I would live, and the numbers brought stress, which ironically compromised the immune system. So the circle was vicious, but we had to find out, we had to get help. We had to get treated for shingles and herpes and mouth sores and lymphoma and ...

The viral load came in the 2000s, a new test that actually measured the number of copies of HIV virus in a milliliter of blood. As the science and pharmaceuticals progressed, a new hierarchy emerged. For many years the distinction between HIV positive people and people with AIDS (PWAs) created striation; now the HIV population was divided between detectables and undetectables. A patient with less than 50 copies of the HIV virus in a milliliter a blood was designated as undetectable and considered unable to transmit the virus. (Undetectable equals Untransmittable or U=U).[3] HIV was still there, still replicating, still in the semen and the spinal fluid and the lymph nodes, but somehow being limited by the actions of these inhibitors. And the hierarchy of stigma continued: 1) AIDS (high viral load, low CD4), 2) HIV Positive (CD4 above 250, detectable load, 3) Positive Undetectable. Dividing practices lead to shunning, while DDF (drug and disease free) gays or those that test negative continued to stigmatize the HIV population at all levels.

Many sexually active men and women or those in a partnership with an HIV positive person, currently take PrEP (pre-exposure prophylaxis), most commonly a drug called Truvada which combines two NRTIs (tenofovir disproxil [aka Viread] and emtricitabine), a blue hot-dog bun that individuals swallow daily to prevent transmission when barebacking (having unprotected anal or vaginal intercourse).

Now in the third decade of the second millennium, one of the new inhibitors that doctors prescribe often is called Triumeq. It combines Epzicom with an integrase inhibitor. Integrase inhibitors (dolutegravir) prevent the RNA strand from merging into the DNA of the host cell. This regimen is one pill once a day.

On the horizon is gene therapy. What is it? And who is this Berlin Patient? Timothy Ray Brown, recently deceased, received a blood stem-cell transplant in 2007 and the donor had in her or his bloodstream a CCR5-delta 32 mutation, a mutation in the t-cell proteins which prevented HIV from attaching to and invading CD4 receptors. Brown was cured of HIV by virtue of the transplant. Doctors have genetically engineered, or reproduced in the laboratory, cells with the CCR5 mutation and infused them into patients' blood streams. Genes have memory and can replicate sua sponte in the system, so the infusion of genetically modified blood cells may allow the body to create its own "medicine" of resistance, its own supply of CCR5, thereby warding off the replication of HIV without the need to constantly swallow costly pills. Some of these gene therapies include cells that instruct the body to produce antibodies to HIV, thus establishing a kind of killing effect. The procedures are not on the market and cost 100,000 dollars per patient. Cost, science, tests, trials and the advancement of death and disease continue to complicate research.

After almost 40 years of the AIDS pandemic, there is no cure or vaccine.

9
PHILADELPHIA

Hindsight can be 20-20. Sometimes the truth about the past can only be understood through the lens of the future, thus complicating the accuracy of memory. Events as initially remembered do not reflect the actuality of what transpired. Like HIV, the memoir complex has its own intricate weave.

Well before the fateful afternoon I found Gil watching *The Golden Girls*, before either of us knew of our *ménage* with the virus, I suddenly came down with a virulent flu. I remembered sheets drenched with sweat, developing a rash on my scalp, losing weight day after day. I thought I had a bad flu and gave myself the requisite two weeks to get over it. Lots of blue Gatorade. Chicken soups. Gil slept in the living room, nervous.

I struggled to get better, had a planned flight to Buffalo to meet my thesis advisor and then a trip to Philadelphia to visit a classmate. I managed, still feeling weak, to board US Air. My friend Thomas found a room in a dorm for me to stay in, found me a mattress on the floor, where I could sweat and run to the bathroom to explode into the toilet. Twelve hours in bed night after night; and the embarrassment of being a sick guest. "You don't look well," my advisor told me when I went to his office. I said, "yeah, I'm getting over a flu bug." I had lost 15 pounds, was pale, and struggled to keep it together. But I didn't think I was dying; I just thought I was sick, sick, bad flu sick. I just kept going, kept staying afloat.

Little did I know that all the malfunctioning body parts that left Prior in *Angels in America* vomiting and shitting in his pants, that left the 25-year-old boys on Fire Island and Castro Street in their beds wasting away, all of the slow horrible breakdowns of flesh and blood were being previewed in my body—unbeknown to my running, working out, jock self. I fought the bug off somehow, apologized for soiling the guy's sheets in the dorm room as I looked down the long dark corridor and waited for my friend Tom to pick me up and drive me to the airport.

An acute or primary HIV reaction takes place usually two to four weeks after infection with the virus. Not everyone suffers from it, only about half of the people who convert. My symptoms were severe: headache, nausea, vomiting, lymph node swelling, night sweats, fever, fatigue. My body was being inundated with the replicating virus, and my white blood cells had not yet recognized their need to fight off the onslaught. I might not have even tested positive for the virus during this period because there were no detectable antibodies measurable yet. If a viral load assay were taken, which rarely occurred—since few knew if they had HIV at this point—the load would be extremely high. Permanent immune damage was taking place during this supposedly bad flu: up to 60% of my infection-fighting CD4 cells could have been wiped out. My gut lining was particularly compromised because the virus replicated most quickly in the gastrointestinal area. Only when antiretrovirals were swallowed did the damage to the immune system get impeded.

I went from Buffalo to Philadelphia to visit Linda, feeling weak but better. I was in a delirious daze of fatigue much of the time. We went to the Philadelphia Museum of Art and The Barnes. Linda had finished her dissertation and was adjuncting at Temple University. Many of my colleagues had spent six years studying and writing about Melville or Hawthorne, only to face the reality that Americans do not value letters, that supply and demand made the pursuit of what they loved unfeasible. They were forced to become lawyers or copywriters or editors or part-timers. Professor Staff we call people like Linda, the exploited class of part-timers. I feared my career change might face the same fate.

I came back from the town whose name would later grace a film dedicated to the disease I didn't know I had. Came back to worried Gil in Newark and gradually regained my strength. I returned to my routine, my commute, my rice and beans with the magic man whom I clung to night after night, amazed at my good fortune to be in touch with a soul who—in spite of all improbabilities of temperament—felt like the perfect fit.

10

ILHA GRANDE

D issociative amnesia accompanies traumatic events. It leads to selective psychogenic recall. It becomes difficult for the rememberer to chronologize. Story dissolves into a patchwork of flashbacks: the long, strange trip out the 1 Broadway train Gil and I took through the Bronx to the Cloisters, our walks through garish lights of Times Square to see *Lethal Weapon* 2, our meandering through Central Park, our quick-paced steps toward museum or subway. The tap of Gil's foot and the fraying of his friendship bracelet, a string around his olive wrist.

Wary of the disarray and inefficacy of western medicine, Gil and I finally decided I should go to Rio to visit a witch doctor in Ilha Grande across the bay from Botafogo, where Victor, having returned to Brazil, would take me to visit the famous healer. Gil had to stay in New Jersey to work. I would acquire the natural remedies that would keep us alive. I booked a flight on United from Newark with the HSBC credit card that kept us afloat.

Mornings later on the early ferry across the bay beside Rio,

Victor and I watched the misty sea rise through an indistinct haze. He had heard of the famed mother healer for years, heard of the pilgrimages of the sick to her humble house on the sand isle off the coast. Looking out over calm and glassy waters, we leaned over the ship rail, bundled up in our jackets, finally landing at the rural pier to inquire where the home of the famous *avó* was. We walked with others, as if in *Red Desert*, out the dirt road toward the white single-story house, a couple of kilometers until we spotted a line outside a home—painted somehow a dirty tinge that seemed almost blue, as if the color of the kitchen glowed from inside. The *fila* consisted of more than 20 people, most women, some with children, all come to find the cure for whatever ailed them—in my case herbs I hoped would, in our desperation, obviate the need to line the pockets of Glaxo-Wellcome and its 3000 dollar a month regimen of AZT—that old cancer drug—overprescribed and almost more toxic than the virus itself—dusted off and thrust in the faces of frantic gay men.

For better or worse, I could not count myself among those out and prouders who had lived it up in the Castro at the baths and bars. I was too shy to go to a bathhouse in the 1980s, before moving to Buffalo, too closeted. I had gone to the White Horse back in the Oakland days. I'd made one-night stands with priests and clarinetists and biologists. Had picked nits off my body, ventured across the bay to The Stud south of Market. I had fought off guys who wanted to fuck me, gotten blowjobs from men I met on the beach in Marin. So there were hook-ups, but I couldn't count myself among the Village People, the cool Fire Island queers who Speedo-ed on rooftops and discoed all night, who fucked in the rhododendrons. I wished I could recount being in those pleasure trenches. I might be dead if I could.

Instead, this parvenu, this man who had just contracted the

deadly virus from the love of his life, stood on an abandoned beach north of Rio, in a long line waiting on a secret cure. What was I thinking? What motions was I going through with my Brazilian cohorts, anxious and impulsive with despair? In line where I spent an hour or two, though they let me through quickly when they figured out how far I'd come. Victor and I outside, and then in the doorway, then in the hall, and then arriving in her blue kitchen, the woman in a chair, a housewife like any other, overweight and long haired in a print dress. Victor told about her SIDA in Portuguese as I listened, told her about my new diagnosis, about my need for help.

She didn't react, implacable as she heard of my journey. She looked around the wooden-floored kitchen and told one of her runners to go to the refrigerator for two large plastic coke bottles of liquid. Another came from the backyard with a plastic bag full of what seemed like dried chard or some long-stemmed plant or flower. Inside were printed directions that explained how to make tea from the leaves, how to drink a spoonful of the liquid for the rest of your life. The entire inter-view took less than five minutes as I stood in the crowded paint-chipped kitchen and remained stoic in the face of my anticli-mactic journey, half in love with the absurdity of my gullibility. To think that this grandmother held the key to an HIV cure. My second-guessing was drowned out by my need to do some-thing, to find hope somewhere.

We were asked to leave donations with a woman at the door. The whole encounter was ironically pro forma, so matter of fact, after all the buildup. The crowded kitchen, the nonde-script healer at her kitchen table with her gray hair in a bun looking up as we squeezed through the doorway into the over-cast morning, me with my *grande* plastic pop bottles full of brown liquid and my bag of brown leaves and stems. Me with hope under my arm. Back we went to Victor's apartment on the hill between Copa and Ipa below the favelas, back to the red bananas and the voice of Caetano Veloso.

I returned days later with the witch's brew—a shopping bag full of unnamable herbs that I carried through customs in Newark. The agent shook his head in disbelief as I laid my cache out on a table and told him it was medicine for a sick friend. The man in uniform was nondescript, pudgy and sorrowful. He seemed sad to see the anxious folly writ large on my burning cheeks as I waited to be detained, waited to have the agricultural products confiscated, waited to have some immigration officer ask me about AIDS. He waived me through customs with a sigh that must have witnessed the desperation of other sick men in the prime of life.

11

RELATIONSHIT

Both Gilberto and I probably wondered how long the domestic bliss of a Brazilian dock loader and a Californian PhD student could continue. I can't remember how our separation unfolded exactly, after a weekend in Cape May—Gil on the rollercoaster, me scared of it. After our return to the upstairs of that cursed flat with its white light and tiny bedroom, we fell into bed and held on to one another. Gil's numbers were not good. His T-Cells hovered in the 200s, but he showed no signs of illness. He could stay in the U.S., but there was no future. He had to go home unless we managed somehow to stay together, unless he moved to Buffalo with me and continued to hang out on the downlow, unless I moved to Brazil and taught English. He hated this country now and wanted to go back to Rio, but he didn't want to break up.

I wasn't sure I could trust Gil anymore. No matter how innocent his mistake. The man whom I threw away my life in Buffalo for, the man whose body was unfathomably beautiful, whose flightiness was grounded in a rough upbringing, who was smart and fun—whom I don't know, who, whom, whose.

Gil was my flight to Passionland. We would try to stay together, but I knew at least I had to go back to Buffalo. I was ABD; I had to finish my dissertation on Love and Desire in Renaissance Romance. I had to get on with my life—had to stay alive to see the millennium. Face the battle between perseverance and despair—Irish gloom and pick-and-shovel stick-to-itiveness. There was my dad in me that kept me going—even if toward some cliff.

We continued our routine, me with my long commute, he with his swing shift in the middle of Nowhere, New Jersey. Carrots and lettuce, rice and beans at night filled our plates when we had time together on the weekends. The cliff got closer as the days moved on. I finally announced that I had to go back in the fall. I was teaching my composition class; I had to finish my thesis. I never invited Gil back. I just expected that we would hang on long distance for a while, that he could come visit, that I could come to Newark on occasion. I felt callous, self-centered. I was balling and bailing, but I was also pissed— my anger, unexpressed, found its outlet in the cool distancing, a laid-back, let's-see-what-happens kind of insincerity. Did Gil understand my resentment at some level? He never articulated any guilt for the positive result. He blamed the testers; he blamed the system; he blamed the world. Finally, he would blame me for leaving him.

The breaking point came one muggy night in the hot summer. Gilberto faced an AIDS diagnosis, his mind unhinged thousands of miles from home as he coped with a shut-down lover, little money, no support, no doctor. A new stigma stuck to him, one much greater than the gay one he had lived with since grammar school. I had the privilege of money, family, friends in Buffalo and California. The privilege of citizenship, a degree coming, a profession to fall back on (lawyering). Even the power of our two egos, the power of our passion, was not sufficient to overcome the material circumstances that governed our consciousness. The stars of Marx's economics controlled our fates in ways that no amount of affection or intimacy could overcome. I was not willing to support Gil even more than I already did with flights and trips and rent money. Not that he ever asked for anything. He did not. But our lives were governed by my American Excess card, as we both knew.

At night we buried the coming decisions in hugs, kisses, movies, and sex. We ended up with barely a sheet over our bodies, the fan turned off in spite of the upstairs stuffiness, windows opened and the night heavy and sweet. It was two in the morning when I rose to pee and clomped through the kitchen over the cool linoleum. He stood at the window and stared into the back outdoor stairway we never used, into the moonlight or streetlight—the light that governs the eastern seaboard at all hours.

"*Como vai?*" I asked him after flushing. He in his cotton briefs, me naked standing in the kitchen. He had a natural, Potato-Eaters pout, a wry ironic wave to his mouth, an arrogant lift to his chin. All of these aspects were pronounced in the blue light.

"This shit," he said. "This bullshit," he repeated. "I cannot live with it. This SIDA. This relationship you call it." He spit out the word as if its Latinate syllabics buried any hint of love it might attempt to signify. "You call it love, this relationshit. You think I don't know you will leave me?"

He suddenly opened a long top drawer and pulled out a carving knife, ten inches long, wooden handled, pulled it out and brandished it at me. His eyes fumed with lucidity and ire, gleamed with awareness of my impending betrayal. He ran through the apartment waving his knife, shoving my books and papers off the table as he threatened me with shouts. His own complicity in this *desastre* was inconsequential, irrelevant.

"Leave now. Get out. Leave me," he yelled, throwing my notebooks at me. He darted from room to room, kicked chairs and lamps, wielded his weapon at the complacent gringo, whose tears and protestations of undying affection were nothing more than theatrics. The gringo was going to pack up his toys and go home once the going got tough. Gil said none of these things other than to scream at me to get out and stop playing games with him. Stop trying to pretend I was going to stay with him. Stop trying to seem nice when in fact I was abandoning him, quitting in the middle of the game of love. The culpa seemed squarely if unfairly to fall on me—the spoiled kid from the unreal suburbs of California.

That summer night in Northern Newark, in my fifth year of endless study on a new career that itself was a total crapshoot, in a new life across the country, uprooted from the Bay Area, uprooted from Buffalo on a lark in love with a man I hardly knew. Out, in school again, on my own at 39. Suddenly HIV positive—a new recruit to the droves of gay men destined to sickness unto death. And why? Because I hung out in a sling at bathhouses on poppers getting happily plugged and sperming wildly? Because I was cruising Christopher Street at 2 in the morning, horny? No, that was not my lifestyle, I told myself self-righteously, implying homophobically that somehow, they deserved it. That wasn't me—me the clean gay—the Puritan gay. I didn't *deserve* it. I was a victim of some cruel joke, I told myself, as I stood in front of my unhinged lover, a victim of wondering what was happening. Why my first experience of opening up to sex and love, my first complete surrender to passion, could turn into a nightmare.

So that night in July, that thick humid East Coast night, all I could do was hold on, struggle to keep myself alive and keep Gil within bounds. I tried to calm him down, for some reason unfrightened by his tantrum. I tried only to defuse, to walk Gil back from some desperate precipice, which happened in less time than I remember.

He in the living room on the couch stared off in the distance, as I sat next to him and began to hold him in my arms, rocking him after he pushed me away once or twice. The knife flung to the carpet floor, stranded with untheatrical consequence. We picked up the pots and pans and bills and notebooks and went back to bed. Only later did I register that my lover had pulled a knife on me. Maybe a couple of days later, during one of my long walks home from the streetcar to our house beside the same worn hedges where months before premonitions had come to me, voices telling me to get out of Newark, voices I fought hard to ignore.

For some reason, the entire blow-up, even as it was happening—ushered not fear into my heart but some kind of strange hilarity, some weird enactment of a telenovela. It seemed so quintessentially melodramatic. The bankers' boxes full of folders, the computer, printer, plastic tin full of bills, duffle bag of clothes, stuffing the Honda wagon, giving notice, and driving off I don't know how soon after our little spat, after the quiet evenings during reruns of *Cheers*, the silence and the heavy truth that neither of us was willing to unpack. For me I had to face the reality that I could not stay in New Jersey, had to go home, regroup, deal with this new twist of fate.

12
SANTOS

By the start of 1991, Gilberto had returned to Rio, and I had booked a ticket for winter-break. I harbored vague thoughts about teaching ESL in the favelas in Brazil even as I somehow realized this trip might be a final reckoning. Ambivalent, I boarded the unfriendly skies to head south—to the sexiest set of lithe humans on earth, the open arms of Corcovado, the raked white sands of Ipanema, the *fio dental* wedged between bumbums on the crowded shores of Copacabana.

The first Brazilian AIDS case was reported in 1982, but the government, once the dictatorship dissolved in the 80s, had since led the most successful anti-AIDS program in the developing world, reducing the expected 1.2 million cases at the turn of the millennium to a mere 600,000. Brazil invoked Article 71 of its constitution, which allowed patented products to be produced locally after three years on the market, to effectively manufacture ARVs (antiretrovirals) in house, which left Merck and Roche in the lurch, in spite of their lawsuits and attempts to convince the United States to implement sanctions. ARVs became free to Brazilians, and condoms readily available. The government embraced needle-exchange programs and refused to denounce prostitution in exchange for US Aid funds. Repudiating the dictates of American "free" enterprise, the Brazilians dealt with the pandemic in ways that rejected, in spite of the predominance of Roman Catholicism and recent evangelical resurgence, the impractical and specious linkage of HIV prevention to abstinence and anti-sexual practices, which is what drives many American politicians.[1]

I knew nothing about AIDS policy when I flew to Rio. Gil picked me up in Victor's car at the airport. We drove to his apartment, nestled in the hillside below the favelas in a section of town that separated Ipa from Copa. We had 14 days to have fun and at the same time figure out what to do with our "relationshit." In many ways, I had already made up my mind, with a selfish, compartmentalized, but unarticulated decisiveness, that this trip probably had to be the last hurrah. I wanted to assure myself that Gil, at some level, knew that my mission was a mercy one. I wanted to be able by some magical key to his consciousness claim that he too knew we could not continue together long distance both geographically and now oddly enough psychologically, insofar as the appearance of the virus had shocked us into different narratives about our levels of trust. I had arrogated a version of the truth to my consciousness that became a kind of armor: Gilberto had recklessly transmitted the disease to me, and under internalized Solomonic mantra that "love is strong as death, jealousy is cruel as the grave," I had naively allowed myself to get fucked. I wanted to say that I blamed the man I loved for ruining my life and at the same time under some code of honor would never accuse him of anything other than a certain victimization by a poor testing mechanism somewhere in the city of Rio. His benign neglect to take extra precautions to make sure he was negative.

I could not condone my indirectness during this venture; in

fact, I found it almost underhanded. It was as if my mind had adopted a stoic façade that I wore to Brazil, facing my lover not as the vulnerable, insatiable hugger in search of the warmth and openness of another soul but instead as a robotic shell of that previous presence. I was there to have fun with Gil for the last time, as a greedy tourist who clutched his passport and round-trip ticket close to his chest. Gil eventually intuited my reserve, my Pinkerton role as the rich American who was toying with his butterfly for the final time.

In spite of this internal drama, I was there to paint the town jungle red, not averse to indulging the joie de vivre that permeated the mosaic of Brazilian life. We spent mornings on the sloped and raked sands of Ipanema—reading and splashing until the heat drove us indoors to naps and food and fucking. I topped with some aggression as a result of all that had transpired, I had become convinced in some pocket of my rationalization process that my boyfriend was really a bottom, that he loved to get fucked and that it was my duty to make sure that he got what he wanted. I was being aggressive, getting back at him, but to his credit, Gil seemed happy with my newfound energy, happy with any and all contact in bed, nonjudgmental of anything but fastidiousness.

There was a moment in a hotel in Santos where we stayed on our way to the enormous city of Saõ Paulo. A moment at the old resort town in the one-story colonial hotel bedroom when I seemed to finally satisfy my lover—to bring him to a climax of ecstasy maybe for the first time. This one time a relaxation and orgasmic release that moved beyond any we had reached before. After we had walked under the shade trees of the cobblestone boardwalk by the sea in Santos, after we'd sauntered through the dappled light of a breeze-fed afternoon, we found the time to *dormir un puo*. This was our finest time, there in the half light of an unlit bedroom, finally with a big bed and no clothes in the warm heat of fanned air. His thighs surround my ribs, I could see rapture in his turned away face, surprised by the pure whiteness of his floss that streamed across his thin torso. It was a moment of completion for us both, one that marked the apogee of our meld, but maybe also its completion.

We drove south from Rio along the magnificent coast, past Saõ Sebastiaõ, where Vespucci landed on the gay saint's day, January 20, in the 16th century. The saint revered for his endurance of torture, his immaculate and defined torso pierced with the arrows of Eros, the uplifted eyes of his placid face imperturbable, sublime in its willing acceptance of its stigmata. I had been pierced by the poison arrow that Gilberto already harbored when we met. Ironically we two, contaminated victims of our own wonderful perversity, one exiled back to his birthplace by immigration laws, the other facing a lethal horizon after five years of preparation for a doctorate and teaching position; the one himself an ex-soldier like the Roman martyr, himself driven from his aesthetic destiny to the fate of a dock loader in Passaic, New Jersey, on the night shift—illegal, alone, strapped for cash until immigration closed the door on his dreams.

"Indeed, to get AIDS is precisely to be revealed...as a member of a certain 'risk group,' a community of pariahs," Susan Sontag wrote in her book on AIDS and its metaphors.[2] Had Gil and I become pariahs to one another? I wondered as we drove in silence. Two outcasts facing one another in the silver sedan on our way to the biggest city in the world. Gil, my tour guide, showed me the place in the park where he had been mugged years before, showed me the museum and botanical gardens, graciously took me to traditional barbecues and colonial towns with palm-shaded lanes and wrought-iron benches, where ice cream vendors ground out music and mothers rolled prams down white and grey mosaic sidewalks.

We had been labeled by the outside world. We were sick, we were homosexuals, we were going to die from a virus, marked as Benetton HIVers. Even as that world had discovered, labeled, and quarantined us, the question that hovered unasked and undiscussed as we sat at stoplights or drove north to Vila to visit Gil's family, the question I avoided in a desperate attempt to save face, the question that followed us around like a familiar through the shrouded rubber plants and the abstract canvases, over the *azulejos* in the sidewalks, the long languid promenades beside the half-moon beaches, the ghost that pointed toward the end of our time together whose graffiti on every wall seemed to ask: are we now pariah to one another? Had the stamp of the syndrome driven a wedge between us? Had the judgment of the world become my judgment, Gil's?

How could intimacy (physical, emotional, domestic) be fraught with such unapproachable avoidances? As if to be close on some level required a requisite refusal to face crucial topics. In my case, to admit to my lover that a routine test at the immigration office which had become an insurmountable obstacle to his path toward citizenship in the United States had also become the impediment to my continuance of our love affair. How could I possibly admit to him that I too had become an immigration officer of sorts, the borders of my state breached by this alien and his tiny weapon, one-sixteenth thousand the size of the head of a pin? The virus which Gil smuggled across the border and injected into me, a poor-unsuspecting dough boy. Maybe I knew our relationship was unworkable long before the virus became the catalyst for my wounded and irreversible extraction, but HIV had come along to give me an excuse—a way to extricate myself from the kind of closeness that the vow "in sickness and in health" exacted from the kind of devotion I could not give.

I knew I had to find a way to blame myself for the impending breakup in order to instigate it. I had to wallow in a certain masochistic irrationalization to do what I had to do, however callous. I had to move on. I had to survive.

The final day arrived. I think I had come clean to Gilberto the night before—as clean as I could come—while we drove through the winding roads and tunnels of Rio. I explained that I had to stay in the US, finish the doctorate, look for a job there. I didn't think it was *feasible* for us to stay together, the word infused with the sterility of pragmatics. What I was saying— and what Gil must have known I was saying—was very simply: "I don't love you anymore." Gil knew it. I knew it.

He got the message, no matter how deftly couched in the irresponsibility of feasance. I doubt I was as definitive as I sound in written prose, but my body language told the story. The next day as we loaded my luggage, the silence between us seethed. A slammed trunk was the prologue to Gil's tantrum— the release of his anguish at my attempt to wrap up our rela- tionship neatly and bloodlessly. A harrowing drive to the airport followed—we passed cars on sidewalks, jolted brakes, my stare out the side window, my white knuckles, our lack of eye contact and the laying of rubber. I was scared, anxious to get into the terminal. I knew I faced the earned consequence of my complacency and noblesse oblige, my carefully managed Dear João *viagem* to the sunny south.

Maybe Gil had the perfect right to take my life into his hands as I asked him repeatedly to please slow down. He floored the compact and passed cars on the highway's apron, glanced at me with a disgust that remained imprinted in my memory. His car skidded to a halt at the departure lane of the airport, my whiplashed head missed the windshield by the grace of a seatbelt. He jumped out of the car, opened the trunk, and hurled my suitcase to the sidewalk. On impact, the latches of the case unclasped, and my dirty boxers were strewn across the sidewalk in front of busy travelers. I stood there stunned, scared and coldly frozen in tropical heat. I waited for him to leave. And he did leave, yelling, "Get out. I hate you. I never see you again. You fucker." His tires laid rubber as he fishtailed madly toward the highway, leaving me kneeling beside my t-shirts.

THE QUEEN CITY

(1990-1991)

13
LAKE ERIE

Back in Buffalo, nominally the rusty armpit of the country, but really a diamond in the rough, I found myself moving into a sketchy neighborhood on Prospect near Lake Erie, where I landed upstairs in an old two-story apartment building. The Queen City was of full brick houses from the 1850s—the Mark Twain and McKinley days—and still featured a great symphony in Kleinhans Hall, a modern museum at the Albright Knox and a park designed by Olmsted. Puerto Ricans, Greeks, Jews, Blacks, all had their enclaves in the admittedly segregated city. The old university, across from Talking Leaves bookstore, was located on the north end of town, but in a moment of architectural panic in the 60s or 70s, when UB became part of the SUNY system, the state built a new penitentiary-like campus in the northeast suburb of Amherst, ostensibly to prevent riots. Renowned for its chicken-wing palaces and blown-out warehouses, the rust belt degradation and Lake Erie charm of Buffalo made SUNY an apt place to study and talk as I hung out under the fluorescent lights on the 9th floor of sterile Clemens Hall.

My place on the Westside of town, a high-ceilinged two bedroom upstairs, looked out onto Lake Erie and Potomac Street. I set up my blonde wooden table in the kitchen where I listened to Afropop Worldwide and cooked curry with home-made ghee. I'd come slinking back from Jersey to this remote but roomy spot, bought a pink couch for the living room and brought my Persian Mauricio home, though the orange cat and the pink couch would soon become points of HIV contention. I returned to my routine of running, swimming, working out, going to my carrel, reading *Orlando Furioso* and *Il Filostrato*. We were all taking notes when Slavoj Žižek, the mad Sloven-ian, came to lecture on Hitchcock. I walked down the halls day or night and found someone talking about Michel Foucault's *History of Sexuality*.

Shortly after my Buffalo re-entry, I was told in no uncertain terms that Mauricio's litter box was a cytomegalovirus hotbed, and since he had become an indoor cat, I was in a fix. Cat feces was at that time a source of considerable panic for immune-compromised pet owners, whose litter boxes signaled blindness and dementia from the handling of decaying excrement. Toxo-plasmosis is a disease caused by a protozoan parasite that is ingested through raw and uncooked meat and vegetables or exposure to oocysts from cat litter boxes. It is the largest DNA virus in the herpes family, which, if contracted by someone teetering on or experiencing full-blown AIDS, can lead to diseases like cerebral palsy. "Get rid of him," Dr. Hewitt said. Get rid of the orange Persian who was my only companion? And who would take him? Jack, my ex-lover, still angry about our breakup, put his foot down. He refused to take the cat back. Sorrowful, I advertised and found someone to take him. Mauricio became the latest casualty in my struggle to survive.

No cats, no Caesar salad, no steak tartare, no grapefruit, no sunny side up eggs. No Mauricio. More tears on the pink couch. My blood work bounced around 400 t-cells, my stress level rose, most of my friends were gone or graduated. I was ABD; I had to finish. No sex, no drinks, no weed. Hewitt was the AIDS doctor in town—young, thirty, and scared. He almost diagnosed a knot in my calf as KS; watched nodes under my arm grow and shrink. He drew blood every couple of months, while I waited with nagging trepidation for a week or two. My happiness depended on some random count of helper cells on a blood slide. I drank carrot juice. I can't even remember what I swallowed beside that horrible Brazilian weed juice. One afternoon I took a walk under the highway toward the lake and couldn't make it back to the bathroom in time. Incontinency loomed ahead, a box of depends on sale at Kmart. Shitting oneself was the ultimate degradation. My body lost control, vulnerable to any foreign substance—any airborne parasite or virus.

Colds, coughs, flu vaccines, rashes, swollen glands, unhealed scratches, fear of blood, mouth ulcers, a slice from a paring knife. The nose-bleed panic, hand washing literal and figurative. In short, the plague. I was contaminated; I could go near no one. Bouncing around a huge old apartment on the west side of Buffalo by myself, a scratchy throat became, in no time, a death knell for a drama queen who featured himself as cool as a California laid-back dude but is in fact a hysteric queer afraid of moths and failure and dying.

14
AMERICAN FALLS

My counselor in Buffalo turned out to be a young priest with wavy gray hair, a marvelous smile, and a willingness to procure for me the words to my favorite prayer:

> Hail, holy queen, mother of mercy, our life, our sweetness, and our hope. To thee do we cry, poor banished children of Eve. To thee do we send up our sighs, mourning and weeping in this valley of tears. Turn thy most gracious eyes of mercy toward us and after this, our exile, show unto us the blessed fruit of thy womb, Jesus. O clement, o loving, o sweet virgin Mary.

Salve Regina, Marian antiphon sung at compline, the close of the day. Canisian hymn among the Benedictines. End of the Rosary. Apostrophic cadence. We banished from heterocentric security, we in the valley of HIV tears. We exiled.

I was in love with him, this therapist, and at weak moments I longed to test his vow of chastity. I knew the monks in St. Mary's were randy. So many gay priests. Father Randall came to my rescue, found me a HIV support group at the Pres-byterian Church, and convinced me to call my sister, Mary, and tell her what had happened. 'I got fucked, sis.' My relationship to my sister, 11 months older, was at that point in my life, extremely close. I trusted her so implicitly that my therapist—who sought naively through his charm to coax me out of my corner, out from under the bed where I hid in the dark, licked my wounds, suspicious of the world, intent on keeping my head down—my counselor called on me to call Mary. To tell someone for Christ's sake—a phrase he obviously did not use, not taking the Lord's name in vain, a commandment he needed to heed.

A week later, Mary flew out from San Francisco to see me after I called and told her. I shuffled through the sliding glass doors of the over-lit Buffalo arrival terminal and headed up its slanting wide linoleum walkway toward the US Air gate where Mary strode toward me. All I remembered was her off-white trench coat. No lapels or huge belts or buttons, just a nonde-script London Fog-like raincoat, one you might see a busi-nessman wear over his suit on Montgomery Street. So unlike her. My cool sister dressed usually with such tasteful flair.

This mental snapshot—this flashbulb memory emblematic of emotional recall—brought to mind my quick assessment of her hurried mission—her white-knight round-trip search and rescue flight to the seedy rust belt to ease the shock to her dear brother's system. The coat evoked. In reality, she was not condescending. She smiled, her deep mahogany hair long enough to reach her shoulders, her face still strikingly petite with a beautiful symmetry. A faint hint of freckles still floated like a speckled ribbon over the ridge of her nose. Her cozy smile and warm greeting. The hug, the "Hi Case," the "you look good," her charming willingness to do the Buffalo thing. No one from my family would venture to this part of the world unless it was a life-or-death situation, but once that eventuality reared its ugly, if hackneyed, head, Mary took it in stride. She knew damn well it was the shits. She knew I needed her empathy to stay afloat.

She would do anything to help, but beyond the assurance of her presence, beyond the raincoat snapshot, there was no serious drama at that point in our history. I can't remember where we ate. I know I took her to the Towne, the Greek place, for rice pudding; I know we drove out to the Falls, the American side, with its crumbling horseshoe, big boulders falling into the gulch. We of course could see the Canadian Falls from the American side—they larger and more majestic, their spray more penetrating, their barrel more unbelievable. Something so deeply suicidal about these cascades. In some way our outing rang a particularly apt bell. I had taken other visitors out on the boat that rode up to the spot where the water hit the river; we had to wear slickers for that. My sis, who clutched her pack of Tareytons, was not game for more than an occasional round of doubles at the Club. She was a rather sedentary sort, she and her penny dreadfuls. We had both read D.H. Lawrence as we toured through Europe together after high school, expiring from the August heat on the train from San Sebastian to Paris with the Seventh Day Adventist sitting across from us. She was an avid reader, but my mother and others moved her into pulp —unless Irving wrote another book. She read quickly and hungrily—with an amazing retention rate she herself never realized. I was envious as I plodded through the complicated periods of Faulkner, relishing each turn of phrase.

I was eternally and unfacetiously grateful that my sister visited, though I can remember little more than that unbecoming trench coat. It wasn't even raining or snowing. People thought Buffalo—bad weather, snow belt. They thought of swinging traffic lights and blizzards. She must have been dressed for success, answering the obligatory stress call of her little brother, bother though it must have been. I think it was a balmy 60s or something when she appeared in her raingear—a beautiful windy Western New York set of days—sharp with color, white caps on Erie, the leaves turning on that wonderful geographic shelf that sat beside the lake.

If the truth be stretched, I was, like my sis, my own brand of snot. I wasn't as cute as she was, did not have the charm, the sweetness and light that was never saccharine, the sentimentality that never dripped, the perfect looks of a *Seventeen* model. But I too had my stuck-up side, had my reticence misinterpreted as arrogance, had my long face and half-moon mouth perpetually frowning at man's inhumanity to man. I had my bitterness, my beauty, my pecs defining themselves under the bench press, my baseball biceps. I had my calves, my Kevin Bacon boyish good looks, more attractive I admit to girls than boys. I couldn't boast a sixpack or more than six inches elsewhere, but I was a standoffish bastard in my own way, sarcastic and intolerant of cellulitis and the uncouth. I admit to a stoic facade, a coolness that kept me from exposing myself to yet another slap down. I had my blue eyes, my Half Moon Bay shuffle, my insouciance. I wasn't perfect, in fact inside a seething mass of insecurity and fear of obscurity. I hid it well.

Mary knew my makeup. She knew my shyness, my independence, my aloofness. She knew she was the one person who could both up with and pierce my façade when I faced the prospect of death within a decade. Her flight across country spoke that knowing. It signaled her love.

15
RED LOBSTER

C all him Larry, Larry who worked at Red Lobster. Larry's story stood out among the 20 people who showed up at First Presbyterian, the big gray church in Buffalo where my HIV support group met in the early 90s. His story got under my skin. It spoke to me in ways that put my trouble in perspective.

Our group leader was a middle-aged social worker who rarely pulled the plug on those who'd come to talk, those who wanted to know where the cure was, what drugs to take, what herbal formula would stave off swollen nodes and that grey film that lined their tongues—the thrush onset which came before the shrivel. We had all genders in the group, we had users, we had ex-cons, we had black guys from the Eastside, we had unwed mothers and homeless teens, we had the out-and-proud and closet dads on the downlow. Talkers and shy boys. Everyone was scared or pissed, everyone was looking a very expensive death in the cavernous face, those still asymptomatic as much as those who were walking skeletons.

Our leader wanted everyone to say something—when we had seroconverted, who knew, what support we had, and of course how we *felt* about our condition. As if a statement of feeling were the same as feeling itself, as if an exclamation of sadness could replace the reality of tears—tears ultimately the place most of us had to go. Not tears at night in the blue light of the window—not in bed biting the pillow and cursing some projected personification of the great dealer in the sky, whose roulette wheel seemed rigged against me. No, tears before my peers, in one of those big anterooms to churches where picnics were planned and laymen gathered to make God into a coffee klatch amid old couches and plastic chairs. Some leaned against the wall, heads between knees; others were loud and cried, weeping in the church annexes of the world where the end approached like a tunnel without an exit.

I could never bring myself to cry in those groups—choked up yes, glassy-eyed, yes. Speechless, cold, sorry, mad. I'm not sure Larry ever cried either during those check-ins once a week —on Wednesdays at 7. Larry was an amalgamation of all of us. Married with children, gay, middle class, alcoholic, suburban, closeted. A heavy-smoking 30-year-old guy—not six feet, not over 180, dark haired, with the Billy Joel look of New Jersey. With humor, he unwound his story while all of us listened to its sheer quintessentialness. The condensation of its Western New Yorkness. Amazingly, he was in good health and had a smile that basked in the pure bravado of his misery, the panache with which he faced the insurmountability of his predicament.

Except Larry's life was also in many ways the opposite of mine. That opposition attracted me, gave me hope. He grew up in the suburbs of Buffalo, in Tonawanda, in an upper middle-class home, in a white high school where he buried his insatiable desire for dick. He had to bury it—what with his Catholic brothers and his bingo parents. In the early 60s with his V-neck sweaters and the white-socks loafers. He had to hide. He married out of high school, went to work at restaurants. Got stoned, drank rum and coke, had two babies, ended up at rest stops and eventually at one of the bars downtown—late before closing at 2, drunk as he sucked cock in pickup trucks and parks.

No one knew; hell, he didn't even know what he was doing other than following the unavoidable press of his prick. He just knew he had to keep flipping steaks on the grill on Sunday evenings when the family ate watermelon and zucchini parmesan, played ping pong and drank Coors. Those dense summer clouds, gray and swollen, dumped rain on the crickets beside the Erie Canal. "I couldn't come out," he told us; "they would kill me if I did; maybe *I* would kill me if I did," he threw in reflectively.

He was fired when his boss came into the restroom and found him jacking off a bus boy in a stall. His wife didn't know; they thought he drank too much, thought he was kind of a wild man. Queer never came to mind. They never saw him put his hand on the delivery man's crotch and get slugged in the face; they never saw him check into the Super 8 with that gym bunny who wanted to fuck, had forgotten his condoms, had too many inches for Larry to take in without pain—plowed and high as he was.

We leaned up against the bike rack on break while he smoked his Marlboro and I told him about ditching the Bay Area for grad school, about coming out, about falling in love with Gil. He leaned on the church wall, took a drag and exhaled. Larry, kind of pudgy, round-faced, not bad looking. Divorced, disowned, and HIV positive. He'd just found out, he told me. He didn't know what the fuck to do; he had no health insurance; he smoked a pack a day but at least was on the wagon—sober, clean, and clear. He was gay, he told me, but the lifestyle for him was impossible. "I have to come to terms with who I am," he told me. "I know that. And now with HIV, shit, I don't know what's going to happen. If they find out, they'll fire me. They won't let me near my kids."

16
LÉOPOLDVILLE

S urvival depended on sympathy. It also depended on knowledge, on finding out. Scientists discovered two strands of the virus: HIV 1 and HIV 2. The first is more virulent, the first most of us contract. Where did it come from? Chimpanzees, gorillas, sooty mangabeys in the Democratic Republic of Congo (formerly the Belgian Congo), from Cameroon, Gabon, the Central African Republic? From a subspecies of chimps called pantroglodytes, troglodytes. But these primates have SIV, a related virus that only exists in nonhuman species and is not necessarily as lethal. How did SIV mutate into lethal HIV? What zoonosis allowed transmission, what phylogenesis led to the transformation of SIV to HIV? There is no definitive answer. The SIV strain of simian immunodeficiency virus tends to mutate in different species and is thought to have a phylogenetic connection to HIV 1. How SIV mutated into HIV is still under investigation, but SIV was probably transmitted to humans through eating raw bushmeat or a meat butcher being cut while skinning bushmeat.

But people have been eating bushmeat for centuries; why would HIV emerge in the 1900s all of sudden? Again the link epidemiologically uncertain, researchers suggest that transmission rates increased during African colonialism, which led to a host of hosts that allowed for mutation of the virus from simian to human.

The current theories begin with Léopoldville (now Kinshasa) in what is the Democratic Republic of Congo, at the turn of the twentieth century and later. Increased migration to the cities, a concentration of railroad workers who traveled long distances and worked in male/male camps for long periods of time led to increased prostitution, increased anal intercourse. The medical history becomes ideologically inflected because prostitution is conflated with men who have sex with men and with promiscuity itself. So same-sex practice equals promiscuity equals prostitution equals.... The Belgian Congo of the turn of the 19th century was not only the scene of Conrad's heart of darkness but a busy crossroad, an intersection of sexed bodies and increased incidence of GUDs, genital ulcer diseases as well—forms of venereal warts and open wounds in the anus —herpes and syphilis. Blood and shit and semen intertwined with penetration—and a lot of the penetration just comes from getting hard and wanting to fuck something or someone. I can't imagine—or can I—this hotbed of horniness, this pleasure in receiving.

At first, I hated the idea of being fucked, couldn't conceive of it—until Gil wanted to go for it and I being a pushover said "sure, *por que não*"—the social stigma notwithstanding. New York in 1990 was no Léopoldville of 1920, I admitted, but I realized workers on the streets of Botafogo in Rio came from rural areas without their wives and were more than willing to have sex with men. Were African men working for queer colonialists like Cecil Rhodes ilk (himself a sorry closet case) of the same ilk? Were they truck-stop cowboys? Were they on the downlow? Like Magic Johnson? Arthur Ashe? Ease-E? There was a high increase in the sex trade in colonial Africa, where the Europeans came, saw, and conquered. And then came the sexual revolution of the 1960s and 1970s.

Much of this history explained transmission rates, explained open hosts for zoonosis. But it did not explain the biological transition from benign SIV to deadly HIV. Nor did it explain why not until 1959 did an extant blood sample from a Congolese man show HIV antibodies, though there was no evidence of symptoms or opportunistic infections in his body. How much assayable blood was preserved before then? In 1969, Robert Rayor, a 16-year-old African American, died of Kaposi's sarcoma in St. Louis and his blood was found to have HIV. He is one of the earliest American cases—the virus thought to have come from Congo to Haiti in the late Sixties. The incubation period for the virus to replicate and undo immune responses could take up to 10 years, which added to the necessary evolutionary mutation period.

Yet none of this anecdotal medical history explained what happened in the 1980s, when Gaëtan Dugas, Canadian flight attendant, the so-called Patient Zero of Randy Shilts's famous but apocryphal *And the Band Played On*, first headed into a New York bathhouse in October of 1982. Dugas was not the founder of AIDS in America even in Shilts's dramatic rendering. A man called Ken Home died in San Francisco in April of 1980 (KS) and a schoolteacher in Brooklyn died the same year of HIV complications. What was, however, discovered about the hook ups of Gaëton (Gay-ton): 240 of the 248 men known to be infected with HIV in 1983 were reported to have had sex with Dugas or had sex with someone he fucked. Eleven unprotected anal intercourse partners a year became a kind of standard for transmitters and carriers of what was discovered later to be HIV.

As I inserted myself into this medical history, I wondered if it really mattered that I wasn't a Gaëtan Dugas, a fly-me steward–that HIV came to me from one partner. Did that make me special? So, what if I contracted the virus after Rock Hudson died, after Surgeon General Koop finally made a stink, after Ronnie Reagan finally threw a few federal dollars at the poor queers, dropping like flies in West Hollywood, Castro Street, the Village, P-town, South Beach, Capitol Hill, the French Quarter? Freddie Mercury and Anthony Perkins. The Brady Bunch and YSL.

Should I be ashamed, having practiced unsafe sex in the late 1980s with Gil, that Montagnier discovered LAV as early as 1983 and 1984—French Nobel Laureate who confirmed the etiological agent now called HIV? Should I be sheepish that these international discoveries, as well as Robert Gallo's in the States, came well before the uncircumcised Gil was on top of me making love so gently so thoroughly so deliciously? I knew Michel Foucault had died in 1984; I knew he was in the Berkeley bathhouses with Thom Gunn. How foolhardy was I? What was I doing living out my wondrous fantasy with the man whom I knew to be negative, considering myself other, so special, not another Ramble statistic, protected by love from the vagaries of anonymous nights at the Midnight Sun, The White Horse, the Stud? He'd been tested. He told me.

17

NEWS AT 11

A decade into the pandemic, I found myself acronymic—belatedly HIV ABD at SUNYAB. In 1991, going to therapy, going to support groups, teaching Eric Fromm's *Art of Loving* to my freshman composition students, making them read "The Ones Who Walk Away from Omelas," the late Ursula Leguin's short short story about an ideal world that has only one catch: once a year these happy people must descend into a dungeon to watch a starving child miserable in a cage. This allegory ate away at my own secret viral cage, the reality that I was part of a new family beyond the nuclear one I had left in the Bay Area, the gay one I had embraced thereafter. I had to do something, now that I was among the positives, even if I wasn't ready to wear the Silence=Death t-shirts or crash Mass at Saint Patrick's Cathedral and lie on the floor between pews.

I decided to join the new chapter of ACT UP Western New York, started by a group of activists from Halwalls, an old warehouse downtown converted into an alternative art space, where poetry readings intermixed with screenings of Derek

Jarman films like *Sebastiane,* in which naked men sat in saunas staring at one another. Watching that movie, I thought back to how Warhol's *Lonesome Cowboys,* which I saw in college at Santa Cruz, had affected me in ways I refused to acknowledge. How mesmerized and simultaneously frightened by my fixation I was then—18, a sophomore trying to fall in love with a Jewish girl from San Francisco, me a young man getting stoned and making chicks with his buddies, suddenly made hot by a campy campfire scene, by the twist that only Annie Proulx would brilliantly bring to fruition with her Wyoming short story about two down-and-out cowboys who went all the way. Between Santa Cruz in 1970 and the lines around the corner in Missoula, Montana, when *Brokeback* opened in the 2000s, thirty years of water had flown through the Erie Canal, under the Higgins Street Bridge in Missoula—a river had indeed run through my life. But at this point in the early nineties, I was just another desperate gay man facing death from AIDS; I was someone I never imagined as a young shy intellectual studying eastern religions and Plato at UC-Santa Cruz. Blown around by fear and denial, I had run from a sexual self, which like death in the parable "Appointment in Samarra," the more I avoided, the closer I approached, the nearer I was to the desire that I was raised to repress.

I found refuge from my death sentence in a motley crew of students and artists starting up a new branch of ACT UP.[1] I shyly attended dark meeting in Hallwalls. One of the directors, a tall thin guy my age, took me in, asked me to join. There were ten of us—all ages, women, men, teenagers. All political types who wanted to prove that silence meant death or a quicker death for New Yorkers outside of Manhattan. Were they positive like me? I didn't know. We organized our chapter of ACT UP, emulated the famous New Yorkers downstate. A lesser version to be sure but still a group bent on needle exchange, on condoms passed out at high schools, on leaflets and fundraisers and announcements at Black churches. Were we idealistic? Were we determined? Were we jumping on a cool political bandwagon? Did we really want to give clean needles to Puerto Rican junkies on the West Side? I didn't know. I was floating through a world I couldn't understand, trying to do something about this virus that had found a home in my soul as well as my body.

We distributed our plastic bags outside high schools. Inside the pouches, a couple of Trojan condoms and a few tubes of lube, a few dental dams. We eventually sponsored a women's drag show entitled Debbie Does Dams on the Westside with Leslie Feinberg, famous author of *Stone Butch Blues*, as MC—a tremendous success in a low-ceilinged meeting hall somewhere near Lake Erie. We used the money to distribute packets and information around town. I had come a long way from the vaulted ceilings and overstated Victorian sofas of my Great Aunt's living room, where on Sunday evenings she would tickle the ivories of her grand piano and sing "East Side, Westside" or "Casey Would Waltz with the Strawberry Blonde." I was in tie and coat as the uniformed dished out pink roast beef and lemon meringue pie at dinner. Aunt Angie's held court beside her 8 by 11 photo of Barry Goldwater on the mantle, her diatribe about the turpitude of the 23rd Vatican Council in scrapping the Latin liturgy always ready. My upbringing, rather obviously, had not prepared me for radical demonstrations, for stone butches in fatigues and jack boots. For the likes of the famous Leslie Feinberg, in tie and coat herself, as she lectured us about Amazons and Transvestite Nuns who joined the conquistadors in Peru in the 16th century.

I found myself outside a Buffalo high school, newly minted member of ACT UP Western New York—me, the man who only years before would regularly curse the approach of homeless strangers in San Francisco. I distributed safe-sex packets to unsuspecting sophomores, many of whom didn't know lube from shampoo and were, for the most part, as ignorant of blow jobs and rimming and fisting and cunnilingus and anal intercourse as I was in boarding school—then a snot-nosed 16-year-old, rubbing mattresses in the morning, humping imaginary Julie Christies, or dreaming vaguely of the dusted muscles of men on the pommel bar.

These packets from Manhattan (the ones I handed out to grinning teens), replete with graphics that explained how to unravel the latex sleeve and pinch its receptacle tip, replete with warnings about unprotected penetrations, did not go unnoticed by the 5 o'clock news, which found these distributions, however well-intentioned under the guise of AIDS prevention, a wholesale assault on the assumed innocence of pubescent children, who, the authorities over-protested, had no intention of doing anything "down there" until epithalamion, atop the marriage bed, and even then only in the obscurity of a darkened bedroom.

News broadcasters interviewed principals, pastors, aghast mothers, and city councilmen. They filmed us on sidewalks beside school grounds watched by the men in blue, camera crews and reporters in a frenzy produced by this sordid scoop. News at Eleven. Radical Sex group descends upon Western New York. The sexuality of children and teens would forever remain fraught with the fictitious projections of adults who wished to erase their own experiments with animals, stuffed or alive, with drunk uncles, with whatever moved or might be rubbable, sex as ubiquitous and sensual as sunshine or rain.

The ACT UP practices, and the days of my participation, put me in a rather awkward mental space. I was raised a devout Catholic and became a Young Republican in high school. I respected men of the cloth and was a bit unnerved by the activists' interruption of the high Mass in Manhattan. I was also an obvious rookie when it came to explaining the uncoiling of the lubricious contraceptive, having myself never used a condom except during some randy moment of self-manipulation, oversexed and salt-and-pepper uniformed parochial boy that I was, rather forgotten by a family wholly concentrated on my older brother, a brilliant bully who played catcher (not in the sexual sense) and batted third in the line-up while his scaredy-cat little brother warmed benches or sat in the bleachers reading Art Linkletter and petting some forlorn border collie.

My parents, I assume, didn't quite know what to do with me then, and in turn I had no idea what to do with me now, faced with a virus I associated with bubble-butted men in Speedos spread out on the sands of Fort Lauderdale, wherever that was. So I understood myself as rather a prude, in my baggy khakis and long white Brooks Brothers boxers. Perhaps I could never be a radical other than on paper—other than the reverse of the trajectory ascribed to one of Churchill's adages—that people are heartless if not liberal in youth, brainless if not conservative in age. I was a bleeding heart who grew more radical as the millennium and my promised demise approached.

My will to survive had radicalized me. My ACT UP group did more than give me support; it brought me out of the political closet. It forced me to fight to end the pandemic.

18

NEEDLE EXCHANGE

O ne of those telling photographic moments, of which I spoke in regard to my Pacific Heights sister, stuck with me during my ACT UP days. Picture a bunk bed in a Lower East Side apartment where our contingent from Western New York spent the night in Manhattan. We had come downstate to take part in an action at the homeless shanties under the bridges of the city. We helped with needle exchange and attended meetings to listen to some of the main movers and shakers in the movement, mostly dykes at that point, people like the late Urvashi Vaid and Kate Clinton, though they may not have been card-carrying members of the coalition. We visited jaw-dropping homeless settlements on the fringes of the richest city in the world, permanent camps made of shopping carts and scrap metal, flapping canvas and old car doors, low campfires and frayed, throwaway overcoats, duct-taped parkas, Dickensian mittens with fingers exposed. We witnessed a world composed of the discarded excess of American indulgence. Kerosene-lanterned and apocalyptic.

Guided by our hosts, mostly women from the still

burgeoning ACT UP chapter in Manhattan, we offered clean needles and STD info. I was discovering I was more attuned to lesbian social consciousness in many ways than the shallow commercialism of gay male culture. But there was one guy in our Buffalo group who belied my knee-jerk assessment. Luke. An idealistic, young, short-haired radical—thin and maybe 5'8", sincere and pale skinned, seventeen with grey eyes and perfect features. A sincere dude who showed up to make a difference in the world, fresh-faced tyro in pea coat and dark jeans, scuffed Chuck Taylors and stocking cap. I fell for him almost instantly.

That night in Manhattan after our work, the six of us who had carpooled to the big city were shown bedrooms in a host's flat. I was assigned to a bunkbed with Luke, me underneath him once he climbed the ladder to the top. I lay there that night for a long time, unable to sleep in a strange room, fixated on the curve of the mattress above me. I wanted desperately to climb up to Luke's perch and hug him in an embrace that would fill the unfillable void in my forlorn chest. I didn't know if he was positive. I didn't know if he was attracted to me sexually. I only knew that his presence above me was electric and excruciating. The compartment of that lower bunk sealed my isolation as a single gay man with HIV, an exile stuck in the dark below my lost youth.

How hopelessly close I felt to this cynical, serious kid—who was hellbent on making some kind of a difference, while I wrestled with my physical attraction to this mix of waif and deer-in-the-headlights who exuded a sincere anger about man's inhumanity to man. I was paralyzed by awareness of his emulation of my assumed erudition as a graduate student. I figured he probably looked up to me while we laughed over our assessment of the media circus and spooned rice pudding together back in Allentown during our weekly planning sections in

Buffalo. Lying underneath him—unable now to even recall if I was hard or getting hard—I remained self-consciously tucked under a rough wool blanket, wanting to reach out with an ache I would never forget, with an unwillingness to break the vision I assumed he had of me, as a political, platonic activist.

Talking to him about my feelings never crossed my consciousness. The talking cure ironically the furthest thing from my mind—or body. How urgently I tried telepathically to make him speak to me, to look down at me, wake up and touch me. My tossing and turning and sighing—my nonverbal attempts to garner attention—were ultimately lost on the reticence of my etiquette. The shell I have never been able to break, hardened by HIV, by the armor of a self-image as stalwart and honorable—as honorable as death.

19

"FAST CAR"

In the winter of '91, I drove more than once from Buffalo to the Himalayan Institute in Honesdale, Pennsylvania—400 acres of rolling trees and farmland in the northeastern part of the state, somewhere south of Cortland. I drove three hours in the rain through the two-lane black top, tree-lined and darkening, as I searched for the entrance to Sri Swami Rama's sprawling ashram, my go-to retreat in an effort to regain my equilibrium, to seek some spiritual support in my struggle to survive.

Sometimes I was the only person in the dormitory rooms— fantasizing that one of the robed permanent acolytes—30, bearded, thin, and devout—might wander into my single bed in the middle of the night after meditation. I was in treatment with Rudolph Ballentine, the famous Ayurvedic medicine man, who, during my series of five-day stints at the institute, prescribed homeopathic tinctures and instructed me in the practices and recipes of his *Diet and Nutrition*, a tome I still possess. I had turned to the Vedas, the 5,000-year-old medical practice of allegiance and surrender to the force of nature, turned to naturopathy, to coordination of mind and body, to yoga and meditation, to ghee and vegetarian curries. I bought my own cumin, mustard seed, turmeric, and coriander. I ate my vegetable medley with lentils and rice and plain yogurt. I drank my twig tea.

I was a good boy, though the lotus position was beyond my hamstrings, though the monkey of my mind would not stop climbing the trunk of the baobab, though as a tree I invariably fell over. There was a ginger-haired man at the brick Victorian Himalayan Institute branch in Buffalo on Delaware Street, where I began my foray into mind/body healing. This short, defined instructor with his red ponytail, this Diggery Venn of sorts, taught yoga and martial arts, wore thick white robes tied with heavy belts. Upstairs in the center at Buffalo he took me on a physical journey, holding my neck rolls and leaning me up against walls. I would go to that urban branch of the Institute once or twice a week, in between support groups, therapy sessions, and long hours in my study carrel in the library, where occasionally a come-on in the men's room left me horny but frightened.

I could not comply; the hurdle of positivity stood in the way of hook-ups, though I was never very attuned to them anyway—always too frightened or unable to perform with anything more than a premature dribble, which finally became too embarrassing for bath houses. I was also working out in the gym at this point in my recovery, swimming and sitting in the sauna watching men and their taut chests, their blond body hair. I was dreaming.

I had a running partner, married to a Columbian, who wrote on Hawthorne and Melville—he was thin and kind and though an excellent runner, willing to put up with my prodding pace. There were times when we were alone in the shower that I had to truncate my ablutions due to indeliberate tumescence.

I think Tim knew I had a crush on him; I think he had a crush on me. But neither of us were in a position to do anything but bond as friends—he married, I positive. We were locked, at least I was, in a reticence amplified by my status as untouchable, contaminated, excommunicated, blood poisoned. Tim would have to know that I had HIV, would have to know that I was struggling to stay alive—would have to know I felt I was hardly worth anyone's investment.

This dismal prospect drove me to the sterile asceticism of the Honesdale campus where I sat thrice a day and listened to the silence of eternity, where I squirmed and once again went through the motions of reverence to the teaching of oneness—the Swami, when present, playing tennis with young girls in their 20s, three of them on one side of the net, he on the other rallying with his followers. I hiked through the deciduous forests, kicked leaves, and listened to obnoxious peacocks. The residents kept their distance from the visitors. I read books about relinquishing attachments and the breath of life. I listened to Tracy Chapman's "Fast Car" on the way down in my Honda Wagon—all nine starting notes on the guitar, the first four traveling up and down, the last four higher, filling me with the most invasive sorrow. I burst uncontrollably into tears as she told me she had a feeling "I could be someone." In a blur, in the rain, in the trees, going 50 in the dark, on my way to the empty ashram—me alone with wipers and tape replayed over and over.

I was 40. My life appeared over—no amount of faith healing, no amount of prayer or wheat grass could—no amount of cleansing, dangerous cathartic bawling, streaks down my cheeks. No amount of journaling or poem-writing could ever, I thought in my weakest moments, bring me out of this tunnel across the border of New York into the scrubby forests of wet Pennsylvania. I had no idea where I was; I had never heard of

Scranton. I never wanted to know Scranton. The two-lane road
—wet and empty and insignificant—like so much of terrain in
the east—thick and dark and so antithetical to the Sierras, to the
boulders of Yosemite or the beaches of Big Sur. How had I
found my way into this darkness, how could I get out? So
unholistic, so unholy, so lonely, so unaligned to my random life.

OREGON

(1992-1994)

20

EUGENE

Eugenics is a scientific term with a vexed history. From forced sterilization approved by Oliver Wendell Holmes to attempts to eradicate the gay gene, the concept has emerged from its racist history to refer to the biochemistry of genetic engineering—the patenting and selling of CCR5 mutations that could potentially prevent HIV from docking into my white blood cells. These costly mutant proteins, when and if feasible, will be able to colonize my blood supply and render the virus sterile.

Beyond etymology, eugenics has no particular relation to the town in Oregon where I was headed to my first university teaching position. Eugene, home of the Ducks on the Willamette River, where Eugene Skinner built his cabin circa 1850. Eugene, home of Nike, Steve Prefontaine, home of a Visiting Assistant Professor of English in 1991, a man who drove his creamy Honda wagon from Buffalo, New York, across the cornfields of Indiana, past the wind caves and Catherian prairies of Nebraska, across the salt flats of Mormon Utah, his wagon loaded, his body viral.

On through Nevada I wheeled until I reached the shores of Tahoe, the lake I called home as a boy in the summer, my nose peeling as I ate salami and cheddar on French bread smothered with mustard chased by a swallow of cold water after a dive off the pier and stubbed toes in the unsettled dust. I got off Highway 80 to drive around the North Shore of the lake. Reliving those days in our cabin on Carnelian Bay, the orange life jackets, the putt-putts, and Chris-Crafts. The long splinters on a barefoot road to the Sierra Boat Company.

The boat company, greasy and redolent of sweet oils, harbored the likes of Jimmy Schwartzman, a short mustached mechanic in overalls. Even then, sexually asleep and socially sidelined, I would lean up against the wall beside the hoist and watch him, smell the solvents, absorb the movements of his short nimble-footed litheness across the hot pavement of August as he took apart the Mercury engine that drove my brother's hydroplane, his Lucky Strike hanging from his lips, his banjo in his pickup, his wife-beater tank top ribbed and soiled. Jimmy ready to pay a visit to our parents' fireplace where Jack Daniels sloshed languidly between heavy cubes cranked from a metal ice tray. The seeds of a nascent gay boy, unaware of his stares, desperately seeking to conform.

Years later when I struggled with coming out in my twenties, I searched for some buried story of unzipped men sneaking out of closets to fondle my undescended testes, searched for—as we queers of a certain age do—some Freudian family drama to explain my penchant for the male form, to construct a narrative of abnormalcy in which I as victim was compelled by some lonely pervert to emerge as I had—staring at the jockey baskets of my cohorts after wrestling in 6th grade. I wanted to blame my love on the external abuse by some horny priest or drunk uncle whose gin led him to tuck me in one too many times.

These were the buried and socially compelled memories that bootstrapped my initial refusal to recognize how fabulous the touch of man for man could be in and of itself. Gil cut those traps. He taught me joy, erased my gay shame even if he gave me another. As I rounded the shore of my childhood, I realized that Freud or no Freud, Father O'Neil or no Father O'Neil, coming out had been one of the bravest and most genuine acts of my life. Could I use that courage to survive HIV?

After a few nights with friends and family at Tahoe, I found my way up north on Highway 5 crossing the Oregon border, past Ashland into the Willamette Valley, onward to Eugene and the University of Oregon, the college strategically placed between the Cascade Mountains and a series of long and wild strands of uncompromising seashore. I lucked into a small two-bedroom house east of campus with a yard to boot, an old clapboard box with refinished floors and a couple of tiny bedrooms on either side of the shower—perfect for an anxious new professor, a one-year replacement for a Shakespearean on sabbatical.

During my first week on the new job, I met Shingles, aka varicella zoster, a kind of chicken pox or Herpes virus that visits those with compromised immune systems. Painful blisters ran down the side of my torso, kept me up at night as I tried to sleep on my back. Acyclovir, a shiny blue football prescribed at the health center, lessened the burning symptoms that lasted for two weeks. The outbreak was clearly related to the admixture of anxiety and my viral nemesis. HIV had followed me across the country, into the bedroom of my bungalow.

I was contagious. No one was to touch my sores, my open wounds, during the weeks I waited impatiently for recovery. I knew exactly why I got it. I was totally freaked out by my first teaching assignment. My viral body spoke my mind. I was teaching the Renaissance Sonnet and a prescribed course on Shakespeare. I was fresh out of graduate school. I assigned 50 sonnets a night and quizzed students on them the next day—along with a set of required critical essays. The kids were in revolt; they went to the chair, a mild-mannered Victorianist who pulled me into his office and told me to temper my grim and insistent rigor—to loosen my grip on requisites, subscribe if I could to some West Coast version of less is more, as if I were in a Zen Monastery in the Marin Headlands. Fuck that shit, I thought, a SUNY graduate accustomed to spending 15 hours locked in a carrel reading Tasso's *Gerusalemme Liberata*. My avidity had become a curse.

The Education Department's teaching effectiveness program suddenly descended upon me. A kind-hearted and slight woman with long skirts sat in the back row and took copious notes. A videographer came to film the laconic and cold delivery of my passion for the complexities of *The Knight of the Burning Pestle*. Who was that un-emphatic lecturer in front of that stupid white board, unable to inspire the classroom of bored English majors who counted the minutes before they could move on to their Cormac McCarthy class? I watched myself—half gay in intonation, falling back into obfuscatory jargon, asking myself questions as I paced in front of the baffled undergraduates, who expected a concise explanation of Othello's jealousy. Who was this weirdo on film? What had I become? There in jeans and wrinkled cotton, pulling my hair, asking questions no one would dare to answer.

21
WINGS

I knew I struggled as a teacher; the Education Department knew too. My body figured it out with the pox, the chicken pox. The pos pox, the return of the invalid, retiring child role I re-assumed whenever another upper respiratory infection, another mouth sore, another fit of anger and depression (replete with torn notebooks and dented dashboards) occupied my indefatigably insufferable consciousness.

After witnessing the disaster that was my classroom, the Teaching Effectiveness Program attempted to remake me in the image of simplicity, turn me into a point-driving, organized professional—in short, a personality makeover. They decided to send me to Wings, a 90s watered-down version of EST, not to date myself (EST is the Erhard Systems Training founded by Werner Erhard in the 1970s in San Francisco), a kind of weekend encounter group that was to allow me and others to change life plans by "being in the world." The university picked up part of the tuition, an underwriting that attested to their desperation with a newly minted PhD from the theory-driven SUNY system.

Twenty-five of us attended Wings that October weekend, many from different companies, some distraught mothers or housewives, some vice presidents, some mid-level managers. On a stool in the front sat our lanky leader, Jim, veteran group guru, in cardigan sweater and casual linen chemise (he was married to Joy) unbuttoned tastefully at the top, his collar open on to a Maui-tanned neck. Most memorably, his craft-fair mug full of herbal tea, steaming out of his thigh where it rested. He introduced himself with the smoothness of Rick Dees on the Weekly Top Forty. But softer, more sincere, more philosophic, more compelling. A trial lawyer perhaps. A step well above a salesman for Charter Communications.

We spent the weekend getting in touch with our angst, lying on the floor listening to Bette Midler. In break-out groups we talked about why we were here now—not in the Ram Dass sense, but more practically. What drove us to Wings? For me, it was my nervousness with my first full-time teaching job. My desire to do well in Eugene, a college town I loved. Big enough to have gay tennis and potlucks. Big enough to hold HIV support groups, but small enough to allow escape to the Metolius River or Yachats, into the woods, down the beach with driftwood and gale-force winds. They even had a gay bar. And Portland was only a couple of hours north. I told none of this to my inner circle, just announced my ineptitude in the classroom, my anxiety about performing for my students. I may have told the Forest Service Rangers and miscarried wives I was light in the penny loafers, but I concentrated on telling the group about my lack of teaching skills.

We adjourned to some yoga stretches, lunch, followed by a couple of front-and-center interviews with willing participants. Jim spoke with new-age eloquence about the baggage of family dynamics, the unclarity of substance intake, the necessity to take the garbage to the dump. To fly on the wings of love, soar like an eagle with Jeffrey Osborne and the gay bath house diva who came to prominence with *The Rose*. Many of us were cathartically weeping to the music which choked up the most cynical and jaded of us gadflies. Post-Sixties derelicts, who still suffocated under the stronghold of Reagan reactionaries—Bush One still in power.

As the afternoon progressed or regressed, we stared into each other's eyes, stretched each other's limbs on yoga matts, danced and chanted. At last Jim, ever observant and perspicaciously attuned to our vibes, assigned us homework. We each had to rehearse a performance for the next day. Rusty, a Forest Ranger, and *moi* were handed tights and a tape of some Tchaikovsky ballet in order to choreograph a five-minute routine. We were to de-butch ourselves, so to speak, to massage the clench of our square Anglo jaws and loosen the constriction of our hips and thighs. Rusty was married with two young children, mustached and wooden in gesture and speech, maybe a bit dull and nondescript (or scripted in his nondescription). He was a model father. He stacked wood and organized his toolbox on weekends in between lawn mowing and short haircuts.

When Rusty and I got back to my place to rehearse, I wanted to make love to him, but of course refrained, the feeling being entirely un-mutual I assumed with my usual reserve, part of which I was being encouraged to relinquish with my *pas de deux avec* the very man I was too shy to kiss. Our packages were pronounced in tights. He changed behind closed doors before we worked on rudimentary choreography that involved some leaps and floor writhing. There might have been some touch but nothing to write home about, though if there had been, home is not where I would be sending my reminiscence, needless to say.

Rusty and I broke a leg the next day, the lights dimmed as we pirouetted across the floor. I did an imitation of a flit, in fact being a flit, as Jim in his infinite clairvoyance saw perfectly. He wanted to bring out my inner sugar-plum fairy and figured Rusty the homo-ignorant hick from Grants Pass or wherever he hailed—southern Oregon being once a Western KKK stronghold—could use some gender bending. Frankly my dear, I don't think Rusty even had queer in his vocab. He was too Methodist, too True Value, too Ford 150 to even have the gay card in his deck. Jim knew that too, knew everything about all of us. All was brewing with his Enlightenment Tea, steeped by the monks in Lhasa. He was the Master, the Seer; we followed his instruction; we wanted to get clear. I flailed my arms around like Fontaine, leapt like Baryshnikov, whom I was lucky enough to have seen jump in *Giselle* back in San Francisco's War Memorial Opera House days. We muddled through, Rusty and I, embarrassed by our little pouches, framed by tight tights. We were a hit.

Then the final debrief. We had to tell our stories to the group. One mother spoke of remorse over her abortion, another spoke of breast cancer, another of valium abuse. Men admitted cocaine and lonely divorces. We became a series of country and western songs, but most of us were crying to hear the travails of our fellow Wingers. I cried at the drop of a puppy, wept whenever Jimmy Carter's voice cracked. Neil Young with his wonderfully off-key Sugar Mountain. Emmy Lou's "Pancho and Lefty." I knew my cue, knew it was not enough to be gay; I had to up the ante. Up the antigen. Had to come clean about my counts, my CD4/CD8 ratio, had to confess my incurable disease, the amazing courage to forge ahead in the face of this plague inside me, to sing like the late Doris Day (homophobe that she was) *que será será.*

What choice did I have? Fold up my tent and trudge down the mountain after lugging all this food and gear up to Lake Shakespeare, full of rainbow trout waiting to be caught by my

Royal Wulff? It was a no brainer. Just keep going until out of gas. But the pity of it, the utter misfortune to have the hamartia of gay love pull the rug out from underneath my pursuit of scholarship and the recognition, the anagnorisis, of this tragic consequence on a Sunday afternoon of commiseration before returning to some random boys yelling faggot out the window of their suped-up '56 Chevy as I walked home from campus to my white clapboard. Back to the disappointments of unproof-read essays and implacable students paralyzed by the intricacies of Hamlet's too too solid flesh.

I had confessed to the Wingers that I was HIV+. Our leader took a long swig of tea and smiled. Rusty hugged me hard and proceeded to confess his part in a failing marriage. Everyone cried for me, maybe even with me. I realized the healing power of disclosure—its relief, its hope. Maybe I had reached self-realization. Maybe not.

22
NOT MIGUEL

The Oregon Citizens Alliance is a conservative Christian political action organization, which in 1992 sponsored Measure 9, a statewide initiative to amend the Oregon Constitution to end special rights for homosexuals, adding a clause that homosexuality, pedophilia, masochism, and sadism were "wrong, abnormal, and perverse." The OCA had its stronghold in the town adjacent to Eugene called Springfield, which passed a local law preventing the protection of homosexuals through any ordinance. I found myself thrown into the middle of this battle the year I began my teaching in Eugene, in part because I was trying to remake myself as an HIV survivor, who, like the virus itself, was able to mutate once it faces the onslaught of antigens in the immune system.

HIV, once it finds a home in the open sore of the vascular anus, replicates so rapidly, according to Dr. Saag's studies, that the probability of its mutation is greatly enhanced. The AIDS virus has 9000 base pairs or strands of RNA as part of its makeup but the error rate in replication is one in every 3000 base pairs, so the virus in replicating is constantly changing its genetic makeup—creating a "swarm of variant viruses" earning the name of a "quasi-species."[1] Hence the difficulty in finding a cure. The discovery of these variants produced a collective sigh of dis-ease among researchers and patients alike. HIV was protean and the cure or vaccine would have to take that mutation factor into account. We were in this for the long—or short —haul, depending on the capacity of our bodies to ward off the massive colonization of the virus, my capacity to treat outbreaks of flu, herpes, shingles, thrush, weight loss, fatigue in order to stay alive for the red ribbon to be unpinned.

I pinned a red loop ribbon next to my rainbow flag when I marched down the streets of Springfield and joined the Gay Men's Tennis group and the HIV support group that met on Tuesday nights in Eugene. I was, in the parlance of the therapy jargon which had suddenly occupied most of my free time, "putting myself out there"—showing up at organizations with my jeans and tennis shoes. I wanted to find someone I could talk to, someone who could love me just the way I was, to fall back on Billy Joel. I was doing some lifting, swimming, playing some tennis in the evening with a gay group that included a man whose name was not Miguel.

He was Mexican, short, thin, handsome, my age or a little younger. We played doubles and rallied at singles together. His lover had died and left him some money. He drove a long black Mustang and had a long, thin boner soon after I met him. We played well together, but I had no idea how to approach any physical contact we might have. Was it acceptable to practice safe sex without disclosing my status? Did I need to say: "Hi, my name is Casey and I have AIDS." Yes, I had my ACT UP FIGHT BACK FIGHT AIDS t-shirt. I wore it once in a while, but I wanted to start anew in the West; I didn't want to begin behind the eight ball, having to announce at potlucks—while I shared a bowl of hummus, dipping my half-eaten celery stick into the paprika-laced chickpea mash—that oh my god I was contaminated. I'm really attracted to you but I'm a fucking pariah.

Miguelito made his move on the bench in the locker room. White towels surrounded our waists as he put his hand on my thigh after we had played two sets. His beautiful clear skin inches from my lips, his piercing eyes peered into mine. His backhand had a top spin I was only beginning to be able to return, his ground game deep and solid and unerratic compared to mine. He proposed a set of singles the following week. I could not bring myself to tell him I was positive; I couldn't ruin my chances of getting to second base with him, my chances of winning a couple of games before he trounced me six love.

I had heard about the lawsuits between soccer players with bloody knees in those days. Hemophiliacs were banned from schools in Florida. Congressmen wanted to quarantine queers and test them. People were still scared about French kissing and dentists were still closing their doors to gay patients. Nurses were masked, sterilization of surfaces was obsessive. My Band-Aid collection was obscene. Bleeding gums and noses; traces of red on toilet paper, dried blood on a razor blade on a sheet—on a counter—anywhere—a source of alarm in spite of the innumerable tests that proved how swallowing a bucket of my saliva or crashing into my scraped knee on the flag football team would not transmit a virus that needed a needle or a penis to make its stigmata. So, speaking of pins and needles, I was hyper-vigilant but also aware that maybe Miguel could be someone whom I could date and with whom I might have some form of intimacy—if only dancing to Bruce Springsteen in the dark. We kissed in the parking lot of the gym on campus after our evening of tennis, our showers, our mutual checking out of appendages—his long and narrow, mine average, mine hidden in the *cabrón* testicles. We took to one another.

The upshot of this match made on the hard courts was a fire lit in my little cottage one autumn evening, just Miguel and me on the floor of the unfurnished living room, on a blanket with cushions over the honey-colored refinished floor. Miguel with his glass of Merlot, me with cranberry juice. I was too scared to even take a drink for fear of hay wiring my helper cells. We were burning scrap two-by-fours and sticks I had picked up in the yard. We were lying on the floor, our palms holding our heads up. We gazed at the flame, gazed at our stretched-out bodies. He reached over, shoved his wine glass aside and kissed me on the lips. He was smaller than me, thin and wiry but strong and very much in control, very much a top I had figured out. I just wanted touch, just wanted to get warm. He planted his knees between my legs, massaged my back. I was getting hard and hot and though he too seemed turned on, he did not display any vulnerability. Our clothes were still on. We headed to the bedroom and I lay on my back.

Another photographic moment. On my bedspread Miguel knelt over my open legs with my pants down, my shirt off. He inserted his long finger into me while I laid back and held my cock in my hand. His penetration was unforgettable, charged, somehow defining. Not since Gilberto had I surrendered, melted so completely, with wonder and the sadness of memory. All of the cultural buttons pushed by the insertion of Miguelito's stone-butch finger into my willing butt and the long jouissant release of semen.

More important than this pornographic moment was its aftermath. Miguel, who hadn't even bothered to get off or let me help him reach climax, stood up and said, "I just wish it wasn't my finger but something else." He smiled slyly, alluding to his desire to fuck me in the future. Jesus was just alright with me, I thought, though somewhat—*cómo se dice*—taken aback by his own unwillingness to submit to my attempts to reciprocate.

Maybe he was nervous, unwilling to open up until the second date.

After this romantic finger fuck, if I might descend into crass alliteration, once Miguel had revved up his Mustang and driven off into the darkness, I had deep misgivings about my failure to disclose my status. We had done nothing unsafe technically. French kissing. His insertion. My emission conveniently absorbed by a Penny's t-shirt. But still I was riddled with guilt and felt I had crossed a felonious line in as much as I had read about lawsuits even criminal prosecutions for knowingly transmitting the virus to another. It was, in many eyes, a form of homicide to expose someone to HIV. My rather expansive imagination spun out a number of penitential scenarios, not only behind bars in this world but also in the next, serving a very long sentence in purgatory or some other undisclosed location. I fretted and remained in a state of deep guilt and remorse. I hastily arranged a meeting with Miguel the next afternoon after school, asked him to meet me for a walk on one of the many wooded paths that meandered through the city. I had to get it off my chest. My consciousness refused to be appeased by assurances from pamphlets and books that stated my behavior was not as egregious as I insisted. I had found another opportunity to indict myself and maybe Miguel's pointed finger had something oddly to do with the excitement of my masochism— as if the simultaneous headlines around the content of the OCA's constitutional amendment had become a self-fulfilling prophecy, Miguel had something of the sadist in his cold refusal to undress. I seemed more than willing to remove the psychological cat o'nine tails from the bottom drawer and, like a Christian martyr, confess my mortal sin on my knees.

The next evening, Miguel and I sauntered through the cattails beside some swampy mudhole in Eugene. "I need to tell you something," I said to him. "I'm feeling bad about not telling you before, even if we really haven't been unsafe. Still, it's not fair that I didn't let you know from the beginning that I'm HIV positive." I stopped there. I paused to glance into Miguel's dark eyes, trying to read his reaction in his handsome features. I stood there, my eyes turned quickly to the walkway, abashed. I glanced up to him again to absorb his reaction. We came to a stop. Miguel in his nondescript black jacket, while I scuffed, looked down, hoping for forgiveness, longing for expiation.

The dim lamplight of the park shined obliquely over his countenance. He paced for a moment and even before he mumbled "you should have told me," I sensed his cold anger and immediate frigidity. "You put my life in danger," he mumbled. I told him to get tested. Now and six months from now. I told him the chances of him contracting HIV were very, very slight, but that did not in any way mitigate the egregiousness of my irresponsibility in not disclosing at the outset, before our fireside massage. Miguelito smothered his seethe in silence. He turned and walked away, left me on the path to go back to his Mustang. I walked away sunk in a sea of self-recrimination.

I saw him later that year. He was negative.

23
LYMPHOPHOBIA

Anyone who had acquired the human immunodeficiency virus, especially if male and familiar with swallowing antiretrovirals, especially those of the early 90s variety like Retrovir and Zerit (d4T or stavudine) were attuned to, in fact petrified by the chance of disfigurement. Either lipodystrophy, a redistribution of fat in the body which included the dreaded buffalo hump or more seriously non-Hodgkin's lymphoma, a cancer of the lymph system that was a common cause of fatality in AIDS in the early days. The clear fluid called lymph runs through vessels and works to filter, stow, and clean white blood cells, but if malignant, the fluid amasses in nodes in the neck, groin, and under the arms, causing diffuse large b-cell lymphoma, a rapid growth of tissue around the carcinogenic area.

HIVers held a holy horror of bodily amorphism, especially since we were already sexually dysmorphic by some social standards. To present as Richard III, no matter how mild the scoliosis, added another layer of alienation to the odd-man-out syndrome that many of gay boys like me had harbored since youth—even as we sought desperately to marry, join the Marines, and accompany our cubs on scouting trips. Our assimilation was an ongoing project though some of us feared extinction as a result.

My first but not my last encounter with lipodystrophy came when I joined the HIV support group in Eugene. As part of my effort to atone for the Miguel mistake, I also saw a social worker, though the HMO that governed my health insurance only allocated six paid (or partially paid) visits for my psychoneurotic depressive reaction. My therapist was an older woman with mahogany hair, a large office hung with mandalas, dream catchers, and knock-off Tiffany lamps. Maxfield Parrish prints of long skirted goddesses floating on air decorated the walls. Sophia's scarves were knitted at craft fairs and she draped long silk blouses of deep mauves and rustic earth tones over her worn Birkenstocks. I reclined in an Ikea rocker and found in her long, gap-toothed Cheshire smile an emanating warmth that almost obviated the necessity of any talking cure, as if just being there with her were enough. I sat and looked and tried to cry. I poured out my litany of woes to this come-to-momma granny, who exuded comfort in ways no cigar-smoking Viennese note-taker could possibly hope to relay. I realized perhaps unconsciously how much more a braided rug, hint of sandalwood, and bubbling aquarium full of angel fish could do to soothe the savage professor, than any incisive Freudian psychoanalysis might induce. I melted in Sophia's arms, dumped out my endless store of self-critique, my soliloquy of self-flagellation. She wept to hear me speak of myself without compassion.

Sophia commiserated. She did not encourage, did not, like Bing Crosby try to persuade me to accentuate the positive or pivot into some Dale Carnegie glad-handing extroversion. She accepted my miasma, traveled with me like Virgil through the circles of my particular form of hell. We wallowed together in my experience, in my pressing through, my performance, my acting out. I found more comfort and clarity with Sophia's approach than I had in all the Jungian, Kleinian, Winnicottian, and Lacanian analyses I underwrote since my days of resisting the gay gene with Karl Gootnick in Marin County.

Finally, I confessed to her my moment of lymphophobia. The HIV support group I attended weekly was not large, maybe sixteen people meeting at six on Wednesdays in some conference center with folding chairs and gray tables. The leader was a young, vivacious woman who let us know that all were welcome—men and women in every stage of the syndrome, from all walks of life, from newly-diagnosed sex workers to men who had come home from San Francisco to die with their recalcitrant families. Understandably, those closer to death became the focus of the group. Our tears flowed most fluently for the emaciated and for the newly diagnosed who feared a life of fear. My attendance at the support group provided another Kodak moment, flashed another overexposed snapshot to scotch tape to the black pages of my photo album.

At the support group, Steve sat on a couch across from me. He was my age or younger, a ginger man with curly gold hair and fair skin, a pudgy man in blue-jean jacket and plaid shirt. There was no way he could not stand out. I was amazed he had the fucking balls to open the door and sit on the couch. Steve had a growth on his neck the size of a grapefruit, a gourd that ballooned above his shoulder, a gnarled lump that no collar was large enough to mask. Steve was a soft-spoken man who had lived in the Castro and worked as a bartender at the Elephant Walk. His low-top Converse All-Stars tapped and his voice cracked when he spoke softly of his exploding nodes.

I stared at him—all of us did, all of us scared to death—afraid, repulsed, saddened, angry. Steve, a mild-mannered man of forty, had less than forty t-cells, but still had the courage to come to the meeting, to tell us he was going to die in the town where he grew up. He was going to die with his parents who had disowned him until he had crawled back to find the only care he could from a pursed-mouthed mother and televisioned father. Over the dirge of his monotone, our eyes glistened, our fear for ourselves grew. I could not look at him. In spite of my self-recrimination, my guilt, I could not return to the group after seeing him week after week in his incurable state.

I could barely countenance my reaction—purely one of self-preservation, thankfulness that Steve was not me. Yet. I was not him; I was not a PWA, just an asymptomatic positive man who happened to be post Shingles. I had graduated from WINGS and was playing tennis with gay men, going to potlucks, having lunch with gay professors at the Honors College. I was beginning to feel good about my videoed self. Milton was emerging a little more emphatically from my lectern. My biceps were beginning to mound again. I was starting to think that *quizás quizás, quizás* even with 490 T-cells I might be able to matriculate for a few years in the world of my Renaissance in spite of the Miguelito misstep.

Sofia heard my story of running away from the sight of that lymphoma, from the horror not just of the support group close-up I faced but of the callousness of my flight response. I felt like a man who turned and ran from the bloodshed of an accident, unwilling to stoop to help, and rode home to save himself instead of staying to offer support. I hated myself for such smallness, such spinelessness. I could not be there for Steve, for the man who came to group for us to hear his story, to smooth his passage to oblivion. Instead, I had slammed my Honda door and drove home to a stack of response papers and waited to confess to my paid pardoner, Sophy.

"I can't go back," I told my counselor. "I can't face him. I know it sounds gutless and hard, but I'm not ready to see that goiter on his neck. It stares at me like fate. I feel like such a jerk, but I can't do it."

She nodded, her eyes glassy. We sat in silence, watched Mount Fuji at dawn in the framed poster. We looked at her maidenhair ferns and motorized waterfall in the corner. She refused to cheer me up. We watched the mobile made of stained glass, motionless. She crossed her legs and folded her large, wrinkled hands, put her fingers through one another and held them to her bosom almost as if in prayer. She smiled at me after a while and finally said, "You are so real. You feel it; you have taken Steve in."

I didn't know what she meant. I wanted to dismiss her New Agey comment as meaningless. A potion of phrases framed almost on purpose to *mean* nothing. Her words, I realized, were her means of our being together, hearing one another, knowing that we both knew what it was like to be alive among the dying and the living. Sophia was the master of the Zen of therapy.

I discovered how difficult it is for HIVers at different stages of the disease to encounter one another. I found out that my reaction was "normal" for those fending off the slow decline of the immune system. I learned that support groups were often divided between PWAs and Asymptomatics and Newly Diagnosed, sometimes divided between gay and straight. There were explanations for my fright and flight; there were official excuses that gave me license to forgive myself, even if I could not forget, even if I could not destroy the photographic evidence, the negative which was stored in a bottom drawer I would, only years later, be forced to pull open.

24

NOT SO WITH JOE

A s my year in Eugene came to an end in June 1992, I found myself jobless, uninsured, and friendless. The threat of thousand-dollar blood tests coming out of my pocket hung over me dauntingly as I searched the Modern Language Association (MLA) Joblist. For most of my professor life, one-third of my salary per month paid for health insurance coverage. I made too much to take advantage of the Ryan White CARE Act. My insurance always had exemptions: co-pays, deductibles, limits on coverage for procedures and hospitalization—loopholes that contributed to increased profits for insurance and pharmaceutical corporations. I was a constant patient in the health care system, a chronic HIV carrier, accessing doctors 10 often 15 times a year, requiring drugs, blood tests, examinations, therapy. My story was a doctor's story. My story required constant medical vigilance, constant payment, constant dollar bleeding. The specter of my financial drowning loomed.

At the last minute, I came up for air and landed two jobs. I grabbed a one-year position with benefits at Lewis & Clark

College in Portland and prepared to head up to grunge city, where I would piece together classes in Renaissance romance as well as the Trial in Literature. Lewis & Clark, in southern Portland, was perched on a hill overlooking Mount Hood, its campus a converted mansion. Wealthy kids intermixed with a scholarship student here and there, one of whom protested Grisham's use of the "n" word in *A Time to Kill*, a novel I admit squeamishly to teaching in the Trial in Literature class.

Joe was my second job. Moonlighting. I met him in the spring downtown at the one-story boxy bar in Eugene, which by ten or eleven at night had a multitude of guys standing around holding up flimsy sheetrock walls. A short, disheveled dude caught my eye—in cut-offs, blonde thinning mussed up hair, torn T, buck teeth, tan, funny, smiling, shy. He had spent the day at the quarry outside of town, nude sun-bathing, perched on a rock with his sari he used as a towel, well-oiled with some brown-bottled Hawaiian tanning oil—with an SPF of minus 10. He was brown, chubby, amicable, reading Daphne du Maurier.

Joe, divorced with two young kids, lived in a shack off Highway 5 in Medford, a flat pear town south of Eugene. Medford with its Mexican migrants, its burrito restaurants low-ceilinged and dark. Joe with his drowning waterbed, whose wooden frame was always somehow out of reach. Joe with his Chopin Ballades, his ten-key, 90 words per minute, fingers running over the keyboard as he practiced for his final exam in Music at Southern Oregon. The Joseph Affair had begun.

He buck-tooth smiled as we tugged at the labels of our Budweisers, looked at one another in the crowded bar, drowned out with Jackson's "Black or White," and Queen's "Bohemian Rhapsody." We checked each other out from a distance for what seemed like a 30-minute eternity, as I inched closer when wall space opened up. And then shoulder to shoulder, he said "hi," and we hooked up. Not that night. That night it was just phone numbers, then a call.

"I'm positive. You might not want to get involved with me. You have a right to leave," I told Joe in the yard of my house, under the moonlight in May, determined not to repeat the Miguel fiasco. Joe pulled my sweatshirt toward him, hugged me, and kissed me on the lips. We went inside and got under the covers of my futon. I was hard. I was hammered with elation to find a guy who wanted to stick with me, a guy with affection and acceptance, a guy who loved to hug and kiss and get off. I jumped in. We didn't always know what to do with his ample appendage, most of the time the two of us just watched it go off like a trip to the moon in Houston. Lift off. He on his back stroking, me watching, he watching. Just spit? Lube? We spooned and slept late. We went to the beach and lakes, got naked. He liked naked. He hung, handsome, the talk of the cruise crowd. We became an item.

When Joe came up to Portland from Medford, we would head out to Sauvie Island on the Columbia River, where I swam and shriveled while the tan and hung Joseph would bake beside the willow bushes, clothing optional men disappeared behind trees for jack offs. We hailed old queens with nipple rings and they stood over us with their go-aheads and slung testicles—reddened in the ultraviolet rays. Joe was good to them; he was interested in gerontology. I tried to read *The Stranger* but was soon distracted by sweat or a set of tanned buttocks.

At LC, I met Annie—a novelist, a deep endless friend—tortured by a lack of love, a penchant for black men, a Holocaust past, a love of old typewriters and ink pens. She helped me find a place, a wooded one-bedroom cottage in the forest of Multnomah—a low-ceilinged, free standing, dark brown job with a big living room, fireplace, tiny kitchen, bathroom, and bedroom. I stayed at her house while she was away for the first semester, and Joe drove up from Medford where we had a marathon massage session in the living room one weekend. He was trying to quit cigs and bourbon. He could care less if I was positive. He was out of shape, out of money—a sweet and caring mess who in his short nimble tumbling body harbored a heart, a sentimental warmth, as big as a delicious apple.

25

DR. ROOT

A job (if impermanent), a boyfriend (if long distance), health insurance (if partial). Things looked brighter in the rainy world of the Northwest. I breathed relief that I was able to continue to pay premiums and copays through Lewis and Clark College. I ventured into the Pearl District—Northwest Portland—to visit a recommended HIV doctor. Dr. Root's fourth floor office in a brick high rise looked out over 23rd Avenue. He was gay, thank God, had a five o'clock shadow and kinky black hair. He wasn't bad looking in a kind of Tom Hanks way, but he wasn't much to ogle. He was a very thorough physician, ordering a plethora of blood tests.

There was no viral load in those days, but his lab tech brought out enough finger-shaped glass tubes with purple, green, and yellow plastic caps to drain the vein in my arm for a couple of minutes. Dr. Root ordered my hemoglobin to be pumped by my systolic system through plastic tubes into vials for the math of the microscope: how many red blood cells were keeping me from anemia, how many clotters (platelets), how many white bloods cells, t-helper cells. He wanted to know about my liver, kidney, fats, and bones. He had to test for lipids (blood fats)—for cholesterol LDLs (those bad low-density fats) for HDLs (those good fats). Then the pee in the cup whether I had to go or not. I slipped into the sterile bathroom and waited for sufficient dribble, so the dipstick could measure glucose levels to find out if my kidney was failing or if I had diabetes. Then the flu shot, tetanus, HEP A, B, and C tests, liver enzymes. Then blood pressure—the constant blood pressure. Systolic rising by the very stress of having to sit in the waiting room looking at Fabio's pecs under a tank top in the pages of a crinkled *People* magazine. The very wait, the clipboard of forms, insurance cards, and my endless date of birth, the last time I lit up a Marlboro. The circles around those genital-less outlines of a body—where it hurt. Those torso drawings like target practice.

Finally, the physical exam. The PA with her computer and flowered scrubs, the pulse, the pressure, the temperature, constant use of antibacterial soaps. The medical waste, latex. My shirt off and the providers checking out my pectorals, feeling my neck and my underarms for growing nodes. When Root came in with his white coat, I was braced. His reputation preceded him; he was known to be "painstakingly systematic," I had been told by others. He was known to do a "complete" exam. He would leave no stone unturned—adages repeated by men in my support group with a raised eyebrow and a smirk—as if they were saying *get ready*. I sat on the exam table with my boxers still up, my ridiculous plaid boxers because I couldn't stand to be bound up with the Calvin Klein fashion industry brief, couldn't be clenched by undergarments even if sold by Marky Mark. I sat up and he (Root that is) with a cold stainless stethoscope told me to breathe normally, ordered me to take a deep breath as he knuckled my shoulders and spine, checked out my eyeballs for increased bilirubin—in search of yellow liver failure.

He put his hand down my shorts to feel for lumps in my groin. "I'm going to have to do a short examination of your prostate and take a rectal swab. It will be brief," he assured me, reaching for the box of blue latex gloves. "I also need to tell you not to worry if the exam causes you to have some reaction. My patients get nervous if they become aroused or ejaculate as a result of my examination. Don't worry; it's quite natural. Could you stand up and lean on the table with your shorts down please?"

I was a good boy. I did what the doctor said. This could have been a Manhunt video. I had seen some porn in my day when I dated a hot St. Lucian who was into chain fucks and watersports, but for me porn was assaulting. It stuck in my head and I couldn't get it out. I tried to steer clear of porn's penetrating images, including the classic doctor patient "examination," but suddenly I starred in a semi-erotic short feature, replete with some kind of lube on the forefinger of Dr. Root, who—had me over—not exactly a barrel—but an upholstered adjustable table. I held on for dear life to the paper cover in the full fluorescent light of an exam room that overlooked a tree-lined sidewalk in Portland, Oregon.

I felt his finger go in. He told me to relax my recalcitrant sphincter. He spent some time in there, stroked my prostate for lumps or size shifts. It hurt; it had dawned on me that what I was experiencing indeed qualified for the "in-depth" and "methodical" descriptors. Perhaps to his dismay, there was not any penile arousal or secretions as a result of his stimulation of my invaded cavity; in fact, I was tremendously relieved when he retracted his index finger. Maybe I wasn't versatile. Maybe I was basically a top who once in a while let a good friend in. Who knows? Positions were hopelessly categorical and rather bonding anyway. Dr. Root removed his lubed gloves with that rubber crackle that seems indescribable in prose, then washed his hands over the sink with a certain satisfaction. He was, after all, just completing his checklist, and my innuendos to the contrary, my insinuation that perhaps his probe provided some ulterior titillation beyond the perfectly respectable provision that he "loved his job," must in the end not rise to any implication that Dr. Root was, in the parlance, rather "kinky" in his practice. An attribution which, were it true, probably garnered him patients rather than frightened them away, certainly with regard to members of my family, which made up the large part of the HIV "community."

I am not a crotch watcher, being much too discreet and, if the truth be known I'm too Catholic for such eye-rape behavior, but from what I can remember (and as you have already gleaned, I am rather lacking in the recall department) Root had no tell-tale signs that his own private parts had reached any ostensible aggrandizement as a result of his journey to the center of my earth. I quickly slipped up my baggy boxers and pulled up my corduroys, feeling rather queasy as a result of the traces of his viscous deposit. Enough said.

26

ELEPHANT MAN

Nomadic academics face tests of their dedication to John Donne or Lord Rochester through the call of small colleges in bucolic but obscure outposts around the country for forlorn PhDs who have spent six years and countless dollars studying the pamphlets of Robert Greene (*A Groats-Worth of Wit*) or the satires of Gascoigne and penning a 300-page dissertation on the use of antimetabole in *The New Arcadia*. The call of these settlements of higher learning was destined to uproot my tendrils from the comfort of Ann Arbor or Berkeley and land me 100 miles south of Rochester, New York, fated to teach Shakespeare and basic writing at a minor state school in the flat limestone shelves of the Finger Lakes. I faced the prospect of living happily ever after upstate, tweed patches ironed on the elbows of my frayed Dress for Less blazer, subsisting on a salary that started at 28,500 a year.

A martyr to the secular scriptures of the humanities, I was trained to educate the masses in the canon of British literature. I was one of the lucky ones to be invited for an on-campus interview at Geneseo State College in New York, a nice little campus in a nice little town with old gray stone buildings and wide windswept walkways through tree-lined quads, all quite languid and contemplative. A good place to study. And Rochester was only hours away, whatever advantage that might have provided—a US Air hub, a Kodak moment. I was flattered to get a call back for a campus visit and delighted to prepare my talk on Milton's lost paradise. Though primarily an Elizabethan, I loved Milton, having gone to bed with *Samson Agonistes* on many a snowy evening during the Buffalo days (a sucker for long hairs).

It was March 1993. My flight was booked for the interview that I feared was probably an exercise in futility because at a Kalamazoo conference, I had met one of the faculty members, an ardent feminist who I presumed would have the ultimate capacity to derail my candidacy. But the prospect of that dim outcome held a certain melodious ring to my defeatist ears, tuned into my notion that Geneseo would be a kind of exile for me, like Ovid to Tomis on the Black Sea.

Dr. Root dug deeply into this narrative of the perils of my job search. His aforementioned probe turned out not to be entirely benign; my road to hell was paved with his good intentions. My stool sample had evidenced some foreign amoebas in my colonic track, in spite of the fact that to the best of my memory no gerbils had recently squirmed into that rectal orifice nor had any juicing carrots or dildonic devices gone once more into that breach. Other than the fickle finger of Miguelito, my port of entry had seen little business after the Brazilian pinnace returned to its native land. But, nevertheless, some bacteria were allegedly extant, and Dr. Root was, well, not to put too fine a point on it, as Snagsby is wont to say in *Bleak House*, hellbent on rooting it out of my system through the prescription of sulfonamide, a synthetic antimicrobial agent slash sledgehammer, that killed every foreign substance in its path. Sold under the name of Bactrim or Septra, "Sulfa" was the drug of choice for Root who was determined through a kind of anti-germ warfare to wipe my slate clean.

It was raining in the spruces of Multnomah. The flimsy particle board bedroom off the kitchen no bigger than a queen-size bed with two-foot aisles on either side exuded the odor of mold and mildew. I tried to stay above water as I taught my classes and prepared for my interview. My plane reservations were made, my tasteful brown slacks, yellow tie, and earth-toned sport coat hung in a zipped garment bag in the shallow closet off the kitchen. I had shined my mahogany wingtips and even ironed a white shirt. I was ready to knock 'em dead upstate. My conference paper, arguing that paradise is always already lost, lay inside a manila folder ready for my presentation.

The night before my flight I dutifully swallowed Sulfa as prescribed. When I rose to yellow the rim of my toilet, I looked into the mirror to find Elephant Man staring me in the face, my head swollen to nearly twice its size, my eyes had become slits, my body ached. It was two in the morning the night before the drive to long-term parking. I was unrecognizable, literally freaked out, alone in that postage-stamp bedroom growing like Alice from what (I didn't even realize at the time) was the taking of that one pill. Those hours until morning while I waited to call the doctor were in themselves a kind of purgatory worse than Geneseo, even if I were ever to get there, could imaginably represent. Rain and the dark forest of Oregon, the world closing in on my depleted immune system. I was in a word, or two words, scared shitless.

Little did I know at that point that 60% of HIV positive

people are allergic to this sulfamethoxazole/trimethoprim combine, which emitted side effects of fever, headaches, rashes, swelling, and more seriously kernicterus (brain damage caused by an overabundance of bilirubin). Was I going to die, be deformed for the rest of my life? What was Geneseo to me? Me to Geneseo? At four in the morning, I held on to my baby blue down comforter with its worn quilts and shedding goose feathers. It was all a blur. Maybe it was Bactrim or Keflex, maybe it wasn't Pfizer's Septra, maybe Root had not gone on an all-expenses paid trip to Honolulu to the Pfizer convention to hear about the "health" benefits of the pharma giant's latest anti-bacterial agent so ripe for use on the immune-compromised butt boys who were dying by the hundreds cross the continent. When in doubt, dose. Not to be confused with Sculptra, the injection that masked the wasted face, Sulfa provided an immediate cure to lipoatrophy—facial ballooning.

I had to postpone my interview for a week, stay at home, go off the drug. I waited for the swelling to subside, hid under the covers with my tears and ibuprofen, with my mint tea, and stack of term papers. With my lovely immemorable self, blown up to a taut, encephalitic, skin-stretched mess. Needless to say, Root was soon rooted out of my rolodex. I tried to joke about it when I called Joe in Medford. I told him I would eventually shrink, that I would cough up the rescheduling fee with US Air.

When I got to New York a week later, I was shuffled down dark hallways to busy professors who had no idea who I was, driven around by a rotund Aemilia Lanyer scholar who asked me if I taught the sonnets of Lady Mary Wroth. She steered her Oldsmobile Cutlass through the sleepy streets of Geneseo. I was treated to an all-I-could eat dinner at The Sizzler. I got the distinct sense that they had already chosen their candidate. I was the perfunctory courtesy interview Human Resources required. I could tell from their complacence that they had already decided to offer the job to some Aphra Behn scholar from Brown or Smith, some young breedable ABD from the Ivies. Dr. C, even without a fat head, was clearly not their man. A collective sigh of relief exhaled from my belly as they deposited me at the Airport Shuttle.

27

CROW MAN

Lusijah Marx started QUEST in 1989. She was an RN turned shaman with long wavy gray-white hair, a tinge of pale beige still extant in the strands held together by her leather beret, fixed in place by long Japanese wooden sticks. In '93, she hadn't gone mainstream yet. She hadn't gone Ryan White on us. She brought HIVers together in a little ramshackle house on Thurman off 23rd, in a neighborhood unconnected to the popular Pearl warehouse/loft/Powell's Bookstore district. Lusijah led support circles on Saturday—a mix of massage, meditation, chant, and psychodrama in the backroom of her single-story clapboard, supplemented by incense and mandalas and music of the spheres. Maybe not tie-dyed, but long flowing skirts and lots of cushions. Lots of flat on our backs, heads toward the center, guided dreams to places outside the self where healing energy could flow through chakras. Where I could run my lavender color through blood and lymph, through walls of my intestines and stomach, muscles of my heart, through nodes and nostrils. Where I could run my pale purple energy from toenails to the excrement of my dirty brown straight hair—bodiless and flat after a wash. Deep breaths. Out with the bad, in with the good.

Lusijah reminded us that the AIDS quilt was coming to the rainy city. In between runs through dripping forests and Japanese gardens over steep hillsides west and south of downtown, hours lost in the stacks of Powell's, and plates full of shoestring fries on Hawthorne Street, I found a parking space at TrailBlazer stadium and peered over the balcony at the homemade patches that covered the entire court. I wandered downstairs, in a daze as I glanced aimlessly at remembrances of dead craftsmen queers, remarkable in their handiness—cowboys, gardeners, decorators, haberdashers, dancers, disc jockeys, divas, junkies, sluts, nurses, baristas, waiters, chefs, plaid-shirted loggers, florists, travel agents, dentists. You name it; they did it all. My dead comrades, memorialized by stitched cloth, by patches of cotton flat on a basketball court.

I thought about Crow Man, a guy who came to Lusijah's support group each Saturday. He spoke to us about the story of his meditation journey. I had a crush on him, on the fabric of his livelihood. He was short with long blond braids and Willie Nelson wrinkles but younger, fairer, more ginger. He was a namaste hippie, a granola who built his own cabin, tanned, and crafted furniture out by Mt. Hood. He was so unqueer, so totally rad—such a mountain man in his run-down pickup.

I wanted to go back to his garden with him and pick greens, mix a kale salad and drink some spearmint tea. I wanted to hang out on his overstuffed couch with cat scratches, socks on, play war on the couch with him and his paint-spattered jeans. I wanted to massage his shoulders as he leaned his tight body into me at the end of the sofa, just hold him close and put my head on his shoulder. Feed the chickens, head out to Tillamook, fish the Metolius for rainbows. I kept seeing him—his 5'7" torso, his 50 years of weathered hands, his wise smile. When I looked at him, I fantasized a life my desk-bound academic career could never embrace. I pictured him gazing up at the snow on Mount Hood, the old Cascade volcano. I could see his canoe, his ax stuck in a stump, the wagging tails of his Labradors. I saw all of that rough, make-ends-meet life—the banjo, and the cookies in the iron-cast oven, the skinny dips and hot tub. Saw all of that Whole-Earth world and wondered about the roads I would never be able to take.

Crow Man had no T-cells. He was wasting away. He couldn't keep food down; he was up all-night sweating, changing sheets, up all night freezing in the summer. Crow Man was alone in the woods with a sister south in Salem, who waited for his phone call, waited to drive up to Mt. Hood and walk him to her station wagon, take him to her suburb before he entered the hospital. Before the life support systems, green blips on the screen gave out from unplugging or just plain expiration, even with the tube in his nose, even with the flowered gown and cranked bed, even with monitors and the railing his sister leaned on. The doctors with their blue outfits slid helplessly around in slippers, and watched as Crow Man flew away into space.

One Saturday Lusijah told us Crow Man wouldn't be coming back. We sensed his going because the dream he related to us the time before channeled crows. He told us about his vision as we shared with each other what we saw when we closed our eyes. I saw lavender run up my spine, saw blue purple of the succulent I kept in my kitchen, that delicious color of the purple sky after a storm at dusk. For me a color running. For Crow Man, circling birds. He saw the gyre of wings; he heard the crows calling. Perched in his trees at home, up in the blue spruce, up in the tall pines, the murder checked, squawked and squealed, beckoning Crow Man to their roost, ominous, foreboding, intuitive. A quilt of crows. They summoned him, these birds, until he had to answer. Our circle grew smaller and Lusijah strong with her glassy eyes saw me stunned and cold as stone. She watched me absorbed by his crow story, week after week, watched me grow stupid and scared as I held on for dear life.

By some uncanny convergence, I was slated to teach John Donne the next Friday afternoon before Easter, "Good Friday, 1613, Riding Westward." I hadn't planned to teach the poem during those holy hours, but the coincidence of events struck my altar boy sensibility as almost prophetic. As I prepared before class, the quietness descended from one to three, and I could feel that suspension in the air. I knew what those hours meant, those hours of crucifixion. I could feel them, feel the sanctity, feel the need to let a heavy nothingness of loss stop the clock, these hours of silence arrested my list of things to do. I thought of Crow Man, how little I knew him, how much I idealized him, admired his spunk. He was dead or dying in a bed with a drip in his arm. I had to write about it.

GOOD FRIDAY, 1994: TEACHING JOHN DONNE

The bell rings at three,
my students sit in a sphere, intelligent—
some moved, some lost in the weekend,
these pupils who know nothing of this scald,
my despair that stares at them.

What good is this Friday anyway,
this end of the Passion?
A man on trial for treason thinks himself immortal—

another dead martyr, his teachings abused
by those who judge my disease,

viral blood turning flesh to ash,
shriveling friends, faces of lovers.
Did He waste away for years
beside those afraid of their fate—
dementia, sarcoma, pneumonia?

Our circle whirls toward the poet's ride—
his back to the face of the crucified man
whose time on earth reminds us of the plot
we'll share when all is undone,
when faith evaporates before the sight

of flesh-stretched bone. I have seen my friend die,
seen men on Welfare, sick, penniless, skeletal,
spit upon in the name of Jesus. I have watched
men soak sheets with sweat, grow grapefruits
on their necks, purple their chests with lesions.

Though these sights, as I teach, be from my eyes,
they still present to my memory.
Teach me to learn from these wounds,
You from whose pain I turn my back
You who kissed the men You loved.

TRADER JOE

(1994-1997)

28

GAY DOG

When Joseph strode down the driveway from the parking lot at Lewis & Clark in the middle of July 1994, he wore the green Montana t-shirt I bought him during my on-campus visit. His buck-toothed grin beamed as he passed through the library sensor and found me hunched over my essay on *Twelfth Night or What You Will*. I saw a certain bounce beyond even the usual spring of his gymnastic step in his nimble-footed stride. What was he doing in the library? He had come to tell me that Montana had offered me the job I had applied for and lost after endless deliberations in May and April. Apparently, the other candidate, the "other woman" as I had affectionately dubbed her, had gotten cold feet and decided to stay put in Britain, leaving me, the maverick Buffalonian, in the cue. It was an offer I had no intention of refusing, even if I was about to enter the jaws of a faculty divided between academic conservatives and progressives, between biographical critic and a queer theorist.

HIV was not even in the mix, other than as a hidden ingredient. I was entering into a period of re-closetization. Why hire a 40-year-old queer man with a life expectancy of five years? What kind of an investment might that be? Why bring that horrible gay disease to our lovely mountain home? When one cancer physician had suggested that Missoula Hospice begin training to take care of terminal AIDS patients, the board looked at him in 1993 like he was a freak. We don't have *that here*, they told him. Yes, a few men had died or come home from West Hollywood or Capitol Hill to pass over in the bosom of their nuclear family, but HIV would never, in the eyes of these shit kickers, reach the bucolic last best place of Missoula, Montana, population 50,000. Home of some radical hippies in the 60s who occupied Main Hall. Yes, home of a drunk writers' society and displaced Indians, of occasional peak baggers and Brad-Pitt fly fisherman—but that "don't mean we got none of those sick fags here."

Joseph and I loaded the U-Haul and the wagon in August and drove up the Columbia Gorge, crossed the big river at Pasco, and headed north to 90 and Spokane. The road descended east from Lone Mountain down the speed-trap freeway into the barren valley of what was left of Glacial Lake Missoula, hemmed in by Mount Jumbo and Mountain Sentinel to the east, the Rattlesnake Wilderness to the North, and opening up to the beautiful Bitterroot to the south, where drainages like Kootenai, Sweeney, Blodgett, and Bass flowed down from the range that kept Idaho at bay but not the polygamous Mormons, who lived in the trees and collected loaded weapons.

One of those Mormons turned out to be a breeder of Golden Retrievers. The sire was a big shorthaired golden and the mother a feathered beauty. Once settled, Joe and I, could not help getting lost in polygamous Pinesdale west of Hamilton, as we searched for the double-wide where pups were for sale. A litter of seven melded together in a cardboard box as they fought for Mom's tits, all chubby but big enough to prance around a bit before they fell and lost what awareness they had of where they were. When one happy camper followed me back to the Honda, I turned and told the breeder, a bearded recluse, that we would take the pup.

Toby became my pet, my survival animal, my life jacket. He also became the department's mascot. He wandered the halls in search of cool linoleum floors for plopping and for yet another student to wag his tail for, his feathered happiness. Sir Toby Belch. During the first year of my tenure track job (in Montana it was called a "tenure trap"), Sir Toby Belch came with me to departmental functions. I had eavesdropped behind a doorway one day, when I heard one of the good ol' boy professors chortle to Bill Kittredge and some others, "I wonder if his dog is gay too."

From 94-96, those first two years I taught at UM, I perished and published, in what order I am not altogether certain. My writing and research, ostensibly removed from any patent self-confession, provided a platform for my hypothetical self-disclosure. My work allowed me to talk the talk in a way that obviated the need to walk the walk or in this case to announce to my Law, Politics, and Literature class that I was not only a happy faggot but also a happy carrier of the virus that causes AIDS. My interest moved from the Renaissance to gay studies. Law, the proverbial jealous mistress, led me to field a course that put American legal literature and politics together—combining cases, political archives, and fiction. We studied individual rights—race, gender, political affiliation, and finally a little section on queer rights. That field was making inroads in scholarship, even though the Supreme Court had upheld sodomy laws in *Bowers v. Hardwick* (1986) and sexual deviancy was still a felony under a Montana statute.

In my vast skimming of law review articles on sexual orientation, I came across the Sharon Kowalski case, the story of a Minnesota women severely disabled in an auto accident, who became the focus of a guardianship battle between her lover, Karen Thompson, and Sharon's parents, a working-class family from the Iron Range. The case had become a *cause célèbre* among the queer legal set because of the prolonged litigation and national spotlight on the courts' decision to award guardianship to Sharon's father, who in turn prevented Karen, a nurse, from visiting her traumatically brain-injured lover for many years. The ten-year court battle ended pyrrhicly when Sharon's father Don finally relinquished his guardianship. Karen Thompson gained legal control without opposition. The case spoke to the HIV in me. It underscored the deep animus that lesbians and gay men faced in relation to their journey through illness and death.

Because there were no marriage rights for same-sex couples, there were no legal presumptions of affinity for purposes of hospital visitation, power of attorney, health directives, inheritance, burial, community property—to name a few of the hundreds of rights and privileges that attached to marriage. Thousands of gay, partnered men entered ICU wards without their lovers having any right to see them. When dementia rendered a 30-year-old adjunct professor in San Francisco incapable of making decisions, only the next of kin, contacted in Abilene years after they disowned their queer son, gained the sole right to decide on his medication or health care. Apartments were emptied by distraught parents driving in from Elko to the Castro while lovers watched, arms folded, in their living rooms. Ashes were removed to Cincinnati. Property sold by lawyers to line the pockets of a father who hadn't seen his son since his boy ran away from home, caught in the shed naked with his roommate. Uninvited to funerals, unmentioned in obituaries— countless deaths from "liver cancer" were recorded.

I decided to write about the Kowalski case. It spoke to me. I was an HIV positive gay man on the verge of legal erasure. I was an assistant professor who spent countless hours in the homophobic halls of the University of Montana with my gay dog.

29
DEEP BAY

The Montana closet accentuated the stress of my trifecta: the stigma of orientation, the stigma of disease, the stigma of passivity, of gender. The stigma of getting fucked and enjoying it. All of it hidden, at times even from myself. The slow pathogenesis of a rapidly multiplying infectious agent that constantly searched for cells under my skin to facilitate its replication. The virulent invisibility of living with this slow killer—the acronymic HIV which, unlike Marburg or Ebola, crept in its petty pace, paradoxically rapid in reproduction, through my system, rotting the host from inside, merciless in its march, its latent reservoir of sub-microscopic colonies whose half-life was thirty or forty months for each particle.

And at the same time, I voraciously read all the name-dropping AIDS memoirs, the Ashes, Sean Stubs, Hemphills, Monettes, Doties, and Feinbergs—the countless heart-wrenching stories of sickness unto death. All of this foundation highlighted my inconsequence, my longing to pass as healthy and undetectable. Zamora, Randy Shilts, *Angels in America,*

Eazy-E—these were the proper names that spelled the years of 1994 and 1995 as breakthrough years on the HIV treatment front. These were the Merck years of nevirapine and indinavir, protease inhibitors and their 23-step process of manufacture for a drug that worked temporarily to stop the leading cause of death of Americans 25 to 44. These were drugs that suddenly found more effectiveness in combination on test cases, sometimes on compassionate use clients who begged for a little more time. AZT, DDI, and DDC had run their course for them. These were the years of Project Inform and buyers' clubs, the years when, in Redwood City, California, two scientists discovered how to measure the amount of HIV in the blood, an advancement that made drug testing phenomenally easier and more effective.

The discovery of viral load testing was deeply chastening. A typical influenza virus produced one million copies of itself in a day while it traveled through streams of the body; HIV made one to ten billion copies of itself in a day. Those with acute sero-conversion like myself had faced exponential duplication during the "flu" period that began the fatal illness. How remarkable that I still had some years to live given the countless hosts I was hosting. Especially, given my stubborn refusal to take these new drugs.

In the mountains of Montana, I hid my syndrome not only by ignoring conventional medicine but also by focusing on my queer veneer. I joined the Gay Men's Task Force (GMTF), became the faculty advisor for the student Lambda organization. I marched in the PRIDE parades, carried a banner down Last Chance Gulch in the Treasure State's great capitol of Helena. I helped to start the Western Montana Gay and Lesbian Community Center. None of these activities–not all the retreats and drag shows, the forums and Judith Butler assignments, the lectures on the two Antonios in Shakespeare, my involvement in our "community's" attempt to drag Montana kicking and screaming into the 20th century even on the cusp of the 21st—none of these diversions could mask the masking of my identity within my identity. I waved a rainbow flag, celebrated diversity, formed the Outfield Alliance to support gay faculty and staff, but avoided like the plague—literally—any mention of my dirty little secret, HIV.

Those first years were a blur, a moment when my mantra was "give it a rest" on the HIV front, expedient as it was to pass. Doctor Seagraves of course knew, my internist at the clinic whose wife apparently gave much of their income to anti-abortion organizations with fetus billboards. Few others knew—besides Joe. I had a partner; I had a job; I had a dog and a fenced yard. My T-cell count bounced around between 400 and 550. I did my gay part in class and the streets.

I had had a moment or two of disclosure. One during a Gay Men's Task Force meeting, when we planned retreats to fulfill the group's mission to build healthier lives for the tortured—literally again—men of our rural last best or worst place. Many of whom were married or mauled in high school, their heads stuck in toilets—their souls condemned in church—disowned and fleeing from ranches in Manhattan, Montana, to studio apartments in Billings or Butte, where they waited tables at the 4Bs or tended bar at the Joker's Wild. They searched for men at rest stops or on levees late at night, stuck with porn if they could find and hide it. Many disowned or damned, many drunk or obese or both. Many skinny, smoking, nervous, acned, addicted, suicidal, shy, campy, bar-fly basket cases our org tried to reach. A large percentage of them would never receive notice of the Gay Men's Task Force because they didn't even consider themselves gay. They were just MSM before that acronym became part of our vernacular. They were guys who got off on guys whenever and wherever they could. They would never come to Deep Bay to sit in a circle and talk about their family or get in a group and draw a map of their life. They would never, after pizza and Pepsi and condom demonstrations, after talks on STDs and hard oatmeal cookies, after guided meditations and flannel sleeping bags rolled out beside the young, horny, and insecure, after all of that, would never in a million years want to hear a 40-something professor at the university in a break-out group disclose after warnings of confidentiality and admissions of fear that he would lose his job or be quarantined, that yes, he was positive.

I stayed in the big-windowed log cabin that overlooked the grand inland, freshwater Flathead Lake beneath the Swan Range that rose from the mercury sheen of the water's vast expanse. I attended the paid-for weekend with macaroni and Mountain Dew. I joined the motley queer crew of thirty men of all ages and all stages of fucked-upness who had come to build camaraderie, learn to love themselves somehow against all American odds of conformity and ostracism. On a cold autumn weekend, on the porch outside—many shivered and smoked in their sweatshirts, most unwilling to go near the water. Most just stared out the picture window in the big open space of the living room, peered out the frosted window at another Montana winter coming to swallow them up, to push them further into their messy and smelly unmade beds with their frozen pizzas and *Will and Grace* reruns. And, if they could afford it, a trip to the mall in Spokane. These boys from Big Sandy and Big Timber, hapless and sick of horseshit, who lived in town with a television and pack of Marlboro Lights, lived with diabetic mothers in La-Z Boys and brothers who had beat the shit out of them. They lived with Jesus and family values.

They faced me, the gay facilitator, afraid to come out as positive until that evening when I found myself in a circle drawing my life map in that big rented cabin on the west side of the lake. It came time for me to show my map and tell my story on the carpeted floor as the sun set on the cold fresh water of that huge inland body where I dreamed of drowning myself in recrimination. I knew I had to tell those boys I was positive. I was living with HIV and I was scared of dying.

MOUNT WASHINGTON

If HIV remained on the down low those first years in Missoula, my sex life did not fare much better. Joseph and I fell into a kiss and cuddle routine. I would not engage in intercourse. I was too anxious, too fearful of transmission, in spite of the assurances of safer sex pamphlets. A gash in my paper-thin Irish skin, a nosebleed from a sneeze in the freeze of frigid Missoula, another outbreak of aphthous ulcers, or herpes simplex, even a hangnail or chapped hand would immediately transport me into infection mode. I thought of Joseph's children who relied on their daddy's affection. I worried about spots drying in the sink, emptied trash cans full of Band-Aids, repeatedly washed my hands with antiseptic soap. I bought a dishwasher, washed clothes on the hot cycle, grew mildly hysteric over cuts while shaving or bleeding gums after a vigorous floss. Given my penchant for worry, our sexual intimacy was soon reduced to frottage and lube-induced masturbation. Our sex was safe. I wondered if it was enough.

I grew hyper vigilant not only about transmission but how these ailments, coupled with the occasional stuffiness of an upper respiratory infection or eczema, might forebode a dreaded OI (opportunistic infection). PCP, KS, Toxoplasmosis, fatigue, neuropathy — the specter of a downturn towards a non-existent hospice continually lurked on my neurotic horizon. I found myself in a regular state of alarm not only about trans-mitting my retrovirus to Joseph but also about transporting myself to the great incinerator in the Big Sky, hoping my good works redeemed me from a Hell that no doubt would resemble a Super Walmart.

One day Joe announced his plan to apply to USC's gerontology program. He longed to get back to The Ice Capades, back to Dorothy Hamill (for whom he had once assembled sequin costumes), back to Santa Monica or wherever he could place his sari in the sun. I proposed to follow him down there by applying to the Center for Feminist Research at USC to work on the Sharon Kowalski case. I was transforming myself from Shakespeare teacher to a queer studies researcher, relying on my law background to write an account of the famous custody case that had clear consequences for people with HIV.

The fellowship came through. I loaded up the Honda wagon in August of 96 and headed south. Joe had moved months earlier, gone down to LA to look for work, where he joined APLA (AIDS Project Los Angeles) as a supplier of home care meals and other needs for patients. He had rented a place for us near Aragon Street close to Cypress Park, a predominantly Hispanic neighborhood wedged between the 5 and the 110 that veered off up to Pasadena. LA was all about freeways, all about traffic. When Toby and I drove up to the grey duplex in LaLa land that summer evening, we found Joe waiting for us in the empty living room. The neighborhood was fairly raunchy. We were on a hill that was populated with one-

and two-story stucco houses and apartments. Fenced Pits lunged upon our arrival and men with bellies that emerged from below their *playeras* (t-shirts) glared as I gingerly climbed out of the wagon after the long drive down 5. A chicken coop next door stood beside a dirt yard full of nervous Chihuahuas. Rancheras blared from the home across the street as shirtless kids kicked a soccer ball. This was not Santa Monica; it was not East LA exactly, but it was not West Hollywood either. I was not greeted by gay men pruning their Ficus hedges and watering cascading nasturtiums. Joe had found a nice remodeled upstairs flat, blue gray in color and quite clean, right smack dab in Tijuana North.

For all my lip service to toleration and love of Mexico, a part of me was still a snobby Hillsborough boy, not ready to live with leashed Rottweilers and low riders, the wafting smell of frying pig entrails and screaming babies naked from the waist down. The noise, aromas, lack of parking, backfiring, the Burger King wrappers, the *pandillas* eyed my Golden with disdain and switchblades—all of this cultural immersion left me a bit uneasy as I walked Toby down the patched asphalt hill where our new apartment stood. Could I adapt?

That challenge, as it turned out, came more compellingly from inside our lovely dwelling, which had little or no furniture. Joe had a mattress on the bedroom floor. After I arrived and walked Toby through the tintinnabulation of the barrio, Joe and I reconnoitered in the kitchen. I was happy to see him; Joe was always the warmest of souls, such a great cuddler, so easy to be around, so laid back, perfect SoCal fare. When we hugged and kissed, however, I detected the scent of cigarette smoke on his breath. He had quit months before when he began running 8 to 10 miles a day. What's up with that? "You been smoking?" I asked him. "No," he answered. I unloaded some of my stuff, lugged a couple of suitcases up the stairs into the bedroom. I fed the dog, scoped out the backyard which was not a backyard but a fenced deck that looked out on a couple of apartment buildings where grilling spareribs and drying underwear provided an apt backdrop to my LA experience.

I had been raised to hate this town, being from the Bay Area, raised to despise the Dodgers, the smog, the superficiality of the bumper-to-bumper life with its Tinsel Town mentality, its amorphous sprawl and barren chaparral hillsides. Of course, there were the beaches, Malibu and Manhattan. Sunny weather when it wasn't socked in. There was Pasadena. It didn't matter. I was at that point in my so-called life still in pursuit of my main squeeze Joseph. I was happy to descend into the glam jam of a place I never thought I would call home, if even for a year. Corsages and OJ were all that came to mind when I thought of USC, the rich little sorority school in the middle of South Central, but I was okay with that too. I was happy to have some time away from Montana, it being, as Joe insisted, rather parochial, and definitely limiting for the queer positive set.

While I cased the joint and wondered if this flat, recently remodeled and manageable, would be sufficient for the two of us and dog, Joe went outside for a few minutes. I had just opened the empty fridge when he came in the door, smiling nervously, that big-toothed grin, self-conscious of his buck teeth, his yellow hair receding, a little mussy, a little thinning, his skin tanned, his short set body always ready to do a flip or handstand. He wore jeans and t, gripped the air with his nervous hands and leaned on the counter. I could smell the smoke from across the kitchen. "You smell like cigarettes," I told him again and he tried to shrug it off. Where there's smoke, there's . . . Joe offered me a beer. I felt like telling him for the twenty thousandth time, "I don't drink, remember; I can't drink because of my fucked up immune system." Maybe a Pale Ale once in a while. My only vices were ice cream and men.

"I got to talk to you," Joe finally mumbled, as he paced over the smooth new linoleum floor. "Look, I've met someone else," he said. I stood there astounded, trying to figure out what he meant. "I've met another guy that I've been dating," he told me. "We've been going out for a while."

I stood in the kitchen trying to absorb this bombshell from my partner, whom I had followed down to Central Los Angeles, after I took LWOP (leave without pay) and an office at USC to write my book while he pursued his degree. I had packed up the fucking Honda wagon, clunked down through Oregon and drove south on the dullest road in the world, Highway 5. I had listened to old Neil Sedaka and Lionel Ritchie songs, flipped the switch in Modesto, in search of something other than Jesus and Johnny Cash. Three days on the road with a dog and a full car. My first night in LA and I had not even unpacked when my lover informed me he's dating another guy, but we could still live together in the gray duplex with the roosters and the Pit bulls.

I wanted out of there immediately. I felt totally rejected, totally freaked out, totally turned off—ready to check-in to some motel. Credit card time. But I was such a nice, cautious man, such a mensch. I said to him, "Okay, we'll work it out; we'll figure it out in the morning." We went to bed, curled up on opposite ends of the mattress. I got no sleep, Toby nervous but hanging out quietly. When we woke up at 6 AM, I told him: "I can't stay here. You can stay. Give the guy notice. We're on a month-to-month. You stay this month. I'm out of here." I'd already paid the rent for that month. I got my stuff back in the wagon, got Toby in, and drove away, in shock, in tears, in panic, in LA. I didn't want to hear his story. I couldn't stand rejection.

There had been too much rejection in my life already. There would be more.

I found my way to the Gay and Lesbian Community Center on Schrader in seedy Hollywood. LA was a mass of long wide streets with stoplights and stucco buildings interspersed with mini shopping centers that sold used appliances and other tchotchkes. An occasional shish kabob restaurant punctuated the strip malls. Parking was parallel and impossible. The homeless pushed shopping carts and hookers wore miniskirts. I left my full car and dog somewhere on the street and waited for *wait* to turn to *walk*, waited to cross some fungible boulevard, dart toward the two-story center with its binder full of housing advertisements.

None of this sudden shock of singleness did much to maintain my immune equilibrium. I envisioned herpes and ulcers in my future in spite of a series of self-conscious time-outs, some superficial deep breaths, and other such ineffectual mind games. I found one room in a house where dogs might be considered, according to an old binder slip. My call was answered by an aging, rather weight-challenged fellow who lived on what seemed to be two acres near the top of Mount Washington, a residential community off the 110, nestled, suspended, peopled by houses in arroyos and hillsides. Apparently, this mail man had inherited a one-story wood-sided modern 60s home from his dead partner, and he lived there alone with a lhasa apso cross. He showed me the small annex off the garage, a long narrow room with a single bed, hardly large enough for the Japanese date I would have months later after a long walk with the queer night hikers in Griffith Park. There was a small desk at the far end, where I could pretend to work. The owner called himself Ed. He was wooed by Sir Toby Belch, whose feathered tail and smile could charm the pants off anyone, though one would not want in this case to have Ed's high-water trousers anywhere but fully pulled up over his ample abdomen. Thank God for figures of speech.

I was trepidatious. The place was a bit remote, the kitchen shared. The owner spun Bert Bacharach vinyl on his old record player. Ed's occasional glance unnerved me initially. I made it clear that I was not interested in a blow job, and his shy approach gave way to a polite distance. He peered up occasionally from the garden with his gloves and trowel in hand. He sauntered into the kitchen while I waited for my toast to burn.

I rented the place out of desperation though it felt a little bit like a potential horror film. The grounds were big and empty. They looked over some steep arroyo. An enormous old stucco mansion loomed over us on the hillside above Ed's yard, home of the Self-Realization Fellowship with its manicured lawns, huge gates, and empty driveway. Occasionally a Madame Sosotris drove her black Mercedes into the graveled entrance. Very spooky stuff. Toby and I did our best. We walked up and down the steep tree-lined and winding roads, avoided as much as possible the alarmed German Shorthairs who howled hopelessly into the reverberate hills.

I had to make do. Ed turned out to be rather naturally removed and self-contained, not someone with the capacity to go postal in spite of the absolute inconsequence of his life, as a single aging overweight gay man—the fate for so many of us, tied as we had become to our mini-series and titillating novels, our lurid trips to Gold's Gym and occasional forays into tears on the couch, bitter widows in dead living rooms. I feared his fate might be my own—were I to live.

31

DON'T PANIC

A two story-building behind eucalyptus trees, painted black. A converted warehouse with concrete floors and overstuffed couches from Goodwill, a long-countered kitchen, a deck that looked out on a curious dirt yard up against the hillside. A garden with walkways and succulents and a path that led to a gazebo, wooden and stained with acorn juice. There were dusty Buddhas and colored Tibetan flags. I had purchased a spiral notebook, smaller than 8 by 10, for the writing group I joined there, at the alternative HIV healing center on Silver Lake Boulevard, in 1996.

The healing center in Silver Lake understood itself as an alternative to APLA (AIDS Project LA), a counterculture option to the new drugs and glitz of West Hollywood, with its Don't Panic gift shop, its trendy bars, its Blue Whale Design Center and Ah Men boutique. This was the hippie queer place in grungier Silver Lake, a place to go for me to meet pos friends who liked to write.

Silver Lake became my refuge on languid Saturday afternoons when smog and fog mixed inconspicuously if the sun did not come out full tilt. I found myself in another survival circle, another ballpoint in my hand, addressing another set of exercises. I described my dream lover, told the story of my virus, imagined a landscape without HIV. We were timed; we had 20 minutes to be clever with language, to hide behind poetics and avoid prosaic anguish, or give up and face our naked loneliness.

One man wrote a column made of license plates for the Sunday *L.A. Times Magazine*. Another was a studio publicist—gray-haired with a dashing mustache who asked me back to his bungalow in North Hollywood. Don had rebounded from a low count and was feeling his oats. I followed him home to his bungalow after our writing group. He brought me a bottle of Perrier that afternoon and plopped down next to me on his lovely off-white couch. He put his arm around me and started sticking his tongue in my mouth as his hand reached for my listless genitals. He wasted no time. I was startled, taken aback. I just wanted to be his friend. I was unattracted to his midriff though he was handsome enough in an aging Burt Reynolds kind of way, a silver fox of sorts. An aggressive one.

I loved to bottom; I loved to top, but thinking back, reminiscing about the men and even women who came on to me too strongly over the years (even the wet vaginas that tried to capture my limp dick), thinking back at my predicament of accommodation, thinking back to some of those unmutual physical moments—none of them amounted to sexual assault I wanted to believe—because I followed these people home whether in a Honda or a Toyota or a Mustang—I tailed them back to their places because I was horny and scared and needed touch. I could never see myself being that forward with anyone. Though I have had anonymous sex with many guys but never topped without their approval, never lost control without a green light.

Don in North Hollywood with his beautiful gray hair and

mustache, in his single-story modern home with plate glass windows that looked out on a clipped green. Don was all over me like more than a wet blanket. He was erect and let me know it. When I told him to stop, to wait a minute, he took time to register my reticence but just kept on, determined to make it happen. His actions were abrupt and frightening. I felt trapped and flustered and scared. His insistence reminded me of Gil. I six feet and worked out and strong but completely unaggressive and hopelessly sympathetic and self-effacing in the face of the demands of others. What about consent and transmission? How often did HIV find its path through the unthinking force of a sex drive, the social pathology of a narcissism that reduced the other to an object? I was the other.

Don backed off eventually and told me his story, told me he hadn't had sex in years, had lost his lover, had finally started shooting up testosterone. His health came back with the aid of the anti-retrovirals. He told me he was desperate, apologized for what he called the call of the steroids. I knew I hurt him with my rejection and began to feel ashamed. But I had to extricate myself from him just as I had as a teenager extricated myself from the clutches of my piano teacher one summer after he squeezed my thigh and asked me to come to his house in San Mateo Park for private lessons.

Post North Hollywood come-on, I avoided the writing group for a few weeks. I still frequented Trader Joe's up the road for my ready-made Oriental Salads and baguettes. I admittedly slunk into the Eagle for a Bud some evenings too early. I held up a wall in the corner and watched the eight ball miss the side pocket. I thought of Gil, of Miguelito, of Joe.

32
CRIX

D r. Gottlieb practiced on the tenth floor of a high rise on Wilshire Boulevard. He was the infectious specialist in infectious diseases who in his ten-by-ten office treated hundreds of impatient HIV patients in 1996. After years of decrying the profiteering of big pharma, I could no longer ignore the evidence of HAART (highly active antiretroviral therapy). The cocktail was saving lives, and I wanted it to save mine. I was ready to abandon the uncertainties of naturopathy and accede to the clear evidence that these new drugs could arrest the multiplication of my viral RNA. I hoped I was not too late.

I called Doctor G, told him what *Project Inform* informed me, that I had to give the $3000-a-month pills a shot, that I wanted to try them. I was willing to take Crixivan three times a day on an empty stomach. I would swallow my Zerit (aka d4t, aka stavudine) with my Norvir booster. I would swallow anything he told me to put in my mouth, my insurance would pick up most of the cost. I would ingest near death to stay alive, weather the side effects just to get better, live longer, cruise through the millennium.

To get to his office in Midtown, I had to enter a multistory parking lot on Wilshire, take a ticket and drive in circles up ramps into dark, low-ceilinged floors of cars, remember where I put my wheels, find the stairs that emptied onto a shopping mall. I was disoriented that summer afternoon in Los Angeles, as I lowered and elevated myself to sit in the crowded waiting room of Dr. Gottlieb, who for all his renown, practiced out of a nondescript set of offices with a number of other doctors. Dr. G was unremarkable too, except for his red curly hair, mild obesity, his blue shirt, and white coat. He swirled on a three-legged stool, quickly checked my lungs and chest, performed the matter-of-fact stethoscoping before he wrote the prescription. A blood test was scheduled a month out.

My first line of defense was Merck's Crixivan (indinavir), only the 8th FDA-approved HIV drug, first on the market in March 1996. I had to take it three times a day on an empty stomach because its effect wore off rapidly after 8 hours, allowing the virus to mutate in response. The side effects were mostly nausea — gastrointestinal — stomach aches that came twenty minutes after ingestion. There was the dreaded Crix stomach, the lipodystrophy associated with the drug as well, the stomach being the center of the six-pack obsession of gay men who were not bears or otters. Crix was the fright of all gym rats like me. I would have to fight hard to keep my stomach flat enough to make tricks, though there were few tricks to make during those days of drugs and disclosure. My Japanese man never proceeded beyond a kiss on the bed, and a walk to watch Hale Bopp's Comet.

The second drug was Zerit, a nucleoside analog reverse transcriptase inhibitor (NRTI). A carcinogen in high doses, Zerit was discovered in the 1960s and reintroduced in the 90s.

It was the kind of antiretroviral that prevented RNA from clinging to DNA generally and more specifically useful in small doses for HIV and Hepatitis B.[1] Zerit caused neuropathy —numbness and tingling in the feet, sharp stabbing pains in the legs or hands. It was also associated with lipoatrophy, facial wasting, localized loss of fat accumulation in the cheeks. The fat atrophy brought pronounced smile lines, nasolabial folds, and deep eye sockets, creating a skeletal-like appearance of age and early onset emaciation. Drug interaction interrupted lipogenesis. Adipocyte (fat cell) maturation was arrested as part of Zerit's larger endeavor to prevent RNA from converting to DNA. Stavudine caused an abnormal apoptosis of adipocytes in the affected areas of the face, killing off lipid cells and creating craters through an apparently accelerated autophagy. The transport of glucose to the areas of cheek fat were "down regulated" by the biochemistry of the drug. While lipohyperdistrophy, such as buffalo humps and increased fat, was associated with AZT and other HIV drugs, Zerit had been signaled out for AIDS face—the sunken expression that told the queer and straight community that I had the plague, that I was anathema.

It didn't take long for my long face to get longer, for the Ichabod Crane syndrome to kick in even as my t-cell count soared into the 500s. The drugs kicked in as Toby and I drove back to the deep north.

UNDER THE BIG SKY

(1997-2011)

33

SUNLITE LANE

W e met at a backyard barbecue. The setting a suburb of
Missoula, west of downtown, across dreaded Reserve
Street, where big box stores sat like bluffs that protected even as
they threatened the scrappy, hand-changing storefronts of
Higgins Avenue, the original downtown of sprawling Missoula
County. Reserve Street was lined with chains like Walmart and
Homo Depot, interspersed among evangelical churches
declaring the vengeance of Jesus—not on moneylenders but
profligate sodomites. Reserve was a broad and easy way full of
over lit outlets with enormous parking lots and interminable
traffic lights. This aesthetic wasteland was the product of a
capitalism that had recast Jesus as a football star from
Oklahoma.

I rarely crossed Reserve unless I was headed to a nursery or
Costco, but that afternoon, a friend from the music school had
invited me to dinner out in the Target Range. Steve was a
pianist whose first partner was one of the early AIDS deaths in
the state but who was now tethered to a horticulturist, a plump
man who raised and sold dahlias at the Saturday market. My

would-be matchmaker showed off his new suburban spread west of Reserve, a gray ranch home that housed his Steinway. The hothouse in the big backyard belonged to his sweet if mildly obese partner, who for many years had blamed his lay-off from the elementary school district on his rather obvious queerness. He never proved it in court; in fact, he never went to court to pursue his case because of his discretion. He wanted to protect his poor mother in Darby who had yet to inform her son that she knew damn well, like everyone else in Montana, that he was light in the loafers.

How gracious of he and Steven to invite me to the queer cook-out that lovely July evening on an ideal Montana summer night, when the sun descended with a lazy glow that suggested maybe one too many pale ales. That soft light was still extant at 10 PM when the temperature hardly warranted a sweatshirt. Sprinklers surrounded us with rainbows as venison sausage and buffalo burgers roasted on the grill, later to ooze juices across Steve's old China from his family in South Dakota. We hoped for a Schubert impromptu in the salon after dinner, but during the bulk of the evening we stood on the lush over-watered grass around smoking coals. I clutched my microbrew as the Marks and Bruces and Brians of our gay gathering gossiped about queer purges in the Fine Arts School during the 80s, about closeted professors who had a penchant for twinks in their twenties, about recent denizens of the Adult Fantasy Bookstore.

AIDS was not in the conversation in our little queer town, not just because 1997 had brought a nationwide decline of 47% of HIV deaths due in part to the "hit early and hit hard" promo of the drug companies pedaling their pricey cocktails, but also because the spread of the virus to 16,000 people a day around the world and the USA and Montana found a greater demographics in people of color (who by the way did not exist in our big state, except for Indians), adding to the 30 million people living with the virus. I am not sure who knew about my demography then—probably none of them. I still held my HIV cards close to my chest, and hoped that my Zerit face would not tip my hand. I later came out as HIV with the self-stories that concluded each chapter of my Sharon Kowalski book, but even after publication, I was amazed at how few knew I was positive. And how few ergo had read the book, how little attention had been paid to writing even if in print, how little recognition we had given to one another.

David came late in his white Toyota Tacoma—a handsome man, thin and tan from running endlessly through the back roads of St. Ignatius, the town north of Missoula on the way up to Flathead Lake, where he lived, even though he had started to teach at Big Sky High, only a mile from Steve's new spread on Sunlite. Freckled, 5 foot 8 or 9, quiet, David was separated from his wife, who had had an affair with their rich neighbor. My blind date showed up late that evening. We were already seated at the long rectangular, folding tables eating our barbecue ribs and potato salad—dripping with the requisite mayonnaise. We were already popping marinated mozzarella balls in our mouth as Bruce went on and on about Byron's bisexuality. We were talking about closeted Philosophy teachers, when David walked in, wearing shorts and a t-shirt.

"Whoever loved that loved not at first sight?" a queer Christopher Marlowe wrote in 1598. I lived with the David I fell for that night for 14 years. I leaned against the side of his white truck door that night while I wrote my phone number on a matchbook cover. I was attracted to this guy with faraway eyes, seven years younger. This high school Spanish teacher was still married, had an adopted daughter and lived in a bungalow in St. Ignatius at the foot of the Mission Mountains, north of Missoula on the way to Flathead Lake. He had transformed his old clapboard into an airy two-bedroom home with refinished floors, a sensual raspberry couch in front of a big fireplace, and a picture window that looked out at the craggy face of the mountain. The kitchen had an original Wedgewood Range where David baked his apple pies. The living room was empty except for his loom (he was a weaver and an artist). The bedroom and pantry were a mess of sheets, blankets, and piles of unfolded clothes. He had built beautiful mounds of rocks and native plants around the perimeter of the lawn. Dave was a drywaller, a painter, a landscaper, a long-distance runner.

During my first overnight in St. Ignatius, I learned that he had dated a couple men since his separation from his wife. One was a dominant Italian who wrote books about safe sex and was not too keen on letting David go. Another was a political consultant in D.C. I didn't know if they were positive, but David seemed undaunted by the prospect of a serodiscordant relationship with me—at least ostensibly. I never knew for sure. I knew immediately I admired his house, which he had completely remodeled single-handedly. The refinished floors glowed with amber warmth. Globes of purple allium lit up the garden. He had collected huge rocks from the riverbeds along the South Fork of the Flathead River, boulders weighing as much as he did that somehow, he leveraged into the back of his pickup. He promised to take me on a rock hunt.

How wonderful it was to find a man I could love again, almost as strongly as I loved Gil. I surprised myself as David and I sat with salmon in our laps before the fire in St. Ignatius. We climbed under his sleek gray comforter that night during summer's end after we scrambled up Mission Falls. Expectation and hope flowed like a river over my tired body that first night. David was a catch.

34

ROCK STEADY

David rescued me from the loneliness of viral exile. With his impenetrable steadiness, he became my prophylaxis, my barrier from the world of despair that hounded a soul in the purgatory of positivity, a drama king like me, who was staving off hopefully forever—or at least until death from unnatural causes—the hell on earth of AIDS. At night I prayed point-lessly for a cure, which remained tantalizingly out of reach with each new World AIDS conference. During the day, I relied on David to allow me to enter into a needed if fey zone of avoid-ance and denial. I was able during those first years of love and happiness, to quote Al Green, to put a rubber on the me=HIV equation that replicated in my psychic cells. I was sick of seeing myself as the man with bad blood, the contaminated man.

Was I able to function normally, teach my queer theory classes and focus my gay activism on petitions for domestic partnership health benefits? Was I living in a latex bubble? Or did the refuge of domestic bliss, knowing like Adam and Eve (or in this case Adam and Adam) to know no more, subtly encourage the long episodes of silence that descended upon us during drives to destinations like Hungry Horse Reservoir or Jewel Basin, places I associated with my Montana man, but places that had become anathema to my rough and ready partner, who longed for the well-lit and temperature-controlled sales floors of Banana Republican in Seattle rather than the golden shores of Yellow Bay. He had been there and done that.

We rarely, if never used a condom the entire time we were together. I was so intensely pleased to have someone to cuddle and kiss and hug that the thought of jeopardizing or contaminating the precious man I had attracted was not part of my thinking when David slept over at my house on Hilda in the University district. David would come back from high school where he taught five or six classes a day, and we would run out the Kim Williams Trail, the river path named after a Missoula naturalist, a kind of local Rachel Carson, her name attached to the road that ran across the south side of the Clark Fork River.

On those first autumn afternoons, we jogged through yellow leaves that clung to cottonwood starts along the bank, me behind David with Toby the Golden as we strode over the narrow trail through leafy spurge and knapweed. On the right, bald eagles hid in the crags below Mt. Sentinel, pines clung to the rich crumbling soil on mossy ledges. On the left, the gleaming river, the noisy highway and railway beside it, freight trains still filled with coal. Beyond loomed the barren mound called Mount Jumbo, the northern side of the gorge, shaped like an elephant's back. David jogged effortlessly, Toby and I clomped nonchalantly after him, solid but slow as we hoofed past unwashed homeless men who lived rent free in the woods and defecated with impunity near the rapids of the wide fork, on its way to the Columbia River via Pend Oreille.

My new boyfriend had my undivided attention. I was elated at last to be able to hang on to another warm body, to kiss and touch and jack off, even if my new partner was the strong and distant type. He had been with a man I called Dominatrix, a pushy Italian whom I heard little about, but who in retrospect must have supplied some needs that I, a vanilla boy who preferred to spoon and cry after a passionate ejaculatory session, could not fulfill. That inadequacy was not at first discernable to my infatuated eyes, so eager—if I can attribute emotion to vision— to please my new love. I had no idea something might be missing in the sex department. I liked to get off together with another guy in bed—maybe some humping, maybe some rolling around and frottage, maybe a little finger fucking here and there. No way was I going to fuck David, with or without a condom. Selfishly perhaps, I didn't want to face all of that shit; I wanted to be in love. And I was—at first.

One night after we moved out of Hilda and bought the place out beyond Reserve Street in the Target Range, I broke down with joy. That night summed up what I wanted, what I loved, what I suddenly had years after HIV arrested me. Our backs against pillows that leaned against the wall, we played with one another up to the point that we were on our way home. We lubed ourselves into the final stages of lift off. My arm around the man I called my lover, I felt the rush up my thighs and watched both of our geysers erupt deliciously in a way that washed over me like a hot wave, so relaxed and relieved and happy I became. Sex was a hot shower, a wave in Hawaii, a Jacuzzi. I was disarmed there in the dark, deeply content as we fell asleep so intimately, so inerasably cloud-nined. Suddenly tears ran uncontrollably from my eyes. I felt like I was in a movie, a love story. I had gone over the top into a place of shivers and sobs about what God had given me—this handsome, loyal, talented man who was willing to be with me.

David heard me cry and asked, "What's going on?"

I don't know how he felt about my meltdown that night in the dark in our new bespackled bedroom with its metal windows that looked out on red berries of the mountain ash in the front yard. He did not move away. He did not speak. He did not squeeze my hand or put his arms around me, though I was leaning against him. The tears welled up, their glistening blur overwhelmed me. In the dark, I knew he was there, knew he wasn't going anywhere. I intuited his solidity beside me—rock steady in its immovability, mysteriously unemotional in its stoniness like Aristotle's god, moving in its unmovedness—devotional in its inanimacy. David was there for me, there with me. He did not gush or cuddle my head in his arms. He did not cradle me like a mother with a crying child. He did not verbalize sympathy like a helpless therapist. He was just there in the dark—not going anywhere—a kind of sounding board with no sound. Just a kind of bolster for my own drama, his cue went unheeded, unseized, his part remained unwritten, still unexpressed in all senses of that phrase.

I finally said, "I can't help it. I can't believe that I'm here in this new house, in bed with you. I can't believe that you're with me. It's just so amazing, so wonderful."

35
FAMILY SYSTEMS

I was in counseling long before and after David and I got together. I was a bit of a therapyholic, actually. I eventually drug him to Molly Miller and then to Petra de Groot over the years. We focused on my discomfort with the implacableness of my Montana-faced partner, who seemed deeply unemotional and removed at some level. Whenever I asked if he would participate in couples counseling, he often felt deeply triangulated. Beyond that, he harbored healthy skepticism about the light-bulb-has-to-really-want-to-change science. Its copays and money-draining side effects were money better spent on trips to San Francisco and Seattle and Spain, better spent on new Hondas and gas ranges.

After trips to Mexico and India, we also amassed substantial credit card debt—a source of worry for me. A wall of silence also began to build between our domestic spheres. David commandeered the kitchen and the garden and the bathtub, lost in the insularity of his do-it-myself mentality. He began to slough off the admittedly tiresome work of reading my essays or poems and commenting on them. Although he was the dedicatee, he probably never entirely read my recently published Kowalski book. In my inimitable, self-effacing way I readily excused him, for the tome was rather specialized anyway. On dog walks, if he bothered to join me, he always walked 20 paces ahead. At the beach in Mexico, he didn't want to swim with me. At home he didn't want me to help with painting rooms in colors he had chosen. In the kitchen, I was purely a Vegematic, prepping for his risottos and paellas. My clothes folding derided, my attempt at cleanliness was dismissed as superficial while he poured Comet and sprayed Windex over all available surfaces. He relished in the potency of chemicals in toilets and lawns, warned his immune-compromised partner to stay out of the way as he sprayed pesticides, ate sushi, or drank another bottle of Merlot. He would not join me at the gym and soon eschewed our canoe.

My litany of accusations attested to a certain arrogance and over-expectation. I wanted Molly to make my lover more emotive, more sharing, more willing to talk about himself, more pliable to my own impossible image of the ideal partner. By some miracle of pharmacological science, I was alive and well in the coolest college town in the west, twenty minutes from Snow Bowl and bordering the Rattlesnake Wilderness. An hour from one of the largest most beautiful inland lakes in the country (Flathead) and only a hundred miles from Glacier National Park. I had a tenure-track position teaching the richest most rewarding texts in English. I lived with the coolest gay man in town—bronze, bilingual, svelte, handsome, artistic, culinary, handy, literary, horticultural, sporty (he ran and swam circles around me), hospitable, and bon-vivant. I led the perfect life—whether gay or straight—with the perfect antidote to the dour doom of the HIV virus. I swallowed the cocktail, got my flu shot, and warded off plantar warts and fungal infections. I staved off herpes simplex outbreaks and politely declined sushi.

From the perspective of external descriptors—all the objective measurements, all the categories by which we were known to judge contentment and connubial harmony—I had found the perfect gay relationship. We found ourselves on the cover of *The Independent,* the local weekly magazine. The photo showed us laying on the grass looking up at the big sky, happy queers in progressive Missoula, who fought for domestic partnership health benefits, ran with our Golden Retriever, drove our Toyota pickup, even raised David's daughter part time. The perfect couple—artists, teachers, swimmers, lovers—on and on the adulating adjectives, the signs of joy and elation, the thesaurus of acceptance and emulation from our friends. What was my problem? Behind the outward trappings, I still felt deeply isolated, unattended, unable to connect with my stoic partner.

HIV came through the backdoor window, like a jealous mistress or an unruly child. Like Rose, David's daughter, the virus wanted attention and through her my condition would out. Five when I met her, Rose saw me as the cause of the breakup of mommy and daddy. On one of our first meetings, she accused me of harming her while we wrestled on the couch in the cabin we rented one summer on Flathead Lake. She screamed and ran to her father. A pattern of play and blame continued. We walked the woods at Kelly Island with Toby, delighted in hide and seek, until tears suddenly drove her back to the house with accusations of abandonment and cruelty. She hid in her room, wanted to go home to her mom, threw a tantrum until her father gave her what she wanted. Shoes at the mall, French toast and lobster, new skis, swarms of loud clothes and phone upgrades. One afternoon, she threatened to jump out of the car as we headed up Brooks Street at forty miles per hour after I lectured her about keeping me waiting for thirty minutes outside the pool. Her father was not pleased, but the battles never ceased.

This acting out was nothing out of the ordinary for an adopted Chilean child in a white and historically racist Rocky Mountain West, a child with a divorced single mom and two daddies. Our conflicts eventually led to Molly Miller's office on the seventh floor of a new ugly highrise in our lovely downtown —a brick box called the Millennium Building with green tinted windows. Molly had moved her office into these new digs, its commanding view a measure of her ascent in the world of American psychotherapy. She was mostly a child-based counselor, one who presumably had read some Winnicott along the way, but mostly studied "family systems." Perhaps I should have studied that subspecialty of therapy more carefully in advance of recommending that our "family" seek Molly's help.

Molly asked to see David by himself for a few sessions after she saw me, as a way of equalizing her attention. She also wanted to talk to our daughter individually. Rose was in middle school at the time, around 12 or 13. David shared custody with her mother; Rose was with us every other week. She hid in her room with dog-eared copies of *Harry Potter* while the television reran sitcoms as she tried to do her math problems. Rose was a fiery prepubescent who cooked frozen Pillsbury Orange Rolls on a cookie sheet at 350 degrees, ate pepperoni pizza delivered from Domino's, and carried her Tic Tacs into our bathroom for long showers. La Princesa—we had our own private teen queen.

Molly was a bit of a slam-bam-thank-you-mam therapist. She he was intent upon getting to the point and liked to ask embarrassing questions like "what are you afraid of?" or "why don't you cry in front of him?" Short, with wiry, unmanageable hair dyed a dark roan brown, Molly wore earth-tone skirts and buckled shoes. She and her husband collected art. She could be seen First Night at the Dana Gallery where David showed his work. Molly was sardonic, funny, almost New Yorky with her spunk and incisive drive to get to the bottom of whatever needed to be mined for some unrecovered truth.

One Wednesday morning at 11, all three of us looked for seats in her office in anticipation of the promised rendezvous. The joint session at last. There were new barrel chairs, an extra dragged in to accommodate four people. I had not been forewarned that we would need to talk about parts of our lives that had not arisen among the three of us. Not that much ever arose since all of us were rarely together for any length of time. Rose was rarely required to eat dinner with us, and if her father requested her presence, a phone call or some other pretense invariably led to her departure to her room upstairs, where she didn't have to face Dad's strict new boyfriend.

Our session was designed to smooth out the wrinkles that my role as the evil stepdad brought into our lives, but I had no inkling that such smoothing involved extracting my dirty little secret. Our counselor began: "Casey is there something about your health that you have not told Rose? Something maybe you have thought about telling her for a long time?" I recoiled in my chair, broadsided. It was suddenly incumbent upon me to talk about HIV to an twelve-year-old who was already very wary of her parents' spoiler.

The answer in my head was an unequivocal "no;" I did not want to tell Rosie I was positive. I did not want to provide her with more ammunition in her stepfather assault. I didn't trust her. She had betrayed me too many times—used my generosity and time-commitment to turn me into some Dickensian martinet or worse some interloper who had ruined her daddy's life. But suddenly I was enmeshed in this family system and had to disclose my status to this angry teenager who ran off to her mother and father every time I asked her to empty a wastebasket. The exposure of my vulnerability, my weakened immune system, had—through some logic of sunlight laws—become the solution to our familial rancor. HIV has suddenly pulled up a chair in Molly's office.

I was being coaxed, even shamed, into telling the child I would die of AIDS once the cocktail party was over. Molly continued to prompt me with her leading questions. "Can you explain to Rosie why you have kept this information from her?" I soon realized I had concealed information from the "family," a cardinal sin in the "family systems" Bible.

Rosie burst into tears when I told her. She promptly became the focus of sympathy for the rest of the session. She was bowled over by the news that her suddenly beloved second father suffered an incurable and infectious disease within the very confines of the house she inhabited. "You can't get it from touching my blood," I assured her, "or from licking my spoon." But that fear seemed much less traumatic than the fact that I had told her at this late date, had been forced to tell her by a therapist. At some mortifying level, I had morphed again into the ogre who had hurt Rose's feelings, both because I underhandedly withheld the news of my impending demise and also, through some Wildean paradox, precisely because I burdened her with the disclosure which, undisclosed, had been equally onerous. I had somehow injured her indelibly by failing to take her into my confidence, as if one of the symptoms of the human-immunodeficiency virus had become my own human deficiency in failing to explain the significance of my ACT UP t-shirt to my middle school stepdaughter, who really wasn't even that, since David and I were not marriage-able at that point.

I hid who I was from her because I did not tell her why I took all those pills in the cupboard. I had lied to her—by failing to reveal my disease. In addition to the opportunistic infections that my diminishing t-cells were being asked to ward off, the load of the virus suddenly extracted its ethical price. I was a sinner in the hands of an angry family. I had to confess the transgression of my selfish privacy.

In the corner, David seemed smug as he watched me squirm with dis-ease. Of course, I didn't know exactly what he thought; I did know, however, what I thought he was thinking. He and Molly had uncovered a breach in the open and affirming system of our family, and they were on a mission to make me atone for my omission. Once I got HIV off my chest and out in the open, the three of us would somehow cement our happy bond. They failed to realize this derelict admission of my vulnerability would augment not allay Rosie's suspicion about me, the evil outlaw.

I felt used, misunderstood, and targeted, as I descended in the new elevator with my "family." In the end though, I came up for air again. Rose, I realized, was just a kid. She was fun to play with in swimming pools, on dog walks. She could learn some discipline from me. We would deal, move on, rise above. I tried to wash my feelings away with clichés. I couldn't tell if it worked.

36
QUEER STORIES

Under the title Gay and Lesbian Literature, in 1996 I taught the first queer studies class at the University of Montana in Missoula, team-taught actually, with my graduate student Mona, who was able to appeal to if not appease the large contingent of Lesbian Avengers who had enrolled. Many had arrived fresh from a fire-eating demonstration outside the University Commons. The class covered various genres— poetry from Judy Grahn to Essex Hemphill, novels and stories from *Rubyfruit Jungle* to *At Home at the End of the World*, HIV literature by Paul Monette and Feinberg's *Spontaneous Combustion*. I was getting in the habit, three years into my assistant professorship, of coming out as HIV positive to classes and high school students where I gave talks to groups of queer kids from locations like Two Dot and Denton. I attended retreats sponsored by the Gay Men's Task Force, and contributed to the Plague Course offered by St. Patrick's Hospital, where I taught a segment on AIDS literature.

How much easier for me to confess to a sea of faces, as a speaker or writer, than to sit down with a high school friend, a brother, a parent and eye-to-eye, flush-faced, and arm-pit sweating as I announced that I was infected. Something about professional anonymity made my confession and extroversion—formal and somehow tied to civic duty—easier for a shy overweight boy who was enamored of his toy soldiers on the stairway growing up—endlessly invested in a world of make believe. Were I to encounter one of my friends from St. Catherine's or boarding school as an adult, a professor, a lawyer, to face one of my parents' cohorts—were I to meet with one of my colleagues in the English Department, disclosure of HIV suddenly became an anxious drama. Whenever I was determined to broach the topic and come clean, some interruption intervened—a phone call or dropped tidbit of departmental gossip. Occasionally, in some awkward non-sequitur, I just blurted it out in the cafeteria over ginger chicken from Noodle Express, threw it out like a green rectangular after-meal mint—to clear the palate. Sometimes a walk by the Clark Fork or up Crazy Canyon ripped it out of me. The closet of HIV was a closet within my queer closet within my shy closet, a kind of Russian doll. The door of self-revelation was opened and slammed shut on a daily basis, especially in a place like beautiful backward Montana. Progressive in the Missoula oasis, but really a place where out gay men did hair and closeted ones did alleyways, darting in and out of dirty bookstores.

I could talk. Mighty Casey headed out to Hellgate High, up to bat, where he discoursed on gay life and literature or headed down to the basement of the public library to welcome our little patch of the AIDS quilt. But before I met the divine David, as my friend MM called him, I too held up walls at AmVets (our gay bar) and visited various M4M porn sites. I found little comfort there. It was isolating in Montana. I had a few dates with self-absorbed survivors who had fled San Francisco and Houston unscathed or unvirused, closeted married men who carried "a few extra pounds." The cute twinks in drag who had joined the Imperial Sovereign Court did not appeal to my rugged Fish and Stream sensibilities.

After the successful offering of the GLBTIQA2SNB course, Mona proceeded to offer a continuing education course that she insisted on calling "Queer Stories." The catalog, widely disseminated to the community, found its way into the hands of the editors of *The Missoulian*, who found the title offensive, and subsequently into the righteous clutches of Daryl Toews, a Republican Senator in the Montana legislature. Toews was a Mennonite from Lustre, a town on the Fort Peck Reservation in eastern Montana. As Chair of the Education Committee, he sent his January 18th letter to all the major dailies in Big Sky country. "As Montanans," he wrote, "we have tried hard to be tolerant of other views. We have tried to understand academic freedom and all it entails. Now UM is asking us to fund and endorse by giving college credit to promote a lifestyle that is by most standards immoral and has significant health consequences." The letter threatened to de-fund the university system if this unhealthy course was approved. This was 1998; this was the United States; this was a state Senator, suggesting that studying *Angels in America* would lead to the spread of HIV, in the same way a course in American Sign Language, one letter writer facetiously noted, could cause hearing loss.

The controversy over Mona's course spearheaded a movement among the faculty to establish a curriculum and pursue a rights agenda. 1998 also brought about the controversial murder of Matt Shepard in neighboring Wyoming. His vigil in hospital created sympathy and huge marches in Missoula. That Matt was probably positive and cruising, that his killers were also probably cruising, added twists to the torturous death of a young man whose beating quickly became more relevant symbolically than any revisionary history would ever be able to undermine. Matthew became the poster boy for every queer that has ever been harassed, assaulted, and beaten in a United States that hid its sadism behind a bill of rights. My country's laws meant little to those who condemned me to hell or sought my quarantine, those who found ways to deny me promotion. Those who stuck my students' heads in toilets in high school, who ignored our 911 calls and referred to us as faggots behind our backs. Those who voted against our tenure because of our "controversial" work. Citizens that proclaimed Christianity gave them the right to send their children to reparative therapy centers. No, I did not live in Uganda or Iran or Russia or even Libby, Montana. Still being queer and positive in 1998 in Missoula was not the most pleasant of experiences, in spite of our trips to parades in the Castro and Capitol Hill in Seattle.

We called ourselves the Outfield Alliance, a coalition of faculty, students, and staff dedicated to the promotion of lesbian and gay academics and civil rights on and off campus. Some of our cohorts ironically seemed to prefer the closet of the infield given their requests for messages in sealed envelopes, but we soldiered on, campaigning for same-sex domestic partner health benefits for university employees. The proposal was financially if not socially modest. It was virtually revenue-neutral given the increased contribution required by employees to add spouses or dependents. The proposal met with little opposition at the campus level, but the buck stopped with the Commissioner of the Board of Regents, who found it politically infeasible given the opposition of the Christian Coalition.

We appealed the Commissioner's decision to the entire Board of Regents, and I traveled north to Kalispell to the meeting at Flathead Valley Community College. The good old boys sat *en banc*, took public comment on the proposal from the likes of *moi*, some students who sided with us, and a long line of

Christian Coalition members, some of whom read from Leviticus. Some likened homosexuals to rapists and murderers and argued—by extension—that same-sex partner health benefits eventually would lead to coverage for horses, border collies, even pet asses. The downfall of western civilization was also prophesied that morning in the junior college auditorium north of Kalispell where shock jock radio hosts regularly cited Fred Phelps of the Westboro Baptist Church in Kansas as the leading expert on abominations. The interested public stood in line, each given five minutes to testify before the busy board members, dressed mostly in gray suits they wore daily at their bank offices.

I was sandwiched between a man in a yoked suede sport coat to match his cowboy boots and a print-dress mother of six who feared for the lives of her children should the homo menace invade her enclave in Ferndale or Big Sandy or wherever she was homeschooling her masturbating boys.

"Our proposal is revenue neutral, and the likelihood that Blue Cross would be inundated in Montana with HIV patients, is frankly unfounded," I insisted, as I turned pink in the neck with a reference to my own condition. "Need I remind the board that the cost of care for a premature infant can easily reach a half million dollars while HIV care rarely if ever reaches that level."

The dark-suited Commissioner Crofts sat like a weight-challenged Christ in the middle of the Regents' table, amid the bored board whose donut quota had long since been met.

"We feel it is our right under the law to have the chance to pay into the system," I continued.

The gray heads of the board members quickly lowered to three-ring binders full of deficits and proposals for the expansion of football locker rooms. The morning Kalispell scene grew more surreal as grimacing ranchers and pursed-lip matrons looked at me like I had just entered the wrong bar. Before I knew it, my pilgrimage north had come to a hollow close. The Regents looked relieved to have done with this three-ring sex circus, counting me no doubt among one of the whackos who tried to legitimize sodomy and its sickness in their home on the range. Ignored by administrators and other faculty at the meeting, I slipped unnoticed through the double doors out to my Honda. It was 10 in the morning. I had risen at 6 to arrive in time. I had been asked no questions during my testimony and realized that the hearing if not proforma was just a necessary nuisance for the suits on the BOR, who would rather discuss the six-figure salaries of Athletic Directors than encounter the tawdry pleas of deviants.

After the Board unanimously voted later that day to uphold the Commissioner's decision to prevent us from paying into the system, our Outfield Alliance sued the bastards. More accurately the ACLU sued and eventually won on our behalf in 2004—six years later, the victory somewhat pyrrhic since by that time the imperious Commissioner Crofts had retired and the state had become interested in granting benefits to all domestic partners (straight and bent) who signed an affidavit. In the interim, two of the lesbian plaintiffs in the case and their son, living in the South Hills of Missoula, narrowly escaped in the middle of the night after their house was set on fire. The community quickly grew up in arms over the hate crime and provided support for Adrienne and Carla. Only a few days after the burning, the police named the plaintiffs and the Director of Pride, a statewide queer org, "persons of interest" in the ongoing arson investigation. After months of supposed inquiry, the prosecutor never charged anyone, conveniently leaving a "cloud of suspicion" in this case of the "queer fire" over the queers themselves. We gained some vindication when the Montana Supreme Court later in *Snetsinger v. Montana*

University System upheld our constitutional right to buy into the health system. In the interim, Focus on the Family had succeeded in the same year (2004) in convincing Montanans to pass a constitutional amendment banning same-sex marriage, a ban not lifted until *Obergefell* in 2015 granted us the constitutional right to avail ourselves of the bundle of burdens and benefits the institution of marriage conferred on citizens.

37
"WHY SO PALE AND WAN"

In 2004, David and I were getting accustomed to our new house in the Target Range at the end of 7th Street, two acres on a corner lot, where the mountain ash out front battled fungal fire blight and the stunted fruit trees were propped up quaintly by weather-beaten two-by-sixes. My intrepid and negative partner taught 5 classes of Spanish at the local high school, while also working on a nascent Gay-Straight Alliance and the local chapter of NCBI (the National Coalition Building Institute). I fielded courses in Shakespeare and queer studies. We were busy boys, and Rosie, who slept downstairs with the Golden, did her homework with her collection of retractable colored pens. Domestic bliss had set in. We were the gay couple de jour, hosting queer activist gatherings in our ample living room, as a fire roared in the hearth and green enchiladas arrived on the dining room table.

I had survived to see the new millennium, a feat I rarely stopped to celebrate during my busy hours. My biochemistry seemed, on the surface, like my relationship, copasetic, under control. My Cluster of Differentiation 4 cells (CD4), also known as T helper cells, hovered around the threshold of 500. These cells, I learned, were actually glycoproteins found on the surface of monocytes, macrophages, and dendritic cells, part of the immunoglobulin superfamily. The number 500 was calculated by measuring within a snapshot of blood the percentage of total number of white cells (immune cells) in relation to the total number of red (oxygen-carrying) and white blood cells. My numbers since conversion had bounced between 300 and 500, one time dropping below 300. I had just enough of these crucial genetic messengers, which were sent to CD8 cells to eradicate infection, to protect me most of the time from opportunistic infections.

An AIDS diagnosis in the U.S. came with consistent numbers below 250, though early survivors in the Eighties like Michael Callen lived and yelled at callous politicians while their T-cell counts hovered in the single digits. Retroviral therapy was being recommended for almost anyone who tested positive. Viral load tests had yet to become readily available in Missoula when I decided to switch physicians and be treated with an infectious disease specialist who practiced out of St. Patrick's Hospital. George Risi worked with AIDS patients in New Orleans before landing in Montana to practice cancer medicine and study hantavirus and other rodent-born pathogens. He was an acclaimed diagnostician—a slight, tall man with a whiskered mustache and an aesthetic sensibility that led to our rather lengthy conversations about Nietzsche and the politics of HIV. George was a cool guy, if somewhat mercurial, and after a number of colloquies about my wishy-washy numerical values as well as my hollow Crix face, he convinced me to try a new regimen. Zerit might also be a contributing factor to the lipoatrophy that had sunk my Kevin-Bacon countenance into early emaciation.

George suggested Viramune, aka Nevirapine (NVP), an

NNRTI, a non-nucleoside reverse transcriptase inhibitor, which Boelhringe Ingelheim had brought on the market originally in 1996. Non-nukes, as opposed to nukes like Zerit, did the work of actually damaging the DNA zipper latch in ways that prevented the RT enzyme from locking into the DNA. NNRTIs had the advantage of keeping HIV RNA removed from the T-cells' DNA altogether. I jumped on it, rather freaked by my increasingly sunken aspect and rather enamored of the quirky and somewhat queer cross-legged physician, who was known to be a ladies' man of some note. The changing of drug therapy required before and after monitoring through blood work and also meant that the drugs I quit using could not be taken again.

Life went on. In the basement where I worked at home, two tables I had constructed with 4 by 4 legs and unfinished doors were covered with unpaid credit card bills and ungraded essays on *The Comedy of Errors*. My desktop also featured chewed Bic pens, unsharpened number 2 pencils, and unfinished conference papers. In the midst of this workload, at school I peered into the mirror of the men's room on the second floor of the Liberal Arts Building one day and admired what seemed to be a new tan in the middle of March. I was pleased to feature a little happy color to mitigate the "why so pale and wan" aspect that usually spoke to me from that unfair wall reflector. The tan seemed a bit tawny like a cat's mane, a bit brown trouty perhaps, but any hue on the spectrum in wintery Montana came as a boon, even if there was a tinge of amber or let's face it yellow in the low light of the faculty-only john. I felt as if I had come out of a bad tanning booth.

In spite of this unlikely and improbable sunshine, my world was admittedly beginning to feel rather heavy. My legs— already rather overworked from running and hiking—suddenly felt like stumps in need of being dragged to the burn pile. I clomped around like the Duchess of Malfi's big-thighed bargeman or a filthy rugby player after one of those pig-play huddles that seemed to my naïve sensibility rather homoerotic. A malaise seemed to be setting in. I hit the sack at 10 and slept until 6 or 7, waking with what felt like a huge 45-pound barbell on my chest. My muscles started to ache more than they usually did from overdoing it on the bench press or running too far out the Kim Williams trail. I had lifted cement bags out of the dump truck when I worked on a Nob Hill condo development one summer back in the Bay Area days. I felt like I was carrying around one of those bags of cement as I walked to class. At first, I just sloughed it off as one of those episodes of fatigue that accompany the pill-popping HIV man. I often got, for example, URIs (upper respiratory infections) that led to a week or two of early-to-bed sleep fests. Surely, in spite of the sniffles, this was just one of those Positive Things, those periodic tests of my survival skills.

I did not recognize the early signs of hepatotoxicity. I did not realize that Viramune was producing liver failure in my corpus, soon to be a corpse. After considerable egging on from the likes of David, I got myself into George's office and after yet another puncture and extraction of blood, found that my gland, the liver, could not metabolize the new drug and rendered my organism increasingly unfunctional. My body was shutting down. Dr. Risi panicked, took me off the drug instantaneously, and sent me home to bed with instructions as to liquid intake. I took my sack of potatoes to the sack and slept through *Kill Bill: Volume 2*. That's how prostrated I had become. Liver failure had arrested my body, and I was heavily chained to the mattress. I pushed and pulled my bones from bed to bath and hopefully not beyond, though at moments I wondered when and if the press would lift. I was almost too weak to register fear.

Two weeks later, I no longer felt I was about to collapse when I opened the RAV4 door. After a month's drug holiday to cleanse the spotted liver, Risi threw me on a new regime of antiretrovirals. I was to take a new cocktail on a full stomach. My new HAART formula started with Bristol Myers trade-named Reyataz (Atazanavir sulfate), s protease inhibitor of first line assault. Its blue and red capsule resembled a tiny patriotic bombshell. Its side effect, ironically enough, was a little jaundice, a little yellowing in the face and especially in the whites of the eyes, as a result of the increased bilirubin levels produced by the drug. Bilirubin, discovered by the Prussian/Polish anti-Bismarck progressive, Rudolf Virchow, in 1847, did the work of breaking down hemes in old red blood cells. This effect created a kind of false positive for the very liver failure I had just avoided. The urine in my cornea after a few months became less noticeable.

Reyataz combined with Epzicom, a drug combination of the NRTIs (nucleoside in this case) Ziagen and Epivil, which had as their side effect increased depression and sleeplessness, the former which I had experienced for as long as I could remember. Even with a partner, I was often so lonely I could die or cry or sing a Toni Braxton song. The fourth drug was Norvir or Ritonavir, Abbott Laboratories' creation, a kind of booster that prevented, through CYP3A4, protease inhibitors from breaking down too quickly, from being metabolized and thus unable to hang around to stop those proteases from breaking up new RNA strands. Norvir kept Reyataz at work for a longer period of time. I had to swallow only three pills in the morning. A miracle of modern science, this new ease of compliance. My new regiment was augmented by a little Murine and a copay for my therapist who I hired to boost, if possible, the ego of the neurotically depressed HIV positive man in his 50s whose financial and romantic troubles lay ahead in the least gay place, namely Montucky. Still I longed to be alive and well, to feel the earth move under my feet.

I was able once again to rant and rave about the stone-faced stoicism of my partner, the anti-intellectualism of my little state university, the manipulations of the child, the weakness of the Americanos at the campus espresso bar, man's inhumanity to queer man. I was able once again to move the malaise from physiognomy to psyche, from fatigue to a weary world. This was one of the great ironies of my discontent. I bemoaned my outcast social fate when my body functioned normally. I felt regret about taking my health for granted, whenever I was bedridden.

38
STOCKYARD ROAD

Once my physical ballast returned, my emotional imbalance began to drown me again. I needed the kind of support I was not getting at home. I had exhausted the stable of therapists in the Missoula bowl, that old glacial lake that held the inverted air of exhaust and sawmill smoke in its concavity during the depressing winter months. David and I had spent enough of his deductibles and my copays on gray-bearded Jungians with their Aleutian Island prints, long-skirted retro-hippy Marianas with their cross-legged Birkenstocks. Even Petra, her dark office hidden in one of the old brick buildings on Higgins, with her grin and indulgence of my partner's abandonment issues, could only partially help us reignite our fire, find new wine in our aging bottles and bottlenecks. After the Molly sessions with Rosie, couples therapy was not a viable option for us.

Still, I remained brainwashed by the lure of psychoanalysis and all of its infinite offshoots. I was into yoga, meditation, retreats, Wings, ACOA, gay community centers, book groups, reiki, and hot rocks. I never lived in Marin, was not particularly touchy feely but I was a Californian. I lived on the Northside of Berkeley for a number of years, hung out at Peet's Coffee and the Cheese Board. I tried to find my way out of the closet back in the 80s, and finally stumbled over the San Rafael Bridge to the offices of Karl 1. He was a corpulent New Yorker who followed Stanley Keleman (*Your Body Speaks Its Mind*) out to the Bay Area. He agreed to take my case, to wit the prosecution of that trespasser into my soul—that old Greek perversion. I, newly minted lawyer and stalwart of the upper echelons of the Peninsula, I was determined to avoid the footsteps of the light-loafered dandies on Polk Street. Karl G, with his dark slacks, golf shirts, and intense capacity to delve into the cavities of the psyche, was willing to cure me of my tendency to gravitate toward the homo section of Cody's on Telegraph Avenue.

The upshot was a series of weekly sessions with my first therapist, who got me hooked on role-playing and assertiveness training. Karl 1, who had submitted to my insurer that I faced a psychoneurotic depressive reaction, suggested that I play the field for a while, switch hit as it were. Now that I was learning how to interact through assertiveness rather than passivity, I was encouraged to experiment. Did I want to date and marry Sue Frattini and live happily ever after with 2.6 children and a home in Montclair? Or would I prefer an intermittent blowjob from a peculiar French Horn player at three in the morning in the back of my Mustang?

It was up to me, of course, though, like the light bulb in the joke, I had insufficient consciousness to even acknowledge that I might want to change, being attuned almost exclusively my entire life to the wants of others. But screwing and unscrewing was another matter, not to put too fine a point on the metaphor. The light bulb that turned on when I unbuttoned the metal circles on a Buddhist's beltless 501s to discover a shitake head buoyant and bobbing told me that no amount of morning pumpage with Sue could possibly measure up to my fascination with Winston. Finally, I convinced Karl that the voltage was too great to ignore. I pulled my therapist into the queer-is-cool age, reluctant though he was to give up his longing to cure me of my perversion. I ended up curing him of his irrational phobia. I never sent him a bill.

Petra mentioned Karl 2 when I wondered out loud if any gay therapists were in Missoula who might be familiar with the perils of HIV. Exacerbated by my friend the virus, I ventured out to Old Stockyard Road, ready as I was to slaughter the demon, not in this case of my dick-love, which by this time was fait accompli, but the bugaboos of my discontent with my "situation" and my disease.

Karl Jr. had established himself early on as one of the few A Gays in our little Montana community. He was a minister in the opening and affirming local church. He hobnobbed with the blond housewives who ran the AIDS organization like a Junior League sorority. They held festive cocktail parties for the upper crust of what was indeed a rather small pie. Karl and his dashing partner wore camel hair sports coats and Perry Ellis neckties to fundraisers in town, where bottled waters and billowing skirts were the order of the evening. I had left San Francisco, of course, in part to eliminate such snobbery from my life of letters, but like the appointment in Samarra, my supposed escape hatch sent me down a tunnel to a lesser version of the Pacific Union club.

Karl 2 had grown up in the family of a popular Los Angeles evangelical. He was the proverbial promiscuous son who lapsed, like James Baldwin, at the sight of exposed phalloi in the chaparral of Griffith Park, where many a tryst completed his sexual education during the hormonal teen years. Dick calls. He had set up his Montana practice in a warehouse office building, near a store that sold automatic weapons to stock-pilers and the workout studio of a personal trainer. He grunted through the walls to the chagrin of my practicing therapist, with his rock collection and abstract art on the big yellow walls of his high-ceilinged space. Voracious reader, capacious remem-berer, nondoctrinaire practitioner, Karl 2 tried tapping, posture, family history, EMDR (a buzzing system) on me. He tried books on meditation, queer trauma theory—tried whatever came his way in an attempt to enlist, expose, and defuse the emotional knots that tied me up.

None of Karl's prestidigitation worked on me, unfortu-nately, for I was the wily client who invariably relied on my critical and unfeeling mind to resist. I shunned primal screams or sobs outside of the privacy of my own home. My nuts uncrackable, I nonetheless engaged in sufficient transference to become deeply attached to this man with whom my sardonic ironies struck a raucous chord in spite of our joint acknowledg-ment of its function as armor. We became fast friends and he quickly recommended that I attend the Thursday night HIV men's support group.

My first time visiting the group left me amazed at its size, given that we were 25 years into the plague. I joined the circle of a dozen men (no women) that first Thursday, introduced by Karl Jr. and warned of our oath of confidentiality, for there were some familiar faces from my days of activism—men I had seen at retreats, at PRIDE weekends in Billings and Kalispell. I recognized faces from the bar before it shut down; men I met at the gay rodeo two Junes ago in Billings. No one attended from the university. The professional stigma was too compelling to risk facing a support group, especially since the injunction to secrecy made confidentiality rules more honored in the breach for even the least catty of gay men.

Of course, this transparent account of my so-called life, this detection of the as yet undetectables at F4 near Reserve Street, is itself an unconscionable violation of all kinds of codes of conduct in spite of the name changes. Memory invaded privacy, planted the flag, lit the green light of the confessional on the juicy and often salacious secrets of the kiss and teller. By its nature the memoir is transgressive, unscrupulous, indecorous, and potentially libelous. Hence its appeal. Hence its invocation of the now iconic AIDS aphorism that silence equals death.

Hence its ironic employment by me, a man noted for recalcitrance, even arrogance in my close-to-the-chest demeanor. My introversion was often mistaken for conceit, for an unwillingness to be detected. That first evening of group, I sat there in my reticence, dressed in my rumpled khakis and overpriced Keen hiking shoes. I listened to the stories of the beaten and exiled and t-cell-less, unrecovering alcoholics and food-stamped survivors, who sat across from me in yet another circle. What a cry baby I felt I had become, as I took in those harrowing stories at group, unable to share my own.

A cast of positive characters had gathered under the tall ceiling of Karl's office, with its recessed lighting and propeller fan. I recognized a bass from the gay chorus who had worked at the white cardboard factory, a bartender from the Joker's Wild. I nodded to jovial Sandy, the accountant activist who helped to start the Missoula LGBT Center and could not stop smoking. I met a farmer from St. Ignatius with a straw hat turned up on one side like Crocodile Dundee. He would later in desperation swallow Interferon, a dangerous cancer drug. I had met him in West Yellowstone at a queer retreat where we bunked together. He was a hippy farmer, scruffy and radical and eminently fuckable. I knew my type. I had to be irreverent and scrappy, had to believe in sweet grass and hot tubs and leaps into deep lakes.

We never managed more than a kiss or two before he disappeared, but this crazy and off-the-grid guy with his torn-jeans had lassoed me from the minute we talked about the fucking Republicans and his trans hens.

There were others in our circle, each with his own story of sickness, ostracism, and travails with the medical world. Each had his t-cell count, each had his "meds"—his Sustiva, his nightmares, his Wellbutrin, his lack of insurance. Each had his story of fear and rejection by citizens of a state that still prided itself on not having that shit in their towns. I heard of parents who gave their sons cash to get the hell out of Plentywood, disinheriting their sick offspring. I heard about a partner who walked away the day his lover Dennis came home positive. I listened to the chain-smoking boy from Hardin who refused to go anywhere near the Partnership Health Clinic and instead drank herb tea and sweated twice a week. There was talk of callous physicians, mouth ulcers and neuropathies, swollen lymph nodes, night sweats, and shingles. Bearded men in hoodies wept openly beside paisley-shirted bank tellers who spat out the dish on every cruel bitch in the community. We were vicious and desperate, bitter and fed with the fear and loathing in and of Montana, a place where most of us were sodomitical ex-felons under the repealed sexual deviancy code, where being positive was still a curse, a death sentence, a chance to fight back, circle the wagons and tell our stories of fierce survival. It was the early 2000s.

39

SANDPOINT

I 'd never seen him before. Few of us had—maybe at the Rhino or The Badlander. This guy who showed up at group one night was pierced, maybe 5'6" with long dark brown hair the color of beef jerky but duller. His was pale and sallow. He carried two silver metal crutches, the kind with loops around the forearms, though he seemed to be walking fine without them. He was nervous and perturbed when he arrived late. He had obviously been pushed through the front door—if not physically then through the verbal shove of an overbearing social worker.

Our focus quickly turned to this new guy, Cyrus. He left his green Army surplus coat on the entire time he was there. He was angry and miserable—physically, mentally, emotionally, socially. Isolated but too irate to take help from any quarter. He told us he was waiting to die in a month or two. If he had had access to one of the Glocks at the ammo shop across the alley from Karl's oasis, he would have been glad to kill himself if it weren't for his ridiculous pups jumping all over him when he came in the door at home. His friends licked his eyes and nose, gleefully wagged their tails like he was their only man. His mutts kept him alive, with their hungry mouths and rollovers on the dirty shag rug in the trailer where he stayed, now that he'd been released from the hospital once the trimethoprim kicked in and knocked the pneumocystis out of his lungs, once he recovered from the stroke that floored him almost simultaneously. Even on the mend from those obstacles, he wasted away right before our very eyes, 110 if a pound. He pumped as much weed as he could acquire into his overdosed body to dull the pain. How could we help him other than to perk up our complacent ears and gossip about him when he didn't show up the next time?

His rage seethed. In an eerie monotone once he settled down, he condemned meds, docs, therapists, hospitals, Missoula, even our fake solicitation. He ranted about his home-town, Sandpoint, home of stockpilers, hoarders, and doomsday preppers on the Idaho Panhandle. He ranted against us. We just wanted to screw him, he glared at us older men in the group. We watched him push the hair out of his eyes with a bony white hand, stared at the floor while he spit out his resent-ment of the so-called gay "community," which he called a bunch of back-biting homos who wanted him to go away now that it wasn't safe to suck him off. He *was* going, he told us. He was on his fucking way. No one stopped him now. His mom didn't even come down anymore from Pend Oreille. He had no fucking friends anyway, didn't want any. And who the fuck would fuck him the way he looked for crying out fucking loud? He shook as his low tones released his bitter fury.

That night I went home from group with a pit in my stom-ach, went home to my diary and wrote:

LOGJAM

The stroke blew his cover.
He landed in St. Pat's for a week,
and his family found out.
He had to learn to walk again,
metal crutches looped through his arms.

His mom drove down from Sandpoint
for a day, but his brothers stayed put,
the ones laid off by Humbird Lumber.
After he got out, he heard nothing
from home and decided to go off the meds.

The doctors gave him two months.
His hate spoke low and halting.
A metal loop pierced his lower lip,
shaking when he mentioned Sara,
the social worker he depended on

until she quit her job. He had two dogs,
one a puppy injured while playing
with the other. Who would take them?
Staring at the carpet, he talked
about his supply of painkillers,

about the closets he lived in,
the mill town he'd left at sixteen,
banged into lockers at Colburn High,
told to go to hell at church. He fled
to hide in our college town. We knew

his face from the bar in the basement
where our county kept its homos
drunk and dark until we came out
in time to get beat up by gangs
of frats emerging from the Logjam.

What we felt near him was fear. For ourselves
more than for him. We didn't want to watch
him die, but were stuck there for two hours,
in that green room. We sat in a circle,
passed cookies, sipped our herbal tea.

Cyrus harbored a raw hate I knew was inside me too though I never bothered to show it to anybody but myself—and my animals. Maybe I didn't have the balls to expose my vitriol—to own up to the fact that I saw myself as a luckless hack who got fucked whenever I tried to accomplish anything substantial or meet somebody I could love. Too scared to open up, too chicken to spill the buckets of self-blame and fist-shaking at a god who seemed to get a kick out of splattering my predicament in my face. I was unhappy, trapped, gay, positive, stuck in a relationship that I lacked the chutzpah to do anything about. Even Cyrus, for all his quiet shaking and pointed control of the evening, was able to convey his resentment towards a world that had fucked him over in ways I would never allow myself to express, contained in my emotional closet, undetectable—trying to be a macho man in front of the world. I crouched on the kitchen floor and sobbed uncontrollably to "Angel from Montgomery." I dreamed back to the promise of my Santa Cruz days, helpless in my search for someone to love.

Language was my only refuge, writing my only catharsis.

40

TUCKER

"Hey, babe, how's it goin' out there? You on your way to work?" Tucker spoke to his partner on his new flip phone, lying on his couch in Montana. Their love had become long distance when Tuck got the pastry job at the new Hilton in Missoula. Brian had to stay put on Figueroa in LA, had his work in Anaheim at the insurance company, had his commute. They checked in almost ten times a day by cell. It was the only way Tucker could hear the voice of the man he'd slept with more years than he could remember—10, 15? They'd been through so much together: HIV, diabetes, heart conditions, pneumonia, transplants, surgeries, 12 steps. Through it all they grew zucchinis and zinnias in the summers, baked apricot pies and apple tarts, raised Westies, threw cantaloupes across the kitchen at each other's heads, cracked cabinets, splattered bowls of heavy cream. They watched *Sunset Boulevard* for the umpteenth thousandth time, over-served their overweight neighbors—Nora and Cliff—with peanut butter bars smothered with Ben and Jerry's. They'd both spent more years than they could remember accepting the things they could not change. They were inseparable.

Tucker heard Brian click on. He heard his love say, "hey there," but then the phone seemed to go haywire—then a smashing sound and then what seemed like a groan or whimper on the other end of the line. "Hello?" Tucker said, repeating the word a few times before he figured they must have gotten cut off. 'Fucking AT&T,' he said to himself as he hung up and dialed again, but this time there was no answer, no message pickup. Brian's phone had gone dead.

Tucker told our group this story from his spot at the far end of the couch. He always sat in the same place, always showed up with a cellophane-wrapped flowered plate of maple blondies, Nutter Butter S'more cookie bars, salted caramel chocolate brownies, poke turtle bars, cream-cheese filled snick-erdoodles—luscious, high fat, sugar-wonderful treats that helped pass the two-hour's time of check-in and tears. Karl 2 always had a pot of coffee going—so caffeine and sugar powered us on from 7 to 9. Tucker—5'8" 140 at best, an ex-smoker, drinker, addict—was a fiery funny irreverent queer, desperate and nervous. He never forgot anything we said but never judged anyone.

His most pronounced physical attribute was the prosthesis he wore on one foot. He had lost half of it to diabetes a couple of years back but his shoe masked most of the damage. His hacking laugh and twinkling eyes told a story of good times and domestic delight. He couldn't eat the sweets he baked for us, nor could he ever tell us exactly how weak his condition was. He had made the rounds of drugs from the AZT days to the current Sustiva craze. He switched regimens whenever the latest inhibitor could no longer inhibit his swollen nodes, unhealed wounds, his prednisone thin skin, and then his creeping lung cancer. These threats stayed hidden beneath the powder sugar sprinkled atop his lemon bars, his rants against right-wing politics, his love of his job, his friends, Karl, our group.

Tucker found out about the fatal collision the next day. Brian had answered the phone while merging into traffic on Highway 5. Tucker, two years later, still lived with the impact of that call every day. He had reached out to his partner and pushed him away forever. He lived with the recognition that he, an alcoholic diabetic HIV+ pastry chef, who had bounced in and out of an AIDS diagnosis for the last 15 years, had not infected his negative partner with the virus but killed him with his kindness. Yet none of the burden of that crushing realization, of the deep irony of the circumstance of his loss, fazed this member of our support group in any way other than a glassy eye, a choked throat, a box of Kleenex, a chink in his chipper, sardonic façade. Ebullient Tucker—one tough cookie. He faced the endless opportunities of infection with his infectious buoyancy.

We must have taken two or three cars even though there were only five or six of us—Chuck, Randy, Karl, me, Richard, James. Some of us lived downtown closer to our destination on Broadway, so we walked home afterwards. We weren't sure they would let us in, but when Karl told us where Tucker was, James suggested we go down and say hi. We entered right next to the sliding doors of the ER at Saint Patrick's Hospital. We stood in the lobby with its stained-glass nuns and statues of praying virgins. It was too late in the evening for any pink ladies, but we managed to cram into an elevator that took us up to the ICU.

I'm not sure I had ever been that close to death. I had seen my dad on oxygen before he recovered from vodka poisoning. I had seen guys in group who were terminal. There were the

Irish open caskets of grandmothers and uncles, but when the nurse finally broke the rules and let us see Tuck hanging out like a pencil on a pillow, his head slightly tilted by the mechanical bed and the placement of the cushion, when he came into my field of vision, I saw my fear. I quickly fashioned a false and nervous cheer that seemed the only genuine way to cope. I faced in the countenance of my friend the unknown but certain fate that this incurable disease adumbrated.

This was it for the gray and shrinking Tucker; this would be it for me. The it, with or without belief, was not ultimately reconcilable with the ferocity of my desire to stay alive even under the most untenable of circumstances. I approached Tucker with a smile and a hand in his. I said hi and asked him how he was doing as if we chatted on Planet Romeo. In the thin air of our small talk hung the certainty of his coming death. He knew; we all knew, but we came to say hi in the ICU, to tell him we missed him at the support group though we all knew— that no one could lend him any more support. Tucker would be dead before the week tolled its seven days and seven nights. He joined the 30 million others who succumbed to the infections that a ravaged immune system could not suppress.

Tucker had just turned 50, this man infectious in mirth and generosity and warmth in ways that few of us could ever emulate. Would he become a piece of cloth spread out on a basketball court? Would his seat on the far side of the couch remain empty, indented, ghostly for the remainder of our Thursday meetings? Would we look back at him with amazement at his struggle to survive in the face of his early frosting?

41

MSENGE

I was supposed to wake every morning to count blessings, thank gods, express gratitude for the light within, show amazement and happiness and delight that I was alive. I who was predicted to evaporate by the turn of the millennium, who contracted the ever-duplicating virus that in 2009 was being squelched by ingested inhibitors. So why did I dwell so regularly on weeds in my garden, dog hair that infested my home, come-ons from 20-something chubs, phone calls from relatives and friends that wanted money, letters, lessons, rides? They wanted everything and anything but a chance to talk to me about my life, to listen to my sadness, to ask about my upcoming trip to Africa—to Kenya for the poetry workshop. Why was I so ubiquitously invisible to my peers, so inconsequent, so easily avoidable except as an advocate or supporter of people and causes other than my own? Why alive and well and yet why extinct and discarded among those—my family and friends (the "f" words)—who only took me off the shelf when I could give them a reference, a recommendation, a legal opinion, a ride to the airport, a shoulder for them to cry on?

By 2008, the first African American President, the phenom Barack Obama, had begun his 63-billion-dollar initiative on world health. A large portion of those funds were destined for PEPFAR, the president's emergency plan for AIDS relief around the world. During the same year, I was in the process of re-inventing myself as a disgruntled poet, and by coincidence I had received a partial scholarship to study and write poetry at the Summer Literary Seminar in Nairobi, one of the hotbeds of HIV in the global south.

The flight to Kenya from Montana went through Amsterdam and took two days, given the long layover. I carried my meds in a cool case in my daypack, concerned about lost luggage, nervous about customs and airport security. I might have been pulled over in Kenya when they recognized the drugs; I feared rejection at customs for being a health risk. Jammed against a window on the flight from Amsterdam. I climbed over unhappy geriatrics as I rose to urinate every forty minutes; I wanted to stay hydrated to avoid headaches that came anyway. I was still leery of raw egg and refused to eat lettuce in foreign lands. Tomato skins, crab cakes, raw tuna, the offer of Caesar salads—all verboten. Fruit juices immediately produced eruptive bowel movements. I also swallowed the requisite malaria medicine and dealt with its side effects. I paid exorbitant sums for dubious bottled waters and elaborate gadgets to ensure my ability to plug in my devices in East African outlets.

I managed to arrive at the rather elaborate pool and terraced hotel in the residential area of Nairobi in a gray van the morning after. Earlier I had found the SLS sign in the concourse of the Jomo Kenyatta airport and stepped into a crammed minivan. Was I the only *shoga* in the group, the only faggot (*msenge*), I wondered, looking at the other passengers? Was I the only one who if by chance crossed the eastern border into Uganda could be stoned to death if discovered kissing another man? I was surrounded by women from the East Coast. I glanced about to confirm my feeling of isolation. I had traveled over poles and across hemispheres only to discover that I still felt like an out-homo teacher in the Rocky Mountains —with HIV.

Of course, water, sleep, and pills were the orders of the day as I schlepped my luggage out of the clunking elevator down to my fifth-floor room, where I closed the door, felt my hunger, noticed the hammer in my cranium. I was both exhausted and nervous even in my insular capsule of a room. Heading downstairs to the buffet, I eyed the sausages that swam in a sea of grease. My stomach almost erupted at the sight of pellucid corners of uncooked and tangled slabs of bacon. I forked my powdered eggs, pale yellow segments that jiggled with desiccation. Was there pepper? There was no butter for the tepid and petrified toast. There may have been jam. Honey was another one of those no-no's, its rawness a host for botulism, easily contracted by the immune-compromised. I sat at a round table of nine chairs, half full. New arrivals spoke of contests and forthcoming novellas, dropping the names of keynote speakers. I had gained permission to join them with stiff nods of assent that seemed to resent my interruption of their brilliant repartee. I sat in tongue-tied silence as the tepid tea slid down my throat with bowel-loosening ease. I had nothing to say for myself. I cringed at my awkward intrusion into the private convo of the literati, excused myself within minutes and headed back upstairs to my cubicle.

KENYA IN MIDDLE AGE

Asifuye mvuwa imemnyea
(*He who praises rain has been rained upon*)
Kiswahili Proverb

In the mirror there are no more imagoes.
What I see are lines, furrows the sonnet warned about.
And in these sockets, two blue fires stare out in fear.
At breakfast, no one asked about my dreams.
They glimpsed at crevices that once were cheeks.
Where could they kiss me? Eyes averted to omelets,
among themselves they talked about giraffes, malaria.

I am at a conference in Kenya, staring at my face,
at the rough road from scalp to grizzle, the rift cratered,
lenses filmed with dust, crumbs. White coffee instant and
    weak.
I couldn't eat that tepid sausage, couldn't join their chat about
    photos,
couldn't feel these lips grow thinner in this simian jaw.
Shrunken. A pounding drum of jet lag behind my mask
told me to bite the stale pastry, spread the butter thick,

wipe my mouth and grin at dropped names. Bare a tooth,
    yellow
and long from gums that have receded. Did I ever belong?
Even when the squash players, splayed in the lounge, locked up
    my eyes,
even then, I knew their stare was sterile. Even then coat sleeves
invited my veined and freckled arms. Five floors up I
    trudged,

eschewing strange and noisy elevators. I climbed to the top
    floor,
my heart burning. I turned the key and smelled my sleep.

In the mirror I see what they would not look at. The graveyard,
strewn with bones. Pill tubes like fingers. Empty bottles
of plastic water, unabsorbed by skin. On the floor spines of
    tomes
unfinished. In the toilet, the ghost flushing three times.
He comes to bed with me. My friend, this jester, his fingers
at work through strands of my hair, his thumbs down my bent
    neck,
palms cupping my blurred vision. This rain, he says, will bless
us.

The next day we were introduced to members of Kwani, the writers' organization in Nairobi. During a Q and A, I had the gumption to raise my hand and ask about the two Kenyan men who had married in London and were disowned by the country as a result. I asked them about the death bill in neighboring Uganda (promoted by American evangelicals). The question came at the end of the session and was answered with the kind of hurried discomfort that accompanies the appearance of elephants in living rooms, a metaphor that could become literal on safari in this part of Africa.

Sodomy was a felony in Kenya, required a 14-year sentence under Section 162 of the penal code, while "gross indecency" (any sexual practices between men) carried a lesser 5-year sentence. Same-sex marriage was banned under the Kenyan Constitution, and there were no explicit protections in the law for sexual orientation or gender identity. Kenya had the fifth highest disapproval rating of homosexuality among 45 countries surveyed by the Pew Global Attitudes Project in 2007. 96% of the polled populace found homosexuality an unacceptable way of life. People who came out were regularly disowned, ridiculed, assaulted, and humiliated. Much of this opprobrium was sponsored by Anglican bishops, Islamic sheiks, and American evangelicals. Men who had sex with men were regularly assaulted by police or local militias called *askaris*. Gay was taboo in Kenya.[1]

The dangers surrounding anything queer in Kenya influenced even the progressive literati of Kwani. The answers I received from the panelists to my question were perfunctory, hushed, and dismissive. I was politely frowned upon as a self-righteous American who imposed his western social and cultural "values," through a colonialist presumptuousness.

Though roseate and somewhat moist under my arms after the conclusion of the panel discussion, I felt no regrets about asking these Kenyan intellectuals about the very oppression which international human rights and AIDS organizations ascribed to the governments of East Africa. I felt actually proud of my audacity, proud of my concern for my fellow sodomites in a way that rather glaringly pointed out one of the prominent paradoxes that had informed the two great developments in my life. Of course, no one bothered to approach me in the courtyard after the session, but I was accustomed to shunning. I cared less if they made the correct assumption that I was a *shoga*, a man who had sex with men, or even a *msenge*, a more formal term that suggested bottoming, for coming out had been the most momentous and courageous act of my life, an act that in fact had brought me the most joy and fulfillment sexually, emotionally, even socially.

For me, being queer was a delight even if a dangerous one— whether in Nairobi or Kalispell, Montana. It had nothing in the least to do with disease—mental or physical. But the irony of this embraced stigma manifested itself in the other momentous event in my life, namely my seroconversion. Being positive about being gay had played a central role in my HIV positivity. I could not deny that correlation even as a railed against archbishops who claimed AIDS to be proof of God's wrath on sick and unnatural perverts. The best thing that ever happened to me—my first trip to a gay bar called the White Horse in 1980— had somehow led to the most calamitous occurrence in my diary—the acquisition of a fatal virus. No matter what silver lining I might ascribe to my long-term survival—in terms of philosophy, meditation, poetry, intimations of mortality, even compassion—I would never be able to make peace with the cruel twist of fate that made my love lethal.

I did not raise my hand at the colloquy and ask about the incidence of HIV in this sub-Saharan country, one of the most affected nationalities by HIV in the world. I did not inquire about the stigmatization of the approximately 1.6 million people living with the virus (almost 6% of the population in 2007). Kenya along with Mozambique and Uganda shared the fourth position as countries with the greatest per capita HIV populations. That statistic persisted in spite of the decline in deaths and the increase in adults who started taking antiretrovirals. Though women and children were also hard hit in this country, new cases found their primary hosts in key populations—men who had sex with men, drug users, and sex workers. The prevalence of HIV was three times greater among gay people than predominantly hetero individuals.

42

KOROGOCHO

My trip to Kenya aggravated the competing tensions of my identity. Even though I came to write poetry, I soon grew preoccupied by my status in an East African country where the gay stigma was almost greater than that of HIV. I needed to find out more. After the seminar, I stayed with friends in Karen, in the suburbs south of Nairobi, a settlement known as the Ngong Hills made famous by Karen Blixen in her memoir *Out of Africa*. During my requisite pilgrimage to Blixen's restored home, I recalled her early 20th-century stories of British colonialists in the "happy hunting grounds," Kikuyu coffee farmers, roaming tribal Masai hunters, migrating Somali Muslims, and Indian merchants who came to Kenya to bank, lend, borrow, and steal. What grabbed me as I sauntered across the cut lawns of Blixen's idyllic farm was another strange and wistful nostalgia. I longed for my Thursday night HIV support group back home. What were James and Randy up to? Was there not a drop-in HIV group in Nairobi where I might go to find queer positive Kenyans?

I suddenly felt compelled to find my HIV people in a

country deeply immersed in the travails of the AIDS struggle—
children, mothers, sex-workers, truck drivers, closeted queers,
MSMers. They were all dying, all vying for unavailable ARVs.
I had to find them, make some contact with them. I knew they
were probably uninsured, probably had little access to the
infectious disease specialists that insisted on a full examination
of my lipoma-strewn body every six months. The phlebotomists
who drew my blood, studied my lipid panels, my liver enzymes,
my glucose levels, my triglycerides. They listened to my heart-
beat and drew wax from my contorted ear canals. What might
it be like to be penniless, to live in Kibera, the largest slum in
the world, to survive shunned and circumspect in the tight
community of red dirt shacks, with its maze of makeshift
dwellings? What must it be like to live without modern incon-
veniences, to live sometimes even without enough food, to wake
up hungry and know too that you were viral, headed for sickness and suffering.

At first, I couldn't discern why I wanted desperately to
connect with others who carried the burden of the HIV virus
nor why I couldn't just enjoy myself with poets and writers and
family and friends that peopled my little safari and beach-
combing visit. The answer had, as its façade, an impulse of
altruism, my rehearsed intention of shedding light on the plight
of others with the virus by writing about my experience. Maybe
I could make the world aware of what we experienced, as if
detailing the lives of HIV long-term survivors (HLTS) across
boundaries could somehow lead to a cure or social acceptance.

But this do-good cover harbored a darker side. Self-promo-
tion. Yes, I wanted to meet some other people on the other side
of the world with my immunodeficiency. Yes, I wanted to find
out more about the untouchable and virtually quarantined
queer with AIDS in Kenya. But I also wanted the light to shine
on myself and my words. I had to ask myself what good, what

value, what need might be met by my finding someone else in my boat. Especially if the person were a mother of three, a son born with the virus, a transfusion victim, a needle user. At first, I could not reason that need.

Eventually I realized that my search for support arose from a deep desire to commune. I longed to be with others like me, to witness and recognize people who felt the burden of this microscopic and invisible load so that I could lighten or help others carry it. Even if it would be difficult for others to understand what I was going through or for me to understand what a single man in his 30s might endure living in Kochi, one of the slums of Nairobi. Could my awareness of his struggle somehow make the hardship of that life or mine any less arduous? The economy of communality, the value of revelation, the release that came from unburdening one's soul among others with similar burdens could not be measured by yardsticks of normal gain or loss. I might have been availing myself of the mystery of human contact as a way of rationalizing my quest, but to justify the ways of AIDS to men and women emerged as my life raft during those days in Karen while I was the lonely guest of a happy family. I was gay and positive and alive in the heart of HIV country. I had to find out more about it.

I was dropped off at the offices of TICAH one morning as a result of my persistence. The Trust for Indigenous Culture and Health was an NGO that promoted alternative health resources for the underprivileged in the slums. The women on salary—some from Kochi themselves—had been asked to accommodate a writer from Montana, to show him the offices and the mission of the organization. I had not read through more than a couple of brochures before I asked point blank if there was an HIV support group I could attend while I was in town. Though decorous but a little shocked, they told me, after some back-room confab, they would try to arrange a special meeting of the group in Kochi for Wednesday morning.

We drove by taxi from TICAH to the edge of the slum, a long drive north toward the city center and east to the township. From the car we could look out to the west at the vast uphill slope of Kibera, one of the largest slums in the world. We were headed to Korogocho, however, another slum on the other side of the city. The driver stopped at a place where the intense iron orange road became too carved by erosive fissures to allow for motor vehicles. I walked with two TICAH women, and as we moved up the road among skillets and goats and smoking old men seated on crates. Sights and sounds of this thriving city within a city amazed me. A couple of times we moved off the wide main road into a maze of man-made alleys that led to dwellings, through a series of sharp angular turns that left me lost in the warren. Alleyways were no wider than three feet, and living spots, almost all unpaved, were cordoned off with corrugated plastic and old lumber. Some had roofs, few had floors. I was shaking hands with some smiling people and quickly shuffled off down the road to our eventual destination, a small maybe 80-square-foot room, where couches and bed had been pushed against the wall and chairs set in a circle.

There were six of us, two guys (including me) and the rest women. I introduced myself as a writer from the United States, a man who lived with HIV for over ten years. The walls of the room were covered with white sheets. I was handed a cup of tea as we began to go around the circle, each person introduced herself to me, since most everyone already was familiar with others in group. I listened to their stories and told my own. I did not mention my queerness, aware of the taboo.

BLOOD WORK

Come to the slum
Kochi, Nairobi
Scrap metal town
corrugated
dirt red.

My nonprofit guides
positive people
who peddle herbs and hope
take me through mazes
"how are yous" from kids
sweet homes built from junk.

This visitor
numb with privilege
shocked smiler
driven from his hotel
to see what he cannot feel.

We wend our way
through warrens
potholes
chickens in crates
charcoal cylinders.

To Mary's place
her door a dead car.
Inside, white sheets
cover walls
light the dark.

She burns incense
translates stories
from Swahili,
six in our group.
Ismael wants to find a lover
now the drugs have kicked in.

Saysa wants me to marry,
share her cabbage juice cocktail,
tell the world we are proud
to be alive with the virus.
She's made her body map
wears her kanga with a message.

Only Jedi quiets banter.
Below her lash
a tear appears.
She calls her brother Deus
the only one who did not shun her.

Her sniffle brings us close
close enough to close the circle.
It slides from duct to voice
speaks deeper than infection
sharper than stigma's sting
the way they stare at you like death
in Kochi, at home, in America.

Her tear immerses us
health workers, mothers
men who have sex
with men, writer intruder
who chokes on asanti sanas.

He took his pills this morning,
He rode the taxi to the center,
He wants to tell their story.
In silence they stand
chapped hands linked
like t-cells.
Blood work.

THE BOROUGH AND BEYOND

(2010-2018)

43
DELETIONS

Mother died February 10, 2010, peacefully in her home —with the help of a morphine drip. With the help of her beloved Tongan women, Lily and Tommi, who had lived in the apartment behind the garage for the last 15 years and had become, for all intents and purposes, her immediate family. Tommi, the butch, was very much in control. She wrote checks and supervised repairs to the house. She hovered in the kitchen and tried unsuccessfully to make herself scarce whenever I or my brother and sisters visited erstwhile Mrs. Full Charge. Fragile Mommie Dearest was no longer able to stand before the gas jet and complain about her ne'er-do-well offspring, with the crucial exception of her eldest daughter who married into considerable Santa Barbara wealth and was living happily ever after in Pacific Heights with Corgis and two beautiful children, both of whom were favorites of Mother. The other three siblings—the gay son with HIV, the belligerent eldest boy who had turned to country music and Harleys, the unmarried youngest daughter who roamed unnamable African countries for independent contracts and gay divorcees—were outcast ingrates. "Sharper than the serpent's tooth" had become the refrain of poor Mother's upper-crust existence.

I was happy to pen Mom's obituary for the *San Francisco Chronicle* given my way with words. I was not happy to learn that my prose had been bowdlerized by the very sister who had come to Buffalo years before to offer succor. I had included the names of David and Rose along with the other survivors in my draft. Those names were deleted in the version that appeared in the paper. This erasure was only the first shock that hit me after Mom died. They came in waves.

Shortly after she passed over, I called my sister Mary, my closest ally since childhood. I told her I would fly out immediately from Missoula to California, but she, in a kind of uncharacteristic monotone, asked me to stay in Montana. She wanted some time alone. Her request surprised me. It was the first sign of the unraveling of our lifelong intimacy. The obituary was still unwritten. I complied with my sister's request. She must be very tired, I rationalized, given the protracted illness.

I flew out to the Peninsula from Missoula a week later, when my little sister had arrived from Paris. I returned to the horrible purple guest room off the kitchen where the visiting children stayed. That hideous hue being the brainchild of the Tongans, who with the death of Mother, were in full funeral mode. They drove the PT Cruiser to Costco for turkey wraps and artichoke dips, commandeered the spoiled spaniel—both of which had been pre-bequeathed to the loving helpmeets. They were not registered nurses, not subject to the ethics code that governed home healthcare workers in regard to bequests.

I woke to black coffee in the kitchen of the one-story Spanish colonial, with its winding driveway and pointless front lawn, its rat-infested palm tree, out-of-place kidney pool, and broken whirlpool. I leaned groggily against white grouted tile countertops and clutched Mr. Coffee, while I admired the hard

wood floors-stained walnut, and wished I had a gas range
island, framed in blue and white tile. As I circled the island
with my second cup of Peet's Major Dickenson blend, my little
sister (fresh from Air France) approached from the inner workings of some sad unused bedroom behind the arras. There were
no arrases, actually. There was a dim dining room and a
morgue-like chintzed living room with couch covers that
mimicked the jungles of Costa Rica. My younger sister
appeared in a tasteful pants suit. "It had been so long" and we
were "so happy to see each other again." She worked for
Lebanese banks, marketed Shea butters, and sold kitchen
knives. Irons were in her fire. She was always on the cusp of big
deals that almost always fizzled but not without some perk—a
trip to a conference in Rome, an exploratory mission in Burkina
Faso.

Kathleen wanted to talk to me about something, wanted to
broach an issue around the funeral next week. Did I really
think that David's daughter needed to attend? Was *that* abso-
lutely necessary; she probed me, tentative at first.

"You're coming with David, yes?" She had begun the
conversation. She liked David. They spoke Spanish together.
My little sister spoke many tongues—French, Spanish, a little
Russian—maybe even Forked.

"Yeah, I guess we'll fly out for it," I answered absently.
"Next week, right? Lots of flights." I dreaded the recurring
smell of Cinnabon in the Salt Lake Airport, the return home to
Montana, only to turn around again. "And you will be here for
a couple of weeks?"

She ignored my mumbled inquiry. "Are you planning on
bringing David's daughter?" she continued her inquiry sheep-
ishly. Was Tommi the Tongan hovering about somewhere, I
suddenly asked myself, as I glanced into the den and out to the
driveway. I tried to digest the slight oddity of her interrogation.

The house was empty but for me, my little sister, and the ubiquitous Pacific Islanders. Kathleen rarely questioned me about anything that I recalled; it was usually all about her. Now she turned my screw in the empty house for some reason. I tried to ignore her.

"I guess so," I said, nonchalantly. "I think she probably will want to come. Break from school. Any chance to come to the Bay Area, you know, get the hell out of Dodge." I opened cabinets, looked for cereals that were not expired.

"Do you think she really wants to come?" Kathleen followed up. I still wasn't paying much attention. There was no two-percent milk in the fridge, just a pint of curdled half and half, only a week after our dearly beloved's peaceful passage to the undiscovered country. And, of course, plenty of butter. Mother loved toast with her butter. I attempted to split open a frozen English muffin. Was there any peanut butter in the house?

"Was she very close to Mom?" Kathleen asked. "I mean, do you think she really needs to fly all the way out here?" I perked up a bit after I noted the archness in this last remark, which I distractedly registered in the midst of my irritation over an unstocked larder. No raspberry jam. No bananas. No juice.

"What difference does it make?" I asked rather uninterestedly, waiting for the interminable toaster to crisp its muffin.

"Well, Susie and Tommi think it might be better to have just the family at the funeral. David's daughter didn't really know Mother very well anyway. They think it might be better to keep it small—immediate family."

She finally gained the response of my full body language with her tenacity. I glanced over at her pinched expression. I ought not to kill the messenger (though my first impulse admittedly), for it didn't take long, after my initial obtuseness, to figure out that poor Kathleen had been deputized to do the bidding of big sister and the South-Sea islanders. I leaned against the kitchen island as smoke rose from the toaster, the muffin trapped in its prongs, the ejector unable to unlodge the oversized crenellations. I came to the rescue with a knife, ready for electrocution. I still had enough sense to unplug the old Toastmaster, its silver sides stained with butter fat and crumbs. The muffins were released like jacks in the box as I turned back to confront my stocky sibling, who held her cup of joe in both hands with intention. She wanted to make her point with force, with conviction. Kathleen didn't know Rose from Adam (or Eve), had met her once or twice, but she was under the bigger one's thumb.

"I think David already made the reservation," I told her quickly, trying to lay her awkward inquiry to rest. "Anyway, I'm not sure how we're defining 'immediate' or 'family' for that matter. David and Rosie seem rather immediate to me—maybe too immediate, if you catch my drift. She will probably behave, though I can't promise anything. If that's what's worrying you. She'll want to shop of course, but we can do that the day after. I can't see why she shouldn't come."

"Well, I'm not sure Mother liked her very much."

"Really?" I asked, suddenly taken aback by Kathleen's categorical assessment. "Well, I did tell Mom about my spats with *la princesa*. I know I was constantly complaining about our knock-down, drag-outs, but Rose is family, for better or worse, and she's growing up. And heavens, I'm not sure Mother liked a lot of people who will be attending the funeral. Take our brother Peter for example. Talk about knock down, with her number one son no less. Let me ask you this," I stated, moving into lawyer mode as I looked her in the eyes. "Did Mother tell you not to invite Rose to the funeral?"

"Oh, I wouldn't know about that," Kathleen retreated. "I..." she hesitated a bit. "We were just thinking it would be a bit much to drag her out here. Mom barely knew her. We just thought it would be less trouble if she didn't have to make the trip."

"We did, did we?" I resorted to even more than my usual dose of sarcasm. "So Mary and the Tongans want to dictate who I bring to my mother's funeral? Since when?" I left it at that, retreated to my muffin.

I was noticeably unfazed that morning; in fact, the full import of the sisters' suggestion didn't really dawn on me as part of a larger orchestration until later. The nooks and crannies of my muffin swam in the melting slabs of butter as I proceeded to the dining room to grade a stack of papers on *King Lear*. I decided not to mention this conversation to my partner, who was already rather leery of the nasty infighting of my family. I later got a call from my sister, who kept her distance up in town. She asked me to consider deleting Rose from the hearse list. "We have only so many seats in the limos," she stated.

"We'll rent a car and follow you up to the ceremony," I insisted. I ignored her new cut but registered this second affront to my gay family somewhere in my consciousness. I stocked up on shock. "Fuck you," was not openly articulated at that point. My honest reaction was muffled under a gentleman's veneer that accommodated being trampled upon with stoic aplomb and a stiff upper lip.

After the shock of discovering the deletions in *The Chronicle*, I continued my self-protective oblivion in a way that characterized the "up with which we put" mindset of many gay men like me, as if complicit in my own continued erasure. As if I were in the closet even after coming out. Some inner narrative apologized for the callous disregard of the hetero-hegemony that had somehow convinced me, playing upon social belittlement, that yes, David and I weren't really married, and yes,

Rose was not really my biological child, and yes, David and I were arguing constantly these days, and yes Rosie was a spoiled brat sometimes. Leaving them out of the obit was really not such a big deal.

Before long, however, insult was added to injury. I found out that I had been summarily removed as executor of my parents' will when I announced my positivity in the late 90s. I was removed as a beneficiary altogether for a period, presumably because my mother assumed I would predecease her. All of this dark side of my "open and affirming" family came to light in the months after Mother's death. I received news of these deletions not with anger but sad dismay. I buried my emotional rage, immersed myself in the mountain of work I had before me at the university. I concentrated on keeping my own relationship with David from disintegrating. All in a day's work, I thought. Until HIV raised its HAND, until the virus took its revenge.

44

THE BARGE

The aggravating affronts that surrounded Mother's death left me on the surface largely unfazed. I was miffed, put out, put upon, pushed out of shape, but these states of mind were always my default. I had made a life out of feeling slighted. I was happy to blame myself if I was unable to find some external source to confirm my suspicion of mistreatment, bad luck, non-recognition, rejection, and—at worst—ridicule. Such self-condemnation coupled with mild depression was visible in my hunched shoulders (mild scoliosis), my slump, my shuffle, my run-in with tree branches as a result of a field of vision largely focused on the icy paths of Missoula's parks I circled with the dogs, a boxer mix who barked relentlessly (sadistically encouraged by David who knew how much quiet meant to his studious professor) and the white yellow lab named Reno, who had come to us not from the biggest little city in the world, but from a kennel in Kansas that trained service dogs with cattle prods on their ears. Reno had been placed with an autistic child in the university district of Missoula, but the match was inauspicious. The child lashed out at the Labrador erratically as part of his symptoms, and after running away for two weeks, Reno was found and came to me. I had been best friend-less since Toby died.

My partner thought Reno, not the child, was the autistic one, and he much preferred the loud and extroverted bitch, our other canine crutch. His aversion for the new Lab was thinly veiled with epithets like "ridiculous tub of white fur" and "shit-eating mutt," while the boxer mix, whom our daughter had brought home from an auto radio shop on a whim, was *la princesa* who could do no wrong. Our multiplying bones of contention were obviously displaced upon the undeserving canines, though to my credit I loved them both, walked and trained them both, and generally took care of the animals. The vet bills, the boarding, hikes in Pattee Canyon, stick throwing, training—all were part of my duties as a responsible if grumbling mensch.

I loved them both as I loved my siblings. I swallowed and shouldered, I hunkered and slouched, with stolid stoicism. I paid the bills, walked with my partner and the child through the mall and Barnes and No Balls, where Rose acquired studded denim at American Eagle and Japanese Manga. I bought the Weber barbecue and the upgraded iPhone for the child. I did it all. But rather than bask in the ego boosting of my largesse and uber-accommodation, instead I wintered in deep discontent and self-abnegation, while my unconscious accumulated stores of resentment and my immune system, unbeknown to me, began to weaken.

I hated clothes with labels; I hated clutter, I hated red leather couches, knife sets. I hated money and yet even with that disdain, I was sucked into the clutches of mortgages and credit cards both at home and at large with the division of the estate in California. David told me to calm down, reminded me that the median debt load of the American family was around

200 grand. Where he got his numbers mystified me, but he brandished his statistics like a sword as he advocated flat screens and electric toothbrushes. Pressure mounted as we waited for my inheritance.

Meanwhile in California the contents of the last will and testament—a document apparently changed by Mother five times in the last ten years—was scheduled for a reading at her lawyer's office in Marin. I soon discovered that once the millennium had come and gone without my death from AIDS, my mother had mercifully inserted me back into the will. Around Will 3, I surfaced as a minor beneficiary, though there was no thought of relying on my legal expertise to be reinstated as executor.

HIV had attacked my economic as well as my physical well-being. My sister became executor and was given a controlling percentage of the estate. I sat stunned in the Larkspur office. I tried to come to grips with the revelations of the Brooks Brother accountant and the rich trust and estates attorney. The grandchildren had all received minor bequeathals; Rose received nothing. The Tongans received large cash bequests. In a Larkspur Landing conference room, the lawyer handed us an enormous document and proceeded to explain the distribution. I should have seethed, but instead sat around the table sunk in astonishment. He explained the complexities of Mother's intricate plan to confer enough power on my sister to remain in control of the entire distribution. Much of the money remained tied up in buildings that our LLC owned and leased. My sister was given full authority over its management, and Tommi was established as her salaried personal secretary for the foreseeable future. My brother did seethe—openly, and the lawyer, in anticipation of a contest, told us we could reconfigure the estate if we were all in agreement.

So my inheritance, the so-called "barge" as David called it, hoping for a windfall to free us from lines of credit with Quicken Loans, turned out to be a dinghy of sorts. My golden years would be plagued with resource scarcity. My great expectation became a raft with leaks. For all my complaining, I managed to eke out around 20% of what was left in the estate after we paid mother's country club and Princess Cruise bills, doled out thousands to the triumphant Tongans, and paid money to the legitimate grandchildren. Sister walked away with almost 40%.

My brother, who took away 15% of the pot, fumed, threatened a will contest, and lobbied me and Kathleen for what he believed would be a more equitable distribution. I found myself —as I always had—in the stressful middle of these competing narcissists. I sought to mediate, to reconcile the differences of my manipulative siblings. I tried to remove any vestige of my own desire from the equation, even as such a discounting continued to accumulate in bio-locations unaware to me. Filling up some psychic dam, my reservoir of goodwill and moderation had beneath its surface other sediments that pressed against the water wall—unbeknownst to my automatic tugboat pilot.

I emailed my siblings in an attempt to have them redistribute the wealth in four equal piles with an agreed-upon subtraction for the funds advanced to my brother over the years. My younger sister and the lawyer were amenable to a mutual re-divvy, but my older sister who was already channeling Mommie Dearest felt compelled to repeat ad nauseam her desire to "carry out Mom's will" in both senses of the latter term. She held the cards, and my brother, with a pair of 8s, had no leverage but the threat of a contest.

The upshot of all this maneuvering came with my rich sister's refusal to budge, to relinquish any control over the power she had gained—the coals that had been sent to her

Newcastle—the money she was to amalgamate with her husband's already substantial holdings. We three other kids had suddenly become the poor relatives, shut out of the life-style to which we had grown accustomed, attending dancing schools and tennis clubs as adolescents. None of this brouhaha mattered to me, I told myself. I had long since run off to Montana, come out of the closet, and invested in cross-country skis, backpacks, and boyfriends. I ignored the deep hurt my sister's rebuff inflicted. That wound would fester.

45

'TIL DEATH DO US PART

Back in Missoula, the march of seasons through 2010 continued. Ironically, the funeral baked meats brought forth the marriage tables. In spite of our struggles over red wine, Tom Cruise movies, and body fat, everyone's favorite gay couple agreed that spring to join the ACLU's Montana marriage case, along with a couple of lesbian couples from Helena and Bozeman. Few knew that our relationship was fraught with tension, but the ACLU case served as a kind of fuck you to the dis of *my family* by the nuclear clan in California. As flawed a historical institution as monogamous marriage was, I felt I should at the very least have access to wedlock. I should have a right to dig my own grave, print my name in obituaries, put flowers on the tombstones of my in-laws. The legal benefits and burdens of marriage within socio-legal spheres represented privileges that even unhappy couples should be able to enjoy, especially those who managed long-term HIV.

Montana's citizens' constitution, ratified in the 1970s, contemplated broad equal protection and privacy rights, and our attorneys relied on the state constitution to challenge the validity of the anti-same sex marriage amendment of 2004. We also sought the right to marry. Our daughter connection, Rose in high school, made our standing even more attractive to the assimilatory rationale of marriage equality, and though David and I saw eye to eye on the wrongheadedness of the costly marriage struggle, we felt too that fighting heterocentrism on all fronts was not a bad idea. John Waters's famous quip came to mind as we mulled over our decision to join the other plaintiffs: "I used to think the two best things about being gay," he was said to have gibed, "were that we didn't have to marry or go into the military." As the neoliberal Human Rights Campaign expended its energy on normalization, battle lines were being drawn between the "we're just like you" LGBT set and more radical queers that shunned assimilation.

David and I were exemplary plaintiffs because of our ability to pass, our swagger instead of swish, our baritones that rarely went into the lisp of a Paul Lynde on *Hollywood Squares*. We were cisgender gay men. We were versatile. We defied stereotypes and hiked in the Bob Marshall Wilderness (at least I did). We were middle-class professionals of good repute. One of us just happened to have HIV, a fact that was not in the legal brief. Some of this Atticus-Finch good guy image of course harbored its own form of internalized homophobia that I acknowledged in moments of reflection.

The pleadings also failed to mention the rancor beneath the façade of our model "marriage." Night after night, I rose to stare out at the blue light of moon on snow while David slept soundly—imperturbable, stolid, unfazed. Depressed and neurotic, I knew romance was slipping out of our years of dedication, if not sex. At three in the morning, the eerie indigo hue across the neighbor's lawn signified nothing but suffused foreboding, building disenchantment. I processed my misery in long talks with my therapist Karl and check-ins with my HIV support group. My counselors listened to my litany of complaints about sarcasm and debt collectors, but never, to their credit, demanded that I quit smoking Davids.

A competing incongruity to my discontent came with some debt relief. The family house in California sold and distributions began. I slowly climbed out of some of the debt we had accumulated—hotels in Seattle and Zihuantanejo, flights to Honduras and SFO. Car rentals. Second mortgages. iPhones and MacBooks. But the waves of bills kept coming and even as I tried to surmount them with checks, anger came instead of relief. I was an unhappy if undemonstrative camper, one without the cajones to let my bitch out and confront my consumerist family, one who instead under the guise of some Robert Mitchum stoicism soldiered on, processing my beefs only behind the closed doors of shrinks who profited from my seethe.

Night after night, I watched the light polluting streetlamps before I curled up on the red leather couch in the living room. I let emotional and financial encounters slide with the ease of an ego-less over-achiever, unable to bring my professional ambition into my personal life, unable to stay "stop, we have too much junk," too much debt, too many easels and new appliances, too many sports coats we never wear, too many Wells Fargo payments. "Stop" dribbled out of the side of my mouth in sarcasm while I watched and waited, grew more trapped, more insecure, more conflicted, more aware of the Gil Newark déjà vu. Helplessly, I grew more aware of the spinelessness of my desire. What I wanted did not matter. What I wanted, even to myself, paled beside the conflicted indulgence I took in letting my "family" pursue their unabashed materialism. I was getting fucked in a different way, and through some masochistic impulse, seemed to enjoy the mess I felt powerless to undo.

46
HUERFANO COUNTY LINE

By 2011 the sphinx factor had fully solidified. For all my attempts to sit down and talk about "us," I could figure out nothing of what David was thinking, and he seemed to have no intention of divulging his "feelings." He loved Mariah Carey and Shakira. He loved to cook and throw parties. He lived and breathed Latin America. But I never saw him cry or emote beyond anger—a dish thrown to the floor, a fist pounded. I was the manic depressive, the downer, the stick in the mud. He was the party animal, the bon vivant, who channeled his energies outside of our mud-stuck dyad.

All of this pettiness, diurnal if mundane, constant if not monumental, came to a head in the fall, while I hung out in a cabin on the Huerfano County line in Colorado, trying to finish a book. I wrote David an email. I told him we had to think about where we were headed with our LTR, told him we had to make changes if we wanted to continue. In many ways the written form of my message allowed me to be clearer about my misgivings, my priorities—my health, our exercise, the outdoors, reciprocal intimacy. The distance allowed me paradoxically to open up about what I wanted and needed—allowed me to delineate the closeness I was missing.

Monday, the 18th of a late fall month brought me home to Missoula to face the red leather couch, face our front room David had painted green, look at myself in the mirror over the piano. We sat down that Saturday morning in the living room we rarely lived in. I perched on the couch and David leaned back in the leather chair that faced our beveled glass cabinets which contained masks and pottery we brought from Mexico.

"I just wanted to set aside some time for us to talk," I started. I knew I would have to do most of the talking. I could never tell what he was thinking. He had replied to my email with a short statement about the weather—and nothing more.

"I guess I'm at a point now that I think we have to do something," I said, couching my disenchantment in vague clichés. "We've both grown apart for a while now." David nodded in agreement but said little about specifics--sex, HIV, food, travel, exercise, money.

"I know we've been to counseling but I'm willing to give it another shot," I finally proposed. "If you want to try it, we could see Molly or someone and talk."

"Pay 150 dollars an hour?" he asked, in so many words. His exact statement escaped me almost immediately. He didn't say much. It was impossible to capture or re-create his voice. He was reluctant, skeptical. "What good would it do?" he wondered. "What is going to change?" he asked.

"I don't know what else to do," I said, exasperated. "We definitely have trouble talking by ourselves. And I'm not sure either of us wants to continue as ships passing in the night."

David grimaced.

"What are our options?" I continued. "I don't want to go on with the status quo. Neither of us is very happy. I don't know if you agree. At least I'm sure we have to make some changes. What do you want to do?"

David looked around the room. He shrugged. He seemed to want to keep going and see where things led. I could not discern. He didn't register, didn't share my urgency.

Frustrated, I finally said, "For me, we either have to try going to a counselor or break up. I just can't see continuing the way we are." I stared over his head onto Second Street. The heavy maple branches drooped over the lawn, leaves about to glow and fall to the ground, where my rake would do the work. My words were not meant as an ultimatum—were they? I just wanted to find a way to bridge our distance. David heard them differently. He may have seen his opportunity in my proposal.

He wasn't going to therapy. He made that clear again. "So, you want to break up then?" I finally asked. He had never used those words.

"Yes," was all he said. His statement seeped out undefinitively but closed the case. He moved out a week later. I took a trip to Mexico.

2011 drew to a close. Gone were Gil, Joe, my mother, my sister. Gone was David. It was just me and HIV now. Me and my long-term lover, the virus that crawled up my spine, ready to hook up with me as I walked the dogs on the river trail. Ready to drive me crazy.

TERRA INCOGNITA

(2011-2013)

4 7

"THE BODY SPEAKS ITS MIND"

What we don't know can hurt us. What we cannot biopsy eludes our study. In semen, yes; in seminal fluids (even pre-cum) yes; in rectal and vaginal fluids, yes; in breast milk, yes. The HIV virus has many tissue-bound reservoirs other than the bloodstream. We know it enlarges lymph nodes; we know it is capable of creating discrete set-ups in parts of the body that are not determined by the viral load in a smear of blood. And we know, from the onset of testing, pre-ARV (antiretrovirals), that HIV has neuro-cognitive effects that start at an early stage of infection. After four months from the time of sero-conversion, HIV has replicated substantially in the central nervous system, and through a process called compartmentalization, the virus sets up shop in places like the spinal cord and the brain, often genetically mutating to establish its own replica of the virus.

To biopsy the brain is a delicate and uncommon procedure. To find out what HIV looks like in the spine is not an easy matter. Hence the indeterminacy of the viral influence on cognition. Hence our ignorance of the interaction of HIV and the unconscious—ignorance of the way the virus influences how the body speaks its mind—even its unknown mind. How little we know about the unknown effect of the shocks that flesh is heir to. Where in the vast recesses of the suppressed immune system, where in dark reservoirs of the HIV colonies, where in the buried emotions of the individual does that psyche meet the virus?

Tremors, incontinence, apathy, withdrawal, muteness, dementia, paralysis. These were the symptoms of early pre-HAART days when weightless men in their 30s circled fountains in Central Park.[1] I had witnessed some of the lost minds and bodies of the Plague Years. Thank God, I had outlasted those horrific days. I was a long-term survivor (HIVLTS), relegated to the status of chronic diabetics who functioned normally when their insulin levels remained stable. HIV was no longer a death sentence. I was walking proof of that miracle, after three decades of wedlock with the virus.

48
MARCH MADNESS

Winters were long in Montana. They began in October, when rain traveled east from Seattle and overcast strangled our atmosphere through June. Big Sky country, if the truth be known, was often socked in. But this day in March 2011, brought no precipitation, no sloppy rain on wet snow, no particular almanac event other than a blue high sky. I walked the dogs—Reno and Coco. I exercised joint custody after the recent breakup with my partner of 14 years.

Our path took us down the path by the Clark Fork, the wide river that ran through my hometown. My route headed west by McCormick Park, where skateboarders whirled into concrete scoops, past baseball diamonds where open fields allowed me to chuck the ball for Coco, who was still in her prime, a tawny white-chested live wire with an endless reserve of energy. Our par course—what with the rubber orange ball and Chuckits that allowed me to fling the thing high in the air and generate some grounders worthy of any shortstop. We crossed the fields and followed the path to a depression that ran under the trestles of an abandoned railroad bridge. Up from under the ties, we emerged to a tall wooden pole that held an osprey nest with its weave of twigs outside the centerfield fence of the baseball stadium, built for our minor league team, which bore the sea eagle's name. On one side of the muddy trail stood the pillars of the grand black statement scoreboard. On the other, the rapids of the mighty river headed west.

I strode along that mid-morning immersed in the exercise of trying to exhaust the canines during my break from reading Shakespeare and grading papers. It was a day immemorable enough—mid-week, mid-morning, mid-semester. I worried about the credit-rating downgrade of one of the retailers our family was invested in, a downgrade that could trigger mortgage payments. Preoccupied with money, schoolwork, reader's reports, grading, grievances, I was nevertheless heady with my newfound independence. I had extricated myself from a troubled relationship. I was excited to be single, relieved to be free from Mother's tight-fisted purse strings (even if she left us with a mess), though bothered still by the betrayal of my siblings during the aftermath.

None of these overarching concerns was center stage as I chucked the ball for Coco. She hunted it up in the tall grass near the nets of the batting practice cage. A poster of a baseball player in designer sunglasses, sliding into third base on his knees struck me as particularly erotic, his white tight butt the focal point of the poster. The packed-dirt trail gave way to pavement as we skirted the stadium and left the river, heading south as part of our daily loop.

The first aura came over me as I rounded the bend. I was transported to a dream state for a half a minute. I had no idea where my mind went, vivid though the dream was. Once I regained consciousness, I found myself still on my feet. I stood on the blacktop, flushed and sweating. I staggered but did not fall. A cold sweat braced my face, I felt confused, scared, uncertain about where I had been. The content of the dream, entirely vivid during its progress, was wholly unrecoverable once I came out of it. When I got home, I jumped into bed, feeling faint and tired. I had an ache between my shoulders, felt heavy, tired, and afraid. Was I going mad?

That March morning seizure would define my life for the next two years. Episodes, quick and unpredictable, began to crop up with alarming regularity. Leaving the gym after a sauna and workout, during the middle of my lecture upstairs in the Jeanette Rankin Building at the university, after a difficult choir practice in which my flat baritone notes became the topic of some discussion among the song-and-dance queers. Nausea, flushed features, fatigue, backaches came after the waking dreams that lasted less than a minute.

Aptly the episodes came on through March Madness—though I had no interest in basketball. There was no warning before the flush, the cold sweat, the transport. Afterwards, I prayed openly to the clouds, to God, to anyone, to tell me what was going on with my body. A professor losing his mind, a gay man now single after 14 years of indebtedness, now free, now ready to travel, see the world, get laid, dance, fuck, scream, and ski—now saddled with uncontrollable mental lapses, waking visions in the middle of class and meetings? Would I have to retire, lose my license, be hospitalized? Was I going crazy?

I saw Dr. Elias, the physician at Partnership Health Center in Missoula, the clinic that served HIV patients. Partnership functioned like a free clinic. The waiting room was crowded with bad dental hygiene, obese women, and homeless men. I was reminded vaguely of my Berkeley days. Dr. Elias was amazingly thorough and caring, perhaps the best doctor I have ever had, and I have gone through 10-15 of them over the years —in Manhattan, Buffalo, Eugene, Portland, Los Angeles, and Missoula. Dr. E considered pre-epilepsy, as he tried to diagnose these short-lived out-of-body experiences. He strapped me into a chest cardio monitor that also recorded EKG impulses. I was to press a button whenever another episode came on the mental screen. I also made notes on the monitor about the episodes.

April proved a merciless month. In class, after music lessons, during play practice (my students performed Shakespeare in the University Commons), I leaned against the wall to recover from an aura. I feigned fatigue, left the classroom and pressed the monitor button. I struggled to maintain my equilibrium, tried to continue my "normal" queer activities, as I rationalized the disassociations as what? Senior moments (though I wasn't 60), stress, general fatigue, dementia, some x-factor Dr. E would discover and cure? Was I to become an incapacitated AIDS victim, shuffled around clipped lawns and fountains by little men in white coats, rocking in wicker chairs with a plaid blanket around my legs, exposing myself to nurse practitioners? I sought desperately to ignore even as I anticipated the next mental trip—to a beach in P.V., poolside in Hillsborough, an apartment on Higgins Avenue—until I recovered and found myself in my office, 216 Liberal Arts, staring at a 200-page thesis draft.

By the end of the month, I had been referred to a ridiculously inattentive neurologist, who drove his clients insane by keeping them seated for an hour in a 10-by-10 waiting room with frayed-edge *Family Circle* magazines as they squirmed on hard plastic chairs. The sliding glass window to the receptionist was shut tight while nurses watched exasperated patients fill out 10-page clipboard questionnaires about diseases our maternal grandmothers may have contracted on a trip through the Panama Canal. Once ushered into the 5-by-10 exam room and blood pressured by some saccharine assistant, who asked me where my smiley face was on a chart from one to ten, I was left alone with boxes of latex gloves and a rubber chest pounder. Once I actually saw the white coat of the 40-something neurologist, I had been driven crazy if I weren't already undone by the absurdities of the visit.

The upshot of course was a quarto script scribbled on a pad. I was sent to CVS down the road for Lamictal. The neurologist—no doubt just back from an all-expenses paid trip to Honolulu for a GlaxoSmithKline "conference" on the latest pharmaceuticals—attempted to be more than a drug dispenser. But for all the time he spent with me as a freaked-out patient, I was hard-pressed to call Dr. S more than a quack. Lamictal or lamotrigine is an anticonvulsant, sulfur-decreasing, mood depressor used for epilepsy and bi-polar disorder, widely tolerated except for an occasional skin rash, and effective for the kind of nebulous schematic events that were currently not only plaguing me but freaking me out. At this point, I also reported some depression around the loss of my partner, mother, sister, and a monthly check from the triple net big box lease. I was also given a prescription of Lexapro, escitalopram, a selective serotonin re-uptake inhibitor of SSRI. Lexapro is a mood elevator with occasional anhedonic and libido-reducing side effects. I wasn't, if I recall correctly, fucking anyone at that point anyway—too preoccupied with my impending psychosis to be interested in boners. There were long bouts of sobbing, knees to chest on the kitchen floor.

For my 60th birthday, I was determined, auras or no auras, to follow through on my planned trip to Manaslu, an 18-day hike in Nepal with the Sierra Club, run by an insufferable know-it-all from the Bay Area, who just happened to be married to the head Sherpa. I somehow made it through the trek. I burst into sympathetic tears beside glacial rivers, walked with fear across span bridges, listened to Tina Turner on my earphones, and wrote sonnets about the breakup with David. Sixty was a big deal. The soundtrack allowed me to wail aura-free under the gray boulders. The perilous rapids below snow-capped peaks reminded me of the Alberton Gorge. I had survived that capsize.

49

SCHEMAS

R emembering is dangerous; recollection can trigger recurrence.

I ended my journey to the Himalayas with a trip to the Great Barrier Reef, a bit out of the way from Kathmandu, but nonetheless a destination I wanted to reach before it was too late. Turtle Cove was a gay resort south of the reef, north of Cairns. Guys hung at the pool in Speedos and ate gourmet food while they sipped their gin and tonics or blue-can Fosters. The beach remained abandoned because of a lethal jellyfish scare, though I swam in the surf anyway. A vinegar bottle stood in a metal cage on a pole up beach in case one were to be stung, apparently the properties of the acidic liquid capable of warding off immediate death. All the talk of deadly chironex fleckeri, the notorious sea wasp, made my dips infrequent though it was not the season for the creatures.

I had a beautiful room in the back of the complex that opened onto a second-floor balcony. The tropical palms that swooshed with a drum-brush rustled at night, enchanted me as I lounged on my king-size bed, alone and lonely, as I recovered from my eighteen days of hiking above 15,000 feet. I was seizure-free and felt my sea legs as I dove from the boat into the cold coral sea during a trip to the Great Barrier. While I stood on the balcony of my room that first night, I saw a man come out of his bungalow as well, a short curly haired guy who waved rather unenthusiastically or maybe shyly, a roly-poly guy from Pennsylvania perhaps.

He and I were the only Americans. There were not many guests at the resort, maybe eight or nine of us at the dining room table under candlelight, the pool romantically lit, while young 30-something partners from Sydney bantered and dished. We had met the night before in the grotto whirlpool, five of us in various stages of undress and inebriation. In the hot tub we chatted and drank, some smoked tobacco, some weed. I sensed that the couple from Sidney were open to some kind of menage, but I didn't pick up on their suggestiveness until after I said goodnight and walked to my room. I also didn't pick up on the cues of the short American man who followed me down the dark path that night, both of us wrapped in beach towels. He seemed pliable, friendly, and sweet, but not really my type. All the paths were dimly lit with foot lamps. The entire complex exuded an aura of luxury and privilege—the kind I had grown up with in an entirely hetero-family context.

"Are you okay?" one of the hotel workers asked as he followed me out of the dining room during my final night. Our entire group had sat down together at a long table, imbibing and laughing with catty banter. We were on dessert, eating lemon cake, when I suddenly discovered myself in another time and place. How could I fight off a brain that wanted to move to a different state, a brain that took me on a trip regardless of whether or not I had bought a ticket, or even wanted to go? The aura came on strong as I sat among the happy homos. Self-conscious, flushed, sweating, I rose suddenly from the table and fled the dining room, half stumbled as I headed toward reception to find my way to my room. The hotel worker who had grabbed me by the arm and righted my stance looked concerned and worried as he inquired after my condition. I joked about having too much to drink, about being tired, about feeling faint. He offered to help me back to my room. I recovered quickly, told him I'd come back and finalize the bill later (I was leaving in the morning).

I went back to my room and collapsed on the beautiful empty bed. It was still warm, still in the tropical 80s. A gorgeous night. I had not been visited by an aura since August. I had spent the fall in Colorado and Nepal without incident. No sooner had I falsely lulled myself into a sense of recovery than I was hit by another wave head-on. This one almost knocked me down—almost turned me into Julius Caesar, the dreaded epileptic. I saw my future writhing on the floor. I began to sob in floods of crescendo for longer than I can remember, propped up against the bed. Travel was not the cure; my neuro-cognitive disorder would follow me to the ends of the earth. Add to my losses of partners and family and trust, another friend: my mind. My longtime companion HIV, however, was going nowhere.

A knock brought me out of my miasma. I went to the door. Bill, the man from Scranton, stood before me. "Are you okay?" he asked. I was deeply embarrassed. I told him I was fine— tired, stressed, fatigued from the trek. Told him not to worry. I was clearly unconvincing. "Please," he said, "come by my room anytime if you don't feel well or want to talk. I'm right across the way." He pointed. He turned out to be a social worker. When I knocked on his door an hour later, he invited me into his dimly lit room. It was smaller than mine and the blue green curtains were pulled. I told him about my life—my breakup, my positivity, my worries. I didn't mention my pre-seizure auras. I didn't tell him I fought a mental condition as well as a retro-virus, that maybe the retrovirus was driving me crazy. That maybe I was losing more than my fortune and fame, that maybe I was losing myself. He didn't care about HIV, he told me. He'd been with lots of pos guys. We laid on his bed together, he in his cotton gym shorts with the long pull strings. We talked about the highbrow eliteness of the clientele at the resort, about his social work practice, his shorts quickly slipped off as he lay naked beside me.

The kindness of strangers, as Tennessee famously called it, somehow rescued me that evening. We hugged and kissed, ran our hands over our sunburned bodies. We watched our genitals grow erect and pressed each other's member in the palm of our hands until the thrill came. Nerves of our electrified bodies gave way to orgasmic release. Liquid gushed from the happy fountains of our arousal, followed by those soft moments of affection, the hand ran down my relaxed thigh, my arm around his spent torso, a towel gentle below his flooded belly button. We stroked and cuddled and I held back my tears as best I could, thankful that this man was able through his random act of kindness to rescue me from my river of sorrow.

50

HAND

In February of 2012, I continued to have a rash of breakthroughs—a dozen, some during sleep oddly enough. A memory about childhood—a nightmare about a priest following me down the halls of St. Catherine's, my brother's friends cornering me on the bunk bed in Tahoe. I couldn't say for sure what happened in those aural seconds. I would wake up in cold sweat, change my t-shirt, deal with the persistent backache, and the heaviness of my spine. Lamictal increased (350 mg pd). Blood tests came more often.

I switched neurologists. This time out beyond Reserve Street in Building 3 of the Community Hospital complex with its metal indoor-outdoor stairway up to Hell. I walked down a long blue corridor that led to door number 666, if I can remember. The waiting room was large and blue, carpeted and entirely empty. Again the sliding glass door, again the clipboard, again the weary receptionist, plastic flowers attached to the pen end, fake fern in the corner. Again *People* magazines from 2010, the photos of Jennifer Aniston, then Brad and Angelina. This time though, I was ushered quickly into an overly large examining room, which had no table or stetho-scope. I sat against the wall and waited for Dr. Lennerd, a thin man in his 60s with ashen skin that hung from his cheeks and dark-rimmed glasses that gave his figure the look of a sad, anorexic soul, half mad himself, his thin legs crossed like Jack Parr in a chair 20 feet from me. Clearly, he had no intention of getting close.

Lamotrigine was also his answer to every ailment that walked in his office, with Keppra as a more expensive backup. He didn't know what was wrong with me. He didn't really care. He talked to himself mostly. In a bizarre monologue, he described the inexactitude of his science, relying on my profes-sorial position to give him license to pontificate about the unsolvable mysteries of the brain. "Take two aspirin and call me in the morning" seemed to be his motto, as his musing, flat tone enhanced the lugubrious insularity of his deserted office. I got out of there alive—barely.

Dr. Elias at the clinic was my go-to, but his thoroughness led me to the harrowing encounter with the psych ward at Providence Medical Center, where the young family psychia-trist Dr. Munjal lorded over psychotic inmates. February turned out to be a sleepless month—torso fatigue, Advil liquid gels, cold sweats, nightmares. Dr. E suggested I enter the sleep monitoring clinic for a couple of nights to undergo some tests, to try to get to the bottom of my cogni-dissociative problems.

I had no idea what I was getting myself into, no real idea that I was entering the psych ward, infamously located at the top of Orange Street right before the entrance and exit to Highway 90. I thought the building a mere adjunct facility to St. Patrick's Hospital, which it was to some degree. It also housed schizophrenics and victims of severe bi-polar disease and manias. I was about to be locked in a room without a computer, without a belt, cell phone, or even a writing implement for three days. I was undressed and given pajamas, my shoes were removed so I couldn't hang myself with laces. I was watched through some hidden window as I lounged on my bed with my copy of *The Duchess of Malfi*. No telly, no communication with the outside world. I signed my Montana Advanced Directive, attested in writing to my potential diagnosis of neuro-cognitive disorder, with early onset dementia or possible epilepsy. I took the precaution of naming my brother personal representative.

None of these frightening features of the so-called "sleep clinic" did more to frighten me than Dr. Munjal himself, with his flaming eyes and Spanish Inquisition goatee. He eagerly examined and tested my memory for an hour or two. He was excited to write down my errors in recall, noting my increased blood pressure. He became fascinated by what he claimed was my wagging tongue, that he found moving uncontrollably in my mouth. His zeal was eerie. His cocky arrogance frightened me in its self-certainty. The more I sat in his dark office and answered his innocuous but sinister questions, the more freaked out I became. I was committed to more of a "nightmare" than a "sleep" clinic. My mistakes on memory tests gave him particular satisfaction as he furiously confirmed his hunch of my neuro-cognitive disorder—my depression, my anxiety, my borderline insanity.

I spent the days in support groups, sat in circles, talked with inmates, drew on butcher paper pictures of my dilemma, expounded on my elusive episodic condition to counselors. I flashed on the real possibility that I would not be released from the ward for some time. Without wallet, without dog, without home, without friends, without computer—stuck in the pea-green bedroom with its wood floor and curved-edged furniture. The windows were long rectangles at the top of the walls. I fantasized about trying to squeeze through them once I was ushered back into my room in the afternoon for my "nap." The nurses patrolled the halls and watched every time I opened the door. I was not allowed out of my room without permission. The ward was a self-fulfilling prophecy. Like a staph infection, it created an atmosphere of Kafka-esque psychosis that preceded the mental state of its inmates. If you build it, they will come, might have been Munjal's motto, so hand-rubbingly pleased to have another victim for his control through examination.

I was released February 28. I didn't know how or why. I didn't care. They upped the Lamictal again and let me keep my driver's license. Dr. E gave me some leeway and more Lexapro, though he sided with the Dr. Munjalstein. Seizure, sweat, fatigue—at the gym, in bed, at my desk—the pattern continued during the second madness of March.

I needed a second opinion. I needed to find out if what I had was related to HIV. I found Igor K in Boston, where I was headed in April to the Shakespeare Association of America. I was still capable to give a paper on the Gentle Way of Punishment in *Measure for Measure* in spite of my impending incarceration in an asylum. Foucault seemed the perfect theoretical apparatus for a man so civilized and so mad at the same time. I called Deaconess Beth Israel and asked the neuro HIV specialist for a consultation during my visit to the Dunkin Donuts capital of America.

I saw Igor in his office on April 11, 2012. He and his assistant, the wire-rimmed diminutive Dr. G, greeted me with starched white coats. Their formality befitted blue-nose Boston, though they were particularly eastern European in their demeanor and thoroughness. Dr. G administered tests (I was able to name 20 animals in a minute) and other games to discover a short-term memory deficit (a cognitive impairment) that she found I was unaware of (who could remember their memory loss?). Her assessment was "non-conclusive for seizures" but consistent with what she called HAND—HIV-associated neurological disorder.

Because HIV entered the brain early on in infection, fooled through a Trojan Horse effect the usual blood-brain barrier (BBB), neurological disorders had followed PLHIV (people living with HIV) since the inception of the epidemic. What was HAND? HIV-associated neurocognitive disorders were neuro-conditions associated with the retrovirus. Most prominent of course was ADC (AIDS dementia complex) as dramatized in *The Hours* and early AIDS films, but HAD (HIV-associated dementia) was also common. Cognitive impairments occurred on a spectrum that ranged from memory loss and poor concentration to symptoms such as depression, apathy, lethargy, and loss of motor function. HAND was not an opportunistic infection but the disorder contributed to conditions like dementia. HAND could lead to delirium—acute confusional states and disorganization of behavior, including hallucinations. All of these symptoms had a variable progression, and spinal and brain taps were only partial indicators of the condition.

Igor and Dr. G decided to do a spinal tap after they examined my test results. I was placed on a gurney and given a local anesthetic as the doctor withdrew fluid from my spine and later assayed it for HIV. As it turned out, almost every PLHIV had the virus not just in their blood, but in many other parts of our watery anatomy. I was no exception.

All of these tests were taking place in between sessions at the Hilton on Shakespeare. A strange *Lear* effect swamped my consciousness. "Oh, let me not be mad, sweet heaven. Keep me in temper." I suppressed my foreboding, conducted myself with the utmost professionalism in conference and doctor's office, treated my disease as a "problem" to be "solved" by the tests and medicines of modern science. When asked about my mood,

I was disoriented. My emotions somehow seemed irrelevant to determining what was causing my hallucinations. In some ways I was more out of body as I sought to find out about my out of body experiences than I was during my short dream-like confusions. Maybe my stoicism, my grace under the pressure of losing my mind—my refusal to "lose it" around "losing my mind"—contributed to the frequent occurrence of the confusional episodes. The balloon effect: push down in one spot and another swelled. I could not know for sure.

I did know I behaved like a perfect gentleman and left the sterile office of Igor with a feeling of being in good hands, secure in the starched, serious halls of learned physicians. I returned to the ambitious Shakespeareans and thought of Macbeth as he questioned of his wife's physician:

> Canst thou not minister to a mind diseased
> Pluck from the memory a rooted sorrow,
> Raze out the written troubles of the brain,
> And with some sweet oblivious antidote
> Cleanse the stuffed bosom of that perilous stuff
> Which weighs upon her heart? (*Macbeth* 5.3.40-45)

In his report, Dr. Igor diagnosed me with HAND. He ruled out seizures, found some cognitive memory impairment, found some neuropathy in my right leg, prescribed Lamictal or Keppra. He ruled out tongue wagging or other motor problems. He ruled in depression. He didn't tell Munjal to go fuck himself, but he was not prepared to go as far as he did, since the amount of HIV in my spine was consistent with other HIV patients in my condition. I was to be watched by Dr. E. I was to be monitored for further deterioration. I was sent home to wait for my delirium to visit me as it wished.

The length of the episodes waned, but in July I had four in

one day. A year later they tapered off, after three years of sudden attacks. Somehow, I seized the seizures, broke through the breakthroughs. I knew they could come back at any time. I knew I would remain under their spell, cast by my constant viral companion.

BEFORE AND AFTER

51

THE WORLD

(2013)

World AIDS day, December 1, and none of the major networks or news services in the United States even mentioned it. Thirty-five million people in 2013 were HIV positive, (about the size of the largest city in the world—Tokyo). Two million people seroconverted every year. Only 1.5 million died of AIDS in 2013 though, a 40% decline from the turn of the millennium. The good news was that the amount of people on antiretrovirals had doubled in the last 10 years from 7 to 15 million. Still, the United States and Russia accounted for almost 90% of the new cases in the developed world, and fewer than half of the men who had sex with men (MSM) even knew their status.[1]

These MSMers were often guys who spelled discreet "discrete" and fucked in the dark at bookstores. These were our soldiers in Camp Pendleton, our miners in the Amazon, our merchant marines. They were our closeted Washington insiders and their escorts. The stigma, mental health issues, disparity in race and gender and class around HIV infections, the difference between poor and rich nations—these factors had perpetuated a pandemic in which material wealth became a matter of life and death.

UNAIDS was proposing to get rid of the epidemic in 30 years under its 909090 plan. In 20 years 90% on drugs, 90% aware of their status, and 90% with undetectable viral loads. The savings to the world economy in reaching such goals was estimated to be $15 billion over the next 20 years.

THE ROPE: DECEMBER 1, 2013

I feel very anchored in/ my various communities/
but I think that/ to use a metaphor, the rope/
attached to that anchor should be long enough to allow
us to move/
into other communities/ to understand and learn
(Angela Davis in *Fires in the Mirror*)

Heavy today with sweat and swollen glands,
with fear and zeros, with the wait
between test tubes and charted counts.
A cotton ball puts pressure on a vein,
tape tears hair from a punctured forearm,
a man's voice cracks and the mayor's red ribbon
is shaped like deletion. Like reflection.
The rope lifts, dripping barnacled,
pulled tight to bind the viral load,
Durban and Montana tied in a knot.

Through a golden grommet in the canvas quilt
a plastic fastener hangs the smiling shroud,
names the Nureyevs of Jackpot and Butte
in the basement of our public library, where Sherry,

mother of a precious girl, looks into the lens
as I have looked at a cave in the mirror,
the ledge from a hollow cheek falling in low light.
She speaks stigmas, the new strand in the cord—
black, female. Thirty million in a tug of war
for drugs. Borders twist fibers, tighten the noose.

Anchored in a community of broken cells,
heavy on the floor of a fluid sea, a guy
is lashed to the rigging of today. "I want to live,"
Nkosi tells his ghostwriter before his death
at twelve, "but I am not afraid to die."
Antibodies linked in a line across ulcers
open onto viscous strands. Our blood twined.
The string of things become a syndrome.
The smell of me incontinent,
an archipelago of wasted bone.

52
OUT, OUT

In '81, I was 30, lived in Berkeley and clerked at the Contra Costa County Superior Court as a newly minted lawyer. I swam in Lake Temescal in Oakland and met a hairless thin man who gave me a blowjob. I wasn't particularly partial to blowjobs; I wanted face-to-face stuff. I kicked a hole in my sheetrock wall a week later, threw my phone through a window. I drove to Marin once a week to therapy, to Karl Gootnick. I played tennis at the Rose Garden. I wanted to be straight. I went out with a blond named Malois, then met the man in the VW van also with blond hair. He taught me gay sex. He lived in Davis, California, and we fucked three times in one morning when I drove there to visit.

Around this time, the Morbidity and Mortality Weekly Report (MMWR) of the Center for Disease Control (CDC) reported five cases of pneumocystis carini (PCP) in Los Angeles gay men (June 5, 1981). In July, *The New York Times* reported cases of a rare cancer, Kaposi's Sarcoma, among 270 gay men, 170 soon to die. Not until the following September— after the Shanti Project began in San Francisco, and word had spread that the CDC would issue a definition of AIDS (the acquired immune-deficiency syndrome)—did Henry Waxman begin to hold hearings in the House of Representatives.

Could it have been more ironic that at the very time gay men in my town were being closed into the darkness of caskets, I was desperately trying to emerge from the darkness of the closet, only to find myself in the midst of this sudden onslaught of loss? I fought to come out—fought myself, my career, my family, my images, and ideals—at the very time HIV closed in on the Castro. After 100,000 reported AIDS cases made the news, after the World Health Organization declared the first World AIDS Day (December 1988). After Mapplethorpe died, Ryan White testified before Congress. After funding finally trickled down from the HRSA (Health Service Resource Administration) and the Office of AIDS Research woke up with the help of ACT UP, the HIV pandemic finally came out to the public. At the same time, I came out as a gay man.

In 1984, I sat on my parents' porch in the Peninsula under a retractable blue and white striped awning as we lounged in those repulsive Brown and Jordan patio chairs near a kidney-shaped pool. When I told Mom and Dad I liked guys, my mother's first reaction was not "Oh honey, whatever is best for you. We stand behind you, sweetheart. You have earned EVERY right to be yourself." Nothing could be further from the tenor of her reaction to my great American coming out story. No, Mother's first reaction: she didn't want me flaunting it. She didn't want me to march down Market Street on the 5 o'clock news. She didn't want me to carry placards behind that horrible New York Jew, Harvey Milk, who had somehow gotten himself elected in the People's Republic of San Francisco. As if I ever would. As if this reticent, Santa Cruz boy with his tagless t-shirts and Earth Shoes would ever in a million years march down—heaven forbid—Market Street. "Please don't get your face on television" her first admonishment. Her second: get thee to a shrink. "You shouldn't jump into these things," she insisted. "It might just be a phase. Why don't you talk to someone first? You've been going out with some wonderful girls over the years."

When I came out as positive a little more than 10 years later, Mother could not pull the maybe-you'll-change-your-mind card. HIV was not a lifestyle choice. She held back the tears as best she could. Her boy was about to die before she did. And then an hour later, "why didn't you tell me earlier?" I had already told my sister, and I think Mom was a little miffed she was not the first to know. I was about to tell my debilitated father, which would further incur her ire. God bless her though. She was the one that encouraged my love of poetry as a lonely boy. She knew I had a way with words if not with deeds.

53
BLOOD BROTHERS

Since the early 1990s, the FDA, through the recommendation of the Health and Human Services Advisory Committee on Blood Safety and Availability, had required indefinite deferral of blood donation by any man who had sex with men (MSM). In the 2010s, the ACBTSA issued revised guidelines. Hemophiliacs and blood-clot sufferers could give blood at any time, but MSM were required to practice one year of abstinence before they were eligible for donation. If you were a gay man or down-low man who had sex with men, you could give blood *if* through presumably some declaration under oath you stated that you had not had sex with another man in the last twelve months.

"Giving blood is not a civil right," one doctor told NPR.

"Discrimination pure and simple," a queer activist countered.

Even though I knew I could never give blood myself, the new rule pissed me off. It perpetuated my stigma. In spite of the fact that the demographics of the HIV population had heterosexualized substantially over the years, the new rule singled out the gay community as contaminated. It assumed most sex between men was unprotected anal intercourse. It endorsed a false metonymy that grafted HIV on to same-sex relations. The guidelines attested to the ongoing animus against gay men who, even if they tested negative, were assumed to be fucking every five minutes and therefore unworthy of donation.

The rule's conflation of *sick* sodomites with eminent homosexuals like Sir Ian McKellen reminded me, as I listened to the radio, of my relations with my "blood brother" Stevie Green at St. Catherine's in 5th Grade. Was I twelve? I had harbored his memory in my conscious cavern for years. It welled up during basement and drawer clearings, during garage sales, funerals, and subsequent boxing and trashing. It arose out of old shoe boxes during summer purges. Moments of discarding, re-organizing, dumpsters and trips to Goodwill turned out to be acts of recovery as much as disposal. I suddenly found myself hidden in a box in the basement as I stared at the pixels of Polaroids. I held one snapshot in my hand—the photo of the sandbox my father built in the backyard, its 6 by 8 frame capped with 2 by 6s and filled with wet granular sand that invariably stuck to the wet knees of boys in jeans. We played with our Matchbox trucks on roads built by smooth, intent hands. We were little adults called kids.

In the album next to the sandbox pic appeared a long shot of the sheds adjacent to our garage, out by the incinerator where we chopped wood behind the pink rose bush splayed in splendor over a sagging fence. Back there stood the toolshed where a belt was removed by Dad for promised and sometimes carried out punishments. For me, the photo called up another kind of belt removal, one that told a different story, the story of my queer struggle to survive in a heterocentric world, a world that still stigmatized positives and their love of perversions.

· · ·

Stevie Green was my best friend in fifth grade. We were blood brothers after a mutual pin prick or two, in the elementary days, the days of Sister Mary Charlene and Father Ward, who exhorted me to swing my Schwinn down the hill at six in the morning during Lent to hit early Mass, to earn my St. Christopher medal, its chain in my mouth. Stevie came from the other side of the tracks. He lived on the flatlands of Burlingame, near the beige stucco school attached to our big church. I could walk to Stevie's after school. We played in his room upstairs, tried to avoid the sadistic slurs and arrows of his juvie older brother Tim, whose notoriety pegged him and his pants as a hood. He was rumored to carry a switchblade.

One afternoon Stevie came over to my house to play in the sandbox. It was before five, but the marine layer had already begun to pour over the hills above Crystal Springs. The two of us motored our toys through the wet malleable sand. After our road building was over, after we had crashed enough cars and buried enough soldiers, we decided to take a break. I took Stevie, the dark brown-haired Irish boy of my height and maybe a little thinner, to the sheds behind the big pink rosebush.

We had been back there before, back to the incinerator, back to the woodpile, but today was different. Today I wanted to share everything with my blood brother. Today I wanted to get kinky, wanted to go all the way. At the age of 12 no less. What was in my head? What compelled me to ask Stevie to take down his sandy jeans that afternoon in the room beside the shed, with its paint-spattered countertops, its cans of latex and the smell of turpentine, with the old rickety door closed? What drove me to ask Stevie to share exposures? Not to do anything really, just to reveal his penis, just to show me his if I showed him mine. As a way to get closer, a way to cement our bond. I just wanted to get closer to him as we stood in the dark. I began to take my belt off and asked him if he wanted to...

Stevie suddenly shook his head. He pulled up his pants over his white briefs. He got scared. He ran out of the shed and jumped on his bike. He rode home and told his mother. She told her son to leave the rich kid on the hill alone. He was sick. He was bad blood. Stevie needed to find other friends.

My first rejection. It would not be my last.

54

"TO PREPARE A FACE TO MEET
THE FACES THAT YOU MEET"
(ELIOT)

I knew the other Steve would eventually come back to haunt me, Steve from the Eugene support group, the man with the grapefruit growth on his neck whom I had run from in fear. As I stared at the hollow divots in my face before the mirror in 2014, I knew I had met my Appointment in Samarra. I had fought to keep my mind sound, but I still had to face my face.

Though the broad category of lipodystrophy (LD) referred to fat redistribution in general and could include the notorious buffalo humps on the neck that HIV engendered, LD-HIV also commonly presented in facial wasting. LD was a bit like climate change; it did not solely include global warming but also involved fluctuation in weather patterns. In my case dystrophy had become atrophy. A loss of fat in the face rendered me gaunt and cavernous and Lincolnesque, even as I had suddenly become a middle-aged man on the market. My indentations ran from high cheekbones down to my simian jaw, creating a skeletal haggardness that added to an already fore-boding downturn of my small domed-mouth. My appearance—although still vestigially handsome with a Nick Nolte-esque flavor—did nothing to mask the natural sourness of my disposition, which grew angrier and more defiant as the country moved deeper into the grips of greed and capitalism.

Though the exact mechanism of the condition called lipoatrophy had not been "fully elucidated," evidence suggested that Zerit contributed to interference with lipid metabolism. Lipid metabolisms synthesized (i.e. produced) and degraded lipids in cells. They were not synonymous with fats; the latter were really a subgroup called triglycerides (saturated and unsaturated). Lipids come from the food we eat and also are endogenously produced by the body to store energy. Upwards to 40% of PLHIVers experienced fat loss from the suprazygomatic (mandibular) and temporal regions of the face severely enough "to impart a stigmatizing emaciated appearance." Most commonly the fat loss occurred in the cheeks (of the face and buttocks), "smile lines" (nasolabial folds), temples, and eyes sockets. Fifty percent of people who, like me, had taken Zerit for 30 months suffered from AIDS Face.

Of course, by 2015, Zerit was in the rearview mirror and I probably had arrested the wasting, but the damage was done, the flattening indentation of the convex contours of my handsome mug indelibly marred. Age was also a factor, the cherubic baby face of young ovular Prince Charles inevitably had given way—HIV or no—to the angular, long face of the weary traveler through life—through a process of natural, slow, and symmetric atrophy. On top of this inevitable brow furrowing, I was also a victim of HAART, which had admittedly saved my life. I was still faced with the psychological ramifications of a disturbing body image rupture, which led in cases like mine to social withdrawal. Walk me into a gay bar, and everyone who got close enough knew I was viral. I wore HIV on my face.

I had visited Costa Rica a year earlier and met a nice man who shared meals with me at outdoor cafes under yellow light and to the sound of howler monkeys in the distance. He asked me why I didn't do something to improve my face. He told me it was obvious that I was positive because of my caved-in cheeks. He was from Chicago; he told me to get some "work" done. The upshot in 2015 was a come-to-Jesus moment, in which—after my dermatologist told me not to worry about it and my heterosexual friends in Montana told me to get over myself—I decided I'd better, before it was too late, do something about the absence of fat between the dermis and fascia of my appearance.

My facial adipocytes had shrunk and spindled, but the science behind the condition seemed too blinding for me to fully comprehend. Though correction of facial fat loss (who would have thunk that I would ever want to gain weight since I'd spent the first quarter of my life as a cute little freckled face chub trying to lose it) was by all accounts crucial for the reduction of stigma and social dysfunction, according to studies, there were few proven findings on the efficacies of particular "modalities of correction." I knew Nufill (aka Sculptra) was not for me. I had no intention of driving to Seattle every six months to have a synthetic if biodegradable plastic inserted into my cheeks and watch a red alchy face give me another stigma. But I was also not ready to close up romantic shop and go gently into my cabin to collect more rejection letters. Not yet, my mantra. I still had a fighting chance of find love, I thought, and gym-going and trip-taking would eventually unmire me from the morass of Missoula—the college town with its underground twink and "discrete" culture—the gay wasteland that seemed weirdly analogous to my facial wasting.

In the end, I opted instead for a fat transfer. The plastic surgeon removed fat from my stomach (what there was of it) and threaded it into the fatless areas—a kind of graft called autologous fat transfer. At least I wasn't injecting a foreign substance into my body, I reasoned. The downside, I was to learn later, was that the fat cells from my stomach would not be able to regenerate because of the metabolic changes in the adipose in the area of wasting. New or transferred cells might not find nutritious soil in the wasted face.

I opted for the two Dr. H's in town, the plastic surgeons. I was destined to cross my leg on expensive waiting room furniture with the other middle-aged ladies, whose hair was done once a week, whose lipstick was glossy and undecipherable, whose eyes had undergone the kind of makeover that reminded me of television anchors. These were the occupants of recessed lit, potted palm waiting rooms of the health providers who augmented and diminished breasts, who treated the Nancy Pelosi's of the Bitterroot, who slipped into ample parking in their black Audis and managed their lustrous yellow hair with a fine-tooth comb. In the waiting room, they found a disheveled professor with duct-taped parka and unstylish hiking shoes, an aging Peter Pan trying desperately to make the scene—so young at heart, so fit and friendly, so eager to find that 40-something airplane pilot who adored older men, silver foxes distinguished, smart, funny, who wanted more than an exchange of penis pictures and a false promise to grab a beer. He was out there; I was doing all I could to find him. I was Grinding and Scruffing, profiling myself on Match and OKCupid and Harmony. I was doing all the right things so judiciously. I was a good guy. I liked to cuddle and wank. I wasn't going to tie anyone up though I didn't care if guys wanted to role play with handles of bull-whips. It just wasn't me.

To maintain my façade, to face the face waste, I found my way to the first surgeon, H1. H1, like so many, was both a hospitalist and a private practitioner. As a result, he moved around and would only be able to see me in one place at one time. He was a small man in his 40s with dark hair, from the

Midwest, rather tentative. He spoke softly with a low squeak. He came in with blue scrubs after his assistant took my blood pressure. I had already drawn large circles around the cheekbones of the silhouette the clipboard presented. I had exhausted Facebook posts on my phone in the exam room. Dr. H had very little affect but seemed competent if not stellar. His face was not ugly but not attractive. He did not have my charisma! He did not rise to comments about alleged rapists on the Griz team, no noteworthy response except in a derisory vein as we shook our heads in response to the Board of Regents attempt to reinstate their indicted quarterback at any cost.

H1 decided to do the work in the hospital under a general anesthetic. Though in-and-out in a day, the process was prolonged by delay and red tape. Blue Cross would only cover the $2000 redistribution of lipids in part and then only if it was done in hospital, which—because of anesthesia and nurse care—added a thousand dollars to the simple transfer of fat cells. The doctor simply took a big hypodermic needle, extracted the turkey fat from the stomach, and put it in a measuring cup to let the fat settle. He scooped out the settled fat and streamed it gingerly with a kind of threading needle up and down the facial wasteland, hoping that the cells would grow in the barren but still extant environment. It was not rocket science, but the gurneys and the waiting rooms and the hospital gowns and the questions about my turmeric intake, the anesthetics and the long wait behind the curtained cubicle while loud nurses joked about their bets at the Claim Jumper and their daughter's soccer matches made me mildly suicidal. I waited on that gurney for 5 hours while Dr. H was held up in surgery.

The results were a week without exercise, a few dissolving stitches, and a golf ball face that made me look like a Baltimore Oriole second baseman with chew in his mouth. The swelling receded after my convalescence, but alas alack mighty C faced strike one. The fat did not take. I went back for a checkup and discovered H1 had left town under rather mysterious circumstances. I was faced with H2, the father of plastic surgery in Missoula, whose reputation was as big as the sky in Mantana where men fish for cutthroats, bag elks, and drive Chevy Silverados.

H2 took over and shot me up with plenty of fat. Most of it drained out; some took. My look appeared comelier. I filled out. Problem was—irony of ironies—I was growing old and the wonderful map of the Antilles was charted from my rowed forehead to entrenched chin, crisscrossed with the dead-end paths I had followed since well before I acquired my viral load from my Carioca lover— more than a quarter of a century ago. I began to look like a Walker Evans photo. Yes, my mug was fuller, but at this juncture few lotions and creams could turn back child-eating Kronos. I looked back at my failure to heed the advice of so many: "moisturize, moisturize, moisturize." I saw the Goya painting in my mind's eye; I heard the winged chariot, the bending sickle of Sonnet 116, the bell tolling another year of struggle. But I marched on, confronted my mirror with wisdom and composure—until the bill came.

I was a new man. And yes, I called the toll-free 1-800 number, yes, my calls were monitored for quality assurance, yes, I recited my group number, disclosed my username, my password—gave up the last four of my Social—even told them my date of birth. They told me my call was important to them— many times they assured me that they would take care of me. I asked to speak to their supervisor, appealed for a variance to the Blue Shield Blue Cross board. On my knees I begged them to use my premiums, to use the $800 a month I paid them, to cover my new face, to realize my surgery was not elective but required, was a side effect of the pharmaceuticals I was asked to ingest to save my life. I told them I had no choice. I tried to stay calm. I spoke slowly and deep-voiced about life savings, about prohibitive deductibles. Once, ashamed though I am to confess, I broke down in a babbling diatribe about corporate profits, executive salaries. Yes, I hung up on them once or twice. There were no more receivers to slam. I could have thrown the cell across the room. I could have ranted about big Pharma forever. But I apologized, called back and squirmed, unctuous and humble, pleaded for Papa Corpo to cover the cost of my new visage.

I did not tell them I was on the market. I did not show them my nude pics. I would not descend that low. I reasoned and pleaded, made asides about almost four decades of an epidemic —without cure, without vaccine. How elevated my cause, how I played the game, how I confronted and appealed to the guilt of their workers. Did I use the word "motherfucker" once in their presence? Did I take the lord's name in vain in the presence of their representatives? Never once did I predict they would go to hell. There was no hell to go to, except the one they created on earth with their changed menus. With their preconditions, their exclusions, their elective surgeries, their deductibles, their ceilings, their replication of the mazes of Kafka.

Did my insurers pay for my outlook? Did they finally cough up some of my dollars to pay for the partial erasure of my stigmata? They did. Two years later I got a check for half the cost of H2's surgery.

55

OBAMA NATION

For a period of time during my initial years in Missoula, I was on the board of the Gay Men's Task Force in the mid-90s and helped organize retreats that combined hook ups with education about the safer way to screw. Almost twenty years later, I was newly single and sane, so I decided to revisit one of the Task Force's Retreats at my ripe old age. Participants ranged in age from 18 to 68. The weekend mixed lectures on chlamydia with roasted marshmallows, Twister and Mountain Dew around the fire ring. Late at night, some bunk jumped and had trysts in the ponderosas. During the course of our weekend in the woods, we watched two 20-year-old men from the B towns of Montana (Billings, Butte, Bozeman, Boulder) present talks about being HIV+ at our rented church camp in Lincoln, home of the Unabomber. I rejoined the ranks of available singles. We had come together to have fun and discuss safer sex while eating Cheetos, drinking Pepsi, and spooning Mac and Cheese from those tin foil vats that gather condensation on their inner saran wrap until unveiled.

When I arrived at the camp Friday evening, I caught a big

brown trout on the North Fork of the Blackfoot while unbeknownst to me a Nakota man watched. He was a 40 something
who had driven from the eastern part of the state to join us.
Conflicted about his sexuality but ready to face it, he worked
on and off for the Department of Transportation up on the
High Line (Highway 2). He came up to me during a break to
admit he had spied on me while I released my catch. We
chatted during the many respites we had on Saturday between
group sessions. He happened to have claimed the bunk across
from me in one of the sparsely occupied sleeping cabins, and
after the evening session, we found ourselves talking across the
divide of upper bunks, eventually joining together for a cuddle
in his narrow bunk. In the course of our quiet convo, I told him
it might be nice to meet sometime halfway between Missoula
and his place in the east. "Maybe Helena," I suggested, just
for fun.

A few minutes later, he suddenly told me he could not
continue our cuddle. Not that I smelled or was unattractive, he
assured me, himself being fairly paunchy even if tall, dark, and
handsome. He was unable to continue, he told me, because I
had asked him to accept a homosexual invitation, which if he
did accept, would render him an "abomination." I was
confused. It was dark, one in the morning, and we were making
out in our underpants (how I hate that word) that October in
Montana before the snows came. We were, I thought, hitting it
off in a state of groggy embrace. I had thought I heard him say
"Obama Nation," after my date invitation. I thought he was
suddenly affirming his pledge of allegiance to our first POC
president, even if Barack was not first nation. I had heard
wrong. My homophonal misunderstanding was a horse of an
entirely different color.

As long as I seduced my Christian friend against his will,
he was perfectly free to pursue his boner, but once I introjected

a date into the mix, he had to make a conscious choice, which, had he intentionally accepted the proposed dinner date, would have landed him presumably in the arena of mortal and not venial transgression, would have rendered him in short an "abomination," rather than an innocent victim of my rather tepid assault. Of course, he had welcomed that "assault" *sub silentio* while we spoke for a half hour before I climbed up to his bunk to partake in what I thought was to be "mutual" masturbation.

My suggestion of a steak at the Outback in the capitol had transformed me into an abominable snowman corrupting a First Nation Christian. I was, in short, a monster on Hell's shortlist. At that point I began feeling my way towards the bunk bed ladder. I figured that we probably did not have much of a future together. I was an egghead from the west, he a road worker from the east. Initially, I thought that difference potentially part of a glue that could lead to some fun camping on the Front Range—halfway between Fort Peck and my hometown west of the Divide. I suppose I should have been heartbroken rather than amusedly flummoxed, but I fell asleep with a head shake.

"We all hear what we want to hear," I smiled to myself the next morning. My truncated liaison reminded me where I was —the Deep Christian North of Montana—and what I was—a single, middle-aged, HIV-positive man who taught Shakespeare. This configuration was not optimal for love and pleasure in the future. First of all, this shitty, inexplicable, random disease, even in 2014, created various problems of disclosure and safety. Add to that my age, my snobbery, my location, my choosiness—the sum of which dramatically reduced my chances of finding Mr. Right in Lincoln, Montana. "Stranger things," I thought, as I went through the motions, hoping to be struck by lightning.

One of the panels that took place during the gay gathering at the rented Christian camp between Missoula and Great Falls featured two catty twinks who were on the HIV circuit. Neither was over 25. Their presentation underscored my alienation. It was not just that the few middle-aged men like me were miffed by our lack of participation or our inconsequence in a queer world that exiled anyone over 40 (at least in the United States where DILFs [daddies I like to fuck] are usually the likes of dark-bearded hunks in their 30s of the Hugh Jackman ilk). It was not that I was jealous or that I felt, as one grey-bearded man stated in an earlier session, "like a young man trapped in an old body that no one cares about." It was not just envy or a sense of superfluity or trouser-rolled, premature geriatrics.

It was their utter superciliousness that irked me as I listened to these boys talk about their recent conversion, as if it were initiation into a Glee Club. In the limelight they regaled us with their tales of disclosure to parents and siblings, with their happy adherence to ARV regimens, swallowed once a day. They delighted in their skinny repartee about cute doctors and friends on PrEP, about texting ex-partners. They flaunted their high counts, their assurance that they were part of the so-what generation who could pop a pill and bareback to their heart's delight.

These young guys were not in the same historical or physical boat as the Prior Walters of the world—not even to speak of the Nkosis and the Ryan Whites. But what they had in common with the hope-and-love PWAs of yesteryear and what I wanted to distinguish from my own experience was a certain smugness about their predicament. They projected a certain insider-ness, a certain excitement and even delight in having found their viral niche and had been able to gain an identity in the contraction of a lifelong chronic illness.

I wanted to yell out at them that HIV was not a brand, not a notch on their belts. I wanted to shout that the virus could bring herpes and shingles, flu and flu shots, blood tests and doctor's appointments, co-pays and head colds. It would bring mouth sores and band aids, caution and condoms, disclosures and rejection, a life of worry and circumspection, of coming out twice and facing the specter of infection for the rest of their fucking lives. Or worse, it could fuck with their heads. It could fuck with their full-cheeked faces. Where was the joy in ostracism? On the stage now with their buddies, yes, they could be Positive and Proud, but take it home and add 15 years. Then what?

The only rock I could add to this cairn of AIDS discourse was that being *positive* was a misnomer. It was a guarded, isolating, unremitting, low-grade nightmare. I didn't want these young men to forget that. I didn't want these kids to make light of this devastating epidemic, even though they had the courage to announce their status. Hopefully they would have the grit to survive, to persevere, to fight for a cure.

EPILOGUE

56
LET'S KICK ASS

June 5 is HIV Long-term Survivor Awareness Day (HLTSAD), a brainchild of Let's Kick ASS, a grass-roots AIDS survivor organization founded in San Francisco that empowered people with HIV Survivor Syndrome. Founded in 2013, the Still Here Collective brings together those who suffer from the emotional trauma of living with HIV, working to fight the epidemic and the political and social stigma that haunts the survival community.[1]

In 2013, over 4.2 million people living with HIV were over 50. One half of the 1.2 million PWHs (people with HIV) in the U.S. were over 50, many of them pre-HAART (before 1996).[2] I discovered I was a pre-HAART PWH, though I had never been a PWA. Call me a pre-HAART HLTS. I was acronymic. ASS (AIDS Survivor Syndrome) was a "syndemic" (Kick Ass's coinage)—a set of "psychosocial health problems" that affected survivors in different ways and different times. The fact sheet with its bullet points—some 20 of them— provided the signs and symptoms, which captured me in psycho-phraseology. Depression, social isolation, cognitive impairment (loss of memory—haha! a memoirist with a loss of memory), emotional numbness, deep sadness, flashes of anger, nightmares, low self-esteem, self-stigma—to name a few of my symptoms.

My investigation revealed I suffered from CPTS (Complex Post Traumatic Stress) because of my passage through the Plague Years, filled with casualties and threats of death, living under the fear of my own illness and demise. To face the terror of aging, the prospect of insignificance, the future of a room with a television and a laptop, a walker and meals on wheels, doctor appointments and a shuffle down the hallway of the nursing home in slippers—that disoriented future, which we all faced—virus or no virus—queerness or no queerness—was coupled with the prolonged fight to survive death that I, as a syndemic survivor, have faced *before* the aging process introduced me to what I have already experienced for so many years. I faced death in the middle of my life. I had grown old at age 40.

Yet "Healthy Aging with HIV" proclaimed itself as the new goal for ASS Kickers! It threw me a lifeline.

57
U=ME

W orld AIDS Day was 30 years old in 2018. No cure.
No vaccine. Vice President Mike Pence, who has
spent his life promoting anti-gay legislation in Indiana and
condemning homosexuality as sinful, gave the AIDS Day
address. He championed faith-based initiatives and failed to
utter the G word.

Meanwhile 77.3 million HIV positive people around the
world mourned the 35.5 million deaths since the 1980s. Long
term survival continued to hold promise for people on ARV.
The one million sero-conversions in 2017 represented a downturn of 52% from 2004. The research horizon, though stalled
with recent setbacks, held promise in various areas of prophylaxis (PrEP), stem-cell research, and viral detection (Unde-
tectable=Untransmittable), injectable ARVs, and even a
possible cure through marrow transplants (the Berlin and
London patients).

It was December 1, 2018. I had survived for almost three
decades. "I've got all my life to live/ And I've got all my love to
give." I had a new face and took one pill a day, Triumeq, six

hours after calcium and two hours before. My coffee was black. I was undetectable. U=U=Me.

We cannot not rest until all are cured, until a vaccine shrinks the percentage of HIV+ South Africans from one-third to zero. Our stories must attest to this resolve: the rapids we have overcome, the hurt we have felt, the bodies we have kept alive, the connections we have made to accentuate the Positives. We will survive.

DISCLAIMER

I have tried to recreate events, locales, and conversations from my best memories of them. Memory can never be entirely accurate. To protect privacy, in some cases, I have also changed names of individuals and places and have altered characteristics and details of situations, people, and locations.

ACKNOWLEDGMENTS

I have Azita Osanloo to thank for convincing me that my HIV story was worth telling. Along the way, I have received help from Annie Dawid, Don Weise, and Lisa Kastner, my editor. I have also had support in the process from David Jeyaraj, Andy Laue, Peter Charles, Mary Akoth Elias, Winslow Lewis, and Eric Haas. Various groups have contributed to my story, including, ACT UP Western New York, TICAH (the Trust for Indigenous Culture and Health), and Let's Kick ASS (AIDS Survivor Syndrome). Lastly, the spirit of my father, Stanley Peter Charles Jr, presides over this story. His message of perseverance (what he called "stick-to-itiveness") guided me through my account of HIV survival.

Running Wild Press publishes stories that cross genres with great stories and writing. RIZE publishes great genre stories written by people of color and by authors who identify with other marginalized groups. Our team consists of:

Lisa Diane Kastner, Founder and Executive Editor
Cody Sisco, Acquisitions Editor, RIZE
Benjamin White, Acquisition Editor, Running Wild
Peter A. Wright, Acquisition Editor, Running Wild
Resa Alboher, Editor
Angela Andrews, Editor
Sandra Bush, Editor
Ashley Crantas, Editor
Rebecca Dimyan, Editor
Abigail Efird, Editor
Aimee Hardy, Editor
Henry L. Herz, Editor
Cecilia Kennedy, Editor
Barbara Lockwood, Editor
Scott Schultz, Editor

Evangeline Estropia, Product Manager
Kimberly Ligutan, Product Manager
Lara Macaione, Marketing Director
Joelle Mitchell, Licensing and Strategy Lead
Pulp Art Studios, Cover Design
Standout Books, Interior Design
Polgarus Studios, Interior Design

Learn more about us and our stories at www.runningwild-press.com.

Loved this story and want more? Follow us at www.runningwildpress.com, www.facebook.com/runningwild press, on Twitter @lisadkastner @RunWildBooks

NOTES

INTRODUCTION

1. PCP (pneumocystis pneumonia) is an opportunistic infection, as is the cancer called Kaposi's sarcoma (KS). Early on in the pandemic, authorities called AIDS the "gay-related immunodeficiency" (GRID); those managing to live with HIV were at one point said to have ARC (AIDS-related complex).

5. SNAPSHOT—1990

1. https://www.avert.org/professionals/history-hiv-aids/overview

8. THE RED SEA

1. AIDS killed 1 million people in 2016; as opposed 1.5 million in 2000. It is now no longer among the five leading causes of death in the world (https://www.who.int/news-room/fact-sheets/detail/the-top-10-causes-of-death)
2. For an illustrated discussion of the HIV replication, see https://www.youtube.com/watch?v=odRyv7V8LAE
3. U=U https://www.preventionaccess.org/

12. SANTOS

1. Brazil's turn to the extreme right with the election of Bolsanaro may have affected AIDS policy https://www.tni.org/en/article/brazils-u-turn-to-the-right-and-backwards
2. Susan Sontag, *AIDS and Its Metaphors* (New York: Farrar, Strauss, Giroux) 1989.

17. NEWS AT 11

1. Formed in New York City in 1987, The AIDS Coalition to Unleash Power (ACT UP) is a grassroots, international organization dedicated to ending the AIDS pandemic. Branches have formed around the globe (https://en.wikipedia.org/wiki/ACT_UP), dramatized most recently in the French film *BPM* (2017, dir. Robin Campillo). ACT UP's motto: "Silence=Death".

22. NOT MIGUEL

1. Michael Saag, *Positive: One Doctor's Personal Encounter with Death, Life, and the US Healthcare System* (Greenleaf Book Group, 2014).

32. CRIX

1. Still used in India and other third-world countries, the patent done in 2008, like Crixivan (retired because of its compliance issues), Zerit has since gone the way of all flesh in America primarily because of its ties to lipodystrophy, for reasons not entirely known or understandable. https://www.aidsmap.com/about-hiv/lipodystrophy

41. MSENGE

1. Kenya Human Rights Commission (2011) 'The Outlawed Among Us' [online] Available from: http: //THE%20OUTLAWED%20A-MONGST%20US%20.pdf]

47. "THE BODY SPEAKS ITS MIND"

1. Highly active antiretroviral therapy (HAART)

51. THE WORLD

1. https://www.unaids.org/sites/default/files/media_asset/UNAIDS_Glob-al_Report_2013_en_1.pdf

56. LET'S KICK ASS

1. https://www.letskickass.org/
2. https://www.hiv.gov/hiv-basics/overview/history/hiv-and-aids-timeline